History
of
Primitive Christianity

History
of
Primitive Christianity

Hans Conzelmann
Translated by John E. Steely

Nashville   Abingdon Press   *New York*

HISTORY OF PRIMITIVE CHRISTIANITY

Originally published as *Geschichte des Urchristentums.*
Translation from the German language with the approval
of the Publishing House Vandenhoeck & Ruprecht, Göttingen.

© Vandenhoeck & Ruprecht, Göttingen.

Library of Congress Cataloging in Publication Data

CONZELMANN, HANS. History of Primitive Christianity.
Bibliography: p.   1. Church history—Primitive and
early church. I. Title.
BR165.C6613   270.1   72-8818
ISBN 0-687-17251-9 (cloth)
ISBN 0-687-17252-7 (paper)

MANUFACTURED BY THE PARTHENON PRESS AT
NASHVILLE, TENNESSEE, UNITED STATES OF AMERICA.

Translator's Preface

This preface provides an opportunity for expressing my thanks to all those who shared in the work of preparing this translation. I am grateful to Professor Conzelmann for his gracious and prompt response to my inquiries; to Professor R. C. Briggs for his initial and continuing encouragement; to the members of the Elm City Baptist Church, for reasons which they will understand; and to my family, whose contribution is evident to me on every page of the completed work.

Wake Forest, North Carolina   John E. Steely
May 1972

Foreword

Jesus' life and teaching are the *presupposition* of church history. The presentation of them does not belong *in* it, but *prior to* it. The history of the church begins after the death of Jesus. She was founded by the appearances of the resurrected One, regardless of how the historian may explain these. This fact poses one of the most difficult problems, a problem besetting theology down to the present day: the primitive Christian faith is oriented in the first place to the person of the resurrected Jesus; not, or only in the second place, to his historical life and his teaching. The content of the faith can be summed up in the one sentence, that Christ died and has risen (see p. 43). Out of this emerges the question: Is the historical man Jesus as the founder of Christianity thus forgotten? Is he concealed by the mythical picture of a heavenly being? This problem in fact emerges early. It is a matter for discussion between Paul and the Corinthians (see pp. 103-4). Even for Paul the individual events of Jesus' life (e.g., his miracles) play no role; and from the teachings of Jesus he cites only a few sentences. But in the face of the tendencies toward mythicizing he stresses the actuality of Jesus' humanness and death; the cross as the saving deed is the historical point of contact for the faith.

The connection of the faith to the historical person of Jesus is kept in another way where people preserved the recollection of his appearance on earth, his deeds, and his words, at first passed along orally, but soon in writing also (on this, see the introductions to New Testament literature). Even where this was done, the resurrection of Jesus is the central content of the faith. From it now the light falls on his earthly appearance, on the history of his suffering and death above all. In this, the unity of the confession of the exalted One and the connection with the historical Jesus appears most clearly; see further p. 72.

Contents

INTRODUCTION
History and the Idea of History

The reader of a "history of primitive Christianity" must be prepared to get more of a presentation of historical *problems* that call for study than a flowing historical narrative which he can assimilate with pleasure. The reason for this lies in the very nature of the case.

1. Of course it is tempting to draw the origin of the most powerful world religion into a broad, world-historical setting, that is, in the heyday of the Roman Empire, the epoch of Roman world peace, into the picture of a politically and, to a large extent, intellectually unified world. And it is tempting to let a ray of light fall from this glowing picture on the young church, which first grows unnoticed on the periphery, but at last is shown to be the more enduring entity. She outlives the empire and the world civilization of antiquity. Indeed, what is still effective today as a legacy of that epoch is in large measure mediated through the church to the present, through the "Middle Ages": political ideas and forms, foundations of law and philosophy, forms of poetry and pictorial art; in short, the foundation of modern civilization and human culture.

Such a view of world history and cultural history has some valid elements: knowledge of the environment of the infant church is indispensable for an understanding of her history, not only because of her external situation, her conflicts and intellectual debates with the state, but also because every movement lives in the life and thought forms of her world, even if she takes a critical position with respect to these. But a detailed presentation of the world of that time calls for more space. It is therefore set forth in a separate volume in this series (*Grundrisse zum Neuen Testament*).

2. Divisions of history are not self-contained units. They are open to their future. Their aftereffects are instructive even for the earlier events themselves. Thus the effect of a politician or a thinker which issues from him—even after his death—is not to be separated from the man himself. Without a knowledge of that effect, even he himself cannot be understood. The same is true of groups. But for the church there exists still another, a direct, connection between the time of founding and the subsequent history. It is placed in the connection of faith and church itself: the church confesses her unity,

not only through the various confessions, but also through the epochs of her history, from her founding down to the present; and she believes in this unity on into the future—because her Lord is *one* Lord.

On the other hand, faith is forbidden to make the look back into history into a means of self-glorification. A glorifying image would distort the actual historical substance, and besides, it is not appropriate to faith. For to faith, the successes of the church are not an achievement of the Christians but a gift of the Lord. Indeed, a historical presentation may not only ask how the Christians saw themselves in the world, what role they assigned to the church here, and to the world there. It must also attempt to see the church from the outside, with the eyes of a Roman official who by virtue of his office had to deal with Christianity; with the eyes of a philosopher who became acquainted with Christian teaching. In the first century the infant religion is not yet a respectable factor, either for the state or for intellectual history. Luke has Paul declare in the hearing before King Agrippa II and the Roman governor Festus (Acts 26:26): "These things were not done in a corner." This is the Christian conviction and also the program of the Christian mission, which is understood as a world mission. But at this time the "world" had not yet taken note of it.

3. A "pleasing" presentation would above all have to follow the course of external events and bring out the dramatic high points: emergence of the church, the leading men, their actions, the crises. But this would remain on the surface. It must be asked: why was the church concerned with expansion from the very first onward? This does not necessarily belong to the essence of a community of conviction. Such a community can also isolate itself as a group of the silent in the land and be satisfied with itself. And *how* did the church expand? It is not as occasionally happens, when an idea, a fashion, or a style emerges and gains ground. Ideas can "hang in the air." They prevail when a group or an age recognizes itself in them. The Christian faith was not "in the air." The Christians indeed believed that God sent his Son "in the fullness of time" (Gal. 4:4). But by this they meant neither that the world in and of itself was ripe to receive the redeemer nor that at that time the world situation was especially favorable for the success of Christianity, but that God determines the times and the fulfillment. The new teaching does not spread, so to speak, by contagion. It is borne through the world by witnesses of the faith because the Lord of the church wills to be recognized as Lord of the *world*. Therein the church knows that the success is not the result of human cleverness; it is the Lord himself who "adds" believers (Acts 2:47).

4. With the expansion, the form of the church, her manner of thinking and speaking, were changed. A large community needs other forms of organ-

ization than a group of twelve men. Does the growth thus lead to the church's being adapted to the "world," to her being thereby secularized even inwardly, so that she no longer is what she was or at least was meant to be at the outset? By what standard is it to be decided what is genuinely Christian possibility of encounter with the "world," and where the substance of the faith begins to be lost? This question as to the norm for believing and acting must guide us in the understanding of church history. The comprehending penetration of the subject is made more difficult thereby, but also more profound, and it becomes immediately topical. For this question is today the life-and-death question for the church, just as it always has been.

The nature of persecution also is to be understood in terms of the whole of the understanding of faith and church. Again one must seek to penetrate beyond the external course of events: why does the church not encounter merely either agreement or rejection? Why is she persecuted? What is the critical point? Is the persecution an accident, or does it result from the content of the Christian message, which is understood as an offense to the world? And how does the church on her part meet the persecution? Here the measure of faith becomes visible: it is necessary to show her Lord to the hostile world—the Lord who uses no power of this world. Hence the believers must bless those who curse them.

5. A further hindrance for a straightforward, coherent narrative lies in the tradition of the *sources* (on this, see the next chapter): from the early period only one single writing is handed down which has as its subject the history of the primitive church, the "Acts of the Apostles" (the title of course does not originate with the author). This lack of early writing of history is not accidental. It is connected with the primitive Christian understanding of faith: the primitive church was conducting a mission, and she was convinced that she would press to the outer limits of the world. But she did not expect that the world would be converted. Quite the contrary! The world would refuse to believe. The believers would remain a little flock which looks toward the imminent end of the world. If one looks at the world thus, then one does not write history for future generations. That the author of the book of Acts then does so anyway is already the result of a development in the Christian view of history: he and his generation—toward the end of the first century—already are reckoning on a longer continuation of the world. How it came to this, and what this signified for the faith and the formation of the church, is to be portrayed in detail later. Here it must be stated first of all that the accounts which we possess are very fragmentary, in spite of the book of Acts. Moreover, the judgment of modern scholarship as to the reliability of the historical

picture provided by the book of Acts is in part skeptical. Long stretches, indeed the longest stretches and the largest part of the area of primitive Christianity, remain hidden to us. And with the extant reports we must continually inquire, as a matter of method, as to how reliable they are. This applies to events, persons, and areas of expansion.

6. The lack of material alone makes it impossible to write primitive Christian history as the history of prominent personalities. Even this is not accidental. There were such personalities, but they are not made the object of hero worship. Faith remains oriented to the message of the faith. The careers of its bearers are not handed down. Only *one* temporally and geographically limited space and the work of *one* man can be taken as a self-contained unit: the mission of Paul. One may even raise the question here whether this is accidental. Of course one will have to move with caution here. For it is quite easy to pass judgment about necessity and accident in world history. On the other hand, one can be reluctant, in view of a Paul, to explain that his work has only accidentally engraved its historical traces. And again: could it not just as well have disappeared from recollection as did the life of Peter and the circle of the Twelve, of whom little more than the names survived?

In the case of Paul, of course, the facts themselves speak their own language. That his epistles were collected, that therewith the recollection of his work survived, is an effect which is situated within his theology. For he did not build his doctrine and his communities on his personal religious experience, but on the confession of faith. Thereby the community is understood as historical association and the church as a unity throughout the whole world. By means of his doctrine of justification through faith alone and of freedom from the law, Paul solved the problem of the unity of Jews and Gentiles in the *one* church, and he solved it not only practically (it was precisely here that there were conflicts), but fundamentally, theologically. Thereby, on the grounds of the pertinence of his theology, his work was designed to last. His labor was continued by his pupils, who applied his insights especially to the understanding and the formation of the church.

7. Finally, one last hindrance is formed by the usual picture of primitive Christianity, which is held down to the present time. Because of this picture the writing of history cannot be content with collecting the knowledge concerning this subject. It must also cast a critical light on prevailing conceptions concerning it. The problem is already indicated in the basic concepts with which people seek to grasp the state of affairs: it is customary to label the first section of church history as "the apostolic period." In this definition two strata of meaning are found, one historical and one "theological," or, better, confessional. The historical thesis runs

thus: there was a time in which the church was defined by *the* apostles
or at least by apostles. The theological one reads: this period is not merely
a first section of church history; it is rather binding on all subsequent times.
The apostles are the foundational authority for the later world also, both
for the development of doctrine and for the structuring of the church.

In this respect Protestants and Catholics are in agreement to a great
extent. But they diverge on the question: *in what way* does the authority
of the apostles continue to work down to the present? For the Protestants
this occurs essentially through the Scriptures, and thus in the immediate
encounter of today's church with the apostolic teaching. The Catholics agree
with this. But in addition they have a continuation of the apostolic office
itself down to the present: the bishops are the successors of the apostles
and represent their authority today. With the continuation of the apostolic
office a continuous further development of doctrine, in continuous connection with the apostolic origins, is also given.

For the time before modern historical research, the picture of the apostolic age of the church and the conviction of the authority of the apostles
were a unity. But this unity has been dissolved; it became evident that
one cannot at all unequivocally assert what an "apostle" was, how many
there were, whether they formed a closed group or were an open circle of
missionaries. It became doubtful whether even a single writing of the New
Testament was written by an apostle—other than some letters of Paul. And
he indeed called himself an "apostle." But he was not everywhere recognized as such, especially since he had no personal associations with Jesus.

The consequences of these facts have not always been drawn with the
desired clarity. The historical discovery was indeed affirmed on details.
But even in critical study the conception of the apostolic period as a historical given was still widely accepted. Thus the pre-critical historical picture was still at work therein, along with the dogmatic theory. Then a "post-
apostolic" age was held to follow the apostolic. This division creates the
impression that this was the time of a second generation which collected
and preserved the legacy of the first generation.

But a methodological distinction must be made between this historical
picture and the historical reality, not only on the details but with respect
to the overall situation of the early church. The investigation of the sources
will show that the view that there was once a time of the apostles is itself
a historical *theory*. To be sure, it goes back to an early time, but not to the
very first. It was sketched out in a time which saw itself already separated
from the founding of the church by a certain distance. This is the period
toward and about the year A.D. 100. In the writings which were composed
in that time one comes upon the traces of a definite self-consciousness:

this generation sees itself as the *third* link in the chain of tradition. It knows itself to be connected with the time of the founding of the church through the mediation of the pupils of the first generation, above all those of Paul. The picture of the primitive church is now idealized: now its peculiar mark of identity is seen in the presence of "the apostles."

This much is clear: the idea of the apostolic age emerged only when people no longer had immediate contact with the early period and had to insert intermediate links. But the idea prevailed and is still dominant down to the present. That it does not correspond to reality, however, can be shown when one asks where the boundary between the apostolic and the post-apostolic age is supposed to run. The normal answer is: the boundary is set by the death of Paul and Peter (thus Knopf, Lietzmann). Up to then the living tradition about Jesus was dominant, the unbroken expectation that he would soon appear, the living sway of the Spirit, of which Paul transmits an intimation in I Corinthians (chaps. 12–14). One may further supplement this view: in the same years the third leading man of the primitive church, James, the brother of Jesus, also died. A visible break is formed also by the Jewish War (A.D. 66-70), which ends with the destruction of Jerusalem and concludes the history of the primitive community.

This picture is not without foundation in the sources. A break does in fact come in the sixties. The years from *ca.* A.D. 60 to *ca.* 100 present a gap in our knowledge, although during them a significant part of the New Testament writings and other writings as well emerged (I Clement; see below, pp. 25-26). But it must be asked whether such a break existed for the consciousness of that generation, whether an immediate, church-wide effect of the death of those three is to be noted. And if one already accepts the conception of the "twelve apostles" as historical: what about the others? those who disappeared from history without a trace? John, who allegedly lived some decades yet and bridged these epochs?

It must be stated that "the apostolic" only little by little was worked out as a normative concept; and only on the basis of this was a break in periods discovered.

The division into apostolic and post-apostolic periods follows (at least presumably) the course of history. Alongside this is another which is oriented to the emergence of the early Christian writings: the distinction between a "New Testament" and a "post-New Testament" period. Here, too, historical statement and dogmatic judgment are intertwined. For the New Testament is indeed not only (historically) a collection of earliest documents of Christianity, but also (dogmatically) the norm of doctrine ("canon"), and this authority is based again on the "apostles."

Even if one acknowledges the proposed historical division in the sixties, one still would get into insoluble difficulties with the assumption of a "New Testament" age. Only a few writings of the New Testament come from this time. And there was not a "New Testament" until a group of writings was elevated as "canonical," around the middle of the second century. And here the measure is not simply that of antiquity: several of the writings of the "Apostolic Fathers" are earlier than several from the New Testament (for example, I Clement is earlier than II Peter).

Thus both of the foregoing schemes of division are proved to be unusable for a historical presentation. Besides, they more or less unconsciously suggest an evaluation which was disseminated especially by Pietism: the primitive period is regarded as the time of the pure church, pure in doctrine and in love. After the time of the apostles it went downhill, into false teaching and strife. But the writing of history must among other things make it clear that there never was the pure church and the pure doctrine. History can only describe how church and doctrine looked at that time. And a theological "evaluation" is possible only through the awareness that the Word of God can be experienced only as historical human word.

For the reasons given, in this book the open designation "primitive Christianity" (Urchristentum) has been chosen. It remains to be asked where its boundary lies. There are a number of objective marks for determining this. But one must go further and search for one in which modern historical reconstruction and the self-consciousness of that time coincide.

Now as we have already mentioned, a clear transition is shown where the church or at least a significant part of the theological thinkers redefine their relation to the tradition, in that they sketch out the idea of the apostolic age and thereby set themselves apart from it. According to this self-consciousness one can draw the boundary at about A.D. 100. Of course the transitions are fluid in nature.

The concept of "primitive Christianity" also demands a further clarification: primitive Christianity is not a unity. It includes gradations and groupings with tensions that go as far as disputes and open breaks. Even in the primitive community in Jerusalem there appeared alongside the earliest group (around Peter and the Twelve, in Acts 6 called the "Hebrews") a new one, the "Hellenists." There follows the transition, decisive for all the future, to the Gentile mission. The juxtaposition of Jews and Gentiles in the church produces problems which are expressed in sharp crises and demand a fundamental, theological solution.

A further problem of substance is indicated by the catchword "early catholicism" (Frühkatholizismus), which recently has been under lively discussion again: where does early catholicism begin? Are there traces of it already in the New Testament? In the center of the debate there stand, above all, the two books of the "Lukan" historical work.

The question is, in itself, a legitimate one. But it must remain strictly historical. It must be kept clear of an involvement, now and then to be observed, with the pietistic view of history, as though one could find *behind* this catholicism a pure original form of Christianity, particularly in Paul. Certainly the differences between Paul and Luke are present. Luke is a typical representative of the third generation. But before he is judged he must be seen in the context where he lives and thinks.

More important than the more concealed element of a depreciation sometimes expressed in this term is a potential defect in method. When one works with such a catchword and does not mean thereby only a statement of facts, but also lets value judgments play a part, then clear information must be given as to what "early catholicism" is and what standards one is using for measuring it.

For an appropriate definition, one should start from the point where the early catholic church as historical phenomenon is fully formed. Its essential features appear in the second century: the organization of the church is no longer free. In the early period a community could be led by "elders" or not; it required no defined offices. The organization was not a matter that affected salvation. But this changed. Already around the year 100, the bishop Ignatius of Antioch connected the concept of the church with the three-level hierarchy of bishop, presbyters, and deacons. Salvation is no longer exclusively connected with the Word, Spirit, and faith, but also with specified transmitters of the saving powers, with the clergy. The sacrament is administered by him. The Spirit is bound to the office. Also the transmission of the tradition, the preservation of the pure doctrine and its correct exposition are under his control. But then the transfer of the office from occupant to occupant must be lawfully and rationally regulated. The idea of "succession" is formed: the successor receives not only the outward dignity but also the Spirit which empowers him to exercise those obligations, and he receives the tradition of the apostolic teaching.

If one proceeds from these characteristics, then it is not correct to label the theology of Luke as early catholic. On the other hand, traces of early catholicism can be seen in the approximately contemporary I Clement, and even more clearly in the barely later Ignatius. Viewed from beforehand and from afterwards, it is confirmed that here is a transition at which one can reasonably conclude the presentation of primitive Christianity.

CHAPTER I
The Sources

1. The situation

The extent and the reliability of the sources are quite different for the individual persons, places, times, events, and issues. For example:

a) *Persons.* For a part of the life of Paul, firsthand material is available in his own letters. In this connection it is necessary to examine the question whether all those attributed to him really come from him. In any case there remains a considerable undisputed body of them. In addition there are the data from second or third hand which the book of Acts affords.

Conversely, for the primitive community in Jerusalem there are only few data from first hand, and these without exception in the letters of Paul, an outsider, who however repeatedly went to Jerusalem. There is above all his report about the "apostolic council" in Gal. 2. All other accounts come from the book of Acts and must be tested from case to case.

In addition, a few items may be lifted—with the greatest caution—from the Gospels: in them are reflected discussions between Christians and Jews in Palestine, persecutions and disciplinary measures, and by allusion also the fate of the community on the outbreak of the Jewish War (A.D. 66). A few fragments from the author Hegesippus (around 180) which are preserved by Eusebius in his *Church History* give reports from the time when James was the leader in Jerusalem. They require sharp historical criticism.

On the whole it may be said that of all the prominent persons other than Paul, only scattered traces have remained.

b) *Places and regions.* About Palestine (Judea, Samaria, the coastal plain as far as Phoenicia) there are only the sketchy statements of the book of Acts. The existence of communities in Galilee can be inferred from the mention of places in the Gospels. It remains hidden how Christianity came, for example, to Damascus (Acts 9:2), and, above all, when and how it came to Rome. A little more light is shed only on the emergence of the community in Antioch. We have firsthand sources and broad portrayals of the book of Acts only for the Pauline communities. Yet even here there are gaps and obscurities: all the extant letters come only from the last years of his activity, from the period after the apostolic council (*ca.* A.D. 48). It

21

can no longer be determined with certainty when the communities were founded to whom the Galatian epistle is sent, and where they were. In later times a number of places and areas are named in which Christianity had been propagated (I Peter 1:1; Rev. 2:1–3:22; Ignatius; Polycarp). But events are only hinted at.

c) *Times.* Here too Paul distinguishes himself, on the one hand from the scanty material about the primitive community, and on the other hand from the darkness which lies over the last third of the first century, although the greater part of the extant literature stems from this period.

d) *Events.* At least in the vicinity of the apostolic council the role of some persons and groups is recognizable: Jerusalem is represented by the three "pillars" (James, Peter, and John), radical Jewish Christians; and Antioch lets itself be represented by Barnabas and Paul.

e) *Issues.* Naturally we have a better picture here. The sources afford abundant insights into a number of types of teaching, struggles over the correct teaching, problems and solutions of the pattern of life: these reflect the church's situation in relation to the world.

2. The New Testament

The most important sources are the writings of the New Testament. For all the historical questions connected with them (about author, time, and place of their origin, historical productivity), reference must be made to the "Introductions to the New Testament" (and the introductions to the individual writings). As already said, the letters of Paul occupy a special position as the only firsthand sources. If one evaluates them in terms of what they yield for a historical presentation, this is a one-sided way of considering them; their doctrinal content is pushed into the background. This is unavoidable. One will always, however, also see the other side of the coin, the theological trains of thought. For it is precisely through these that Paul's letters have their historical effect, which leaves its result in the post-Pauline writings. But it is fruitful to make a methodological distinction between the two possible ways of exposition. One can read a document for the sake of its content. In that case, understanding itself is the ultimate aim: the reader expects immediate benefit from his reading. A document can also be employed as a historical source. Then exposition is a means to an end; the end is the reconstruction of history. One can make clear for oneself the relationship of the two possibilities in the Galatian epistle. The substantive center of gravity lies in the exposition of the doctrine of justification in chapters 3 and 4. This can be regarded as a direct contribution to the basic theological questions. For the historian, it is interesting first of all in terms of what effects it set off in history. In the Galatian epistle he will apply himself above all to the account of the apostolic council in chap. 2.

With this example we have already touched another point: the critical evaluation of the sources. A second presentation of the apostolic council is found in Acts 15, and this differs in essential points from Paul's account. Who is correct on which points?

To arrive at an assured judgment, one should begin with the fact that Paul is an eyewitness, while Luke must rely on second- or thirdhand accounts (he does not possess a direct eyewitness report). Perhaps his accounts are only scanty anyway, and he attempts to fill them out by means of his own reflections into a complete picture. On the other hand, it must be taken into account that Paul sets forth just *his* view of things, and that his presentation thus is one-sided, and perhaps even intentionally incomplete. He is in open conflict with the Galatians and possibly mentions only what can serve him as an argument for his polemic.

Now if one follows this conflict of Paul with several communities, then the chapters on the doctrine of justification also—in addition to and beyond their systematic doctrinal content—take on interest as sources not only for Paul's later impact but also for the history of his own time. They disclose the depth of a struggle between two different views of faith and the way of salvation which raged through the church on a major scale.

An important difficulty lies in the fact that, in part, our study must move in a circle. The circumstances of composition (author, time, place, occasion, and any of the more specific circumstances) are not known for any of the New Testament writings other than Paul's letters. The study must infer all this from internal features. But we become acquainted with these precisely from the writings themselves. Then, moving now in the opposite direction, we gain from those features a picture of the epoch in question, for example a picture of the church in Asia Minor from the period around the year 100 from I Peter and Revelation, supplemented from the letters of Ignatius.

Now this does not mean that study is suspended in midair and does not arrive at assured results at all. There are objective points of contact, for example with assured historical dates, with recognizable literary connections. We know the rough outline of Paul's life after his conversion until shortly before his death.

Many later items can be related to that event. Later epistles and the book of Acts clearly look back on his death. The latter work is not only an invaluable source for the events which it relates, but also for the thinking of the period after Paul. The Gospel of Luke is connected with it. Both books were written by the same author. The Gospel of Luke is dependent in turn upon the Gospel of Mark. With this book we go back a bit further in time. It is disputed whether Mark's Gospel was written before or after the Jewish War. The decision depends on whether the fall of Jerusalem is reflected in it; divergent opinions are possible on this. In any case, Luke has made a clarification on this point (cf. Mark 13:14 with Luke 21:20). With him it is clear that he is looking back on the fall of Jerusalem. Therewith is given a point of time after which the book was written. The book of Acts presupposes the Gospel, and thus was written after it. The Gospel of Matthew also belongs to this same period; it stands in a relation of dependence to Mark like that of Luke and likewise unmistakably refers to the fall of Jerusalem (Matt. 22:7).

John 21 looks back on the martyr's death of Peter; I Clement (and Ignatius likewise) on the death of both Peter and Paul. There are various other literary connections. Two epistles—by different authors—were written in the name of Peter. The second is acquainted with the first (II Peter 3:1), as well as with the Epistle of Jude and a collection of Paul's epistles (II Peter 3:15-16). If one follows such traces, points of contact may be gained for arranging in temporal sequence and for substantive connections.

3. Sources outside the New Testament

The most important of these are the writings of the "Apostolic Fathers." Under this designation (it does not come from the early church but was first coined in the seventeenth century) are collected a group of writings which in point of time are adjacent to the later writings of the New Testament, and indeed overlap with them. Thus I Clement was probably written about the same time as I Peter, and thus earlier than II Peter.

These sources allow us to recognize events only in a limited range. Most of all, they open up insights into the forms of church life and into theological thought currents. For understanding the transition from the primitive Christian to the early catholic epoch, they are foundational.

Counted among the "Apostolic Fathers" are the following:

a) The *"Teaching of the Twelve Apostles to the Nations"* (*Didache*). It is composed of two parts. The first is a catechism on proper conduct (chaps. 1–6). It is constructed so that the two "ways" of life and death are contrasted. This catechism is a Christian revision of a Jewish catechism. This can be demonstrated: the same Jewish catechism has been worked into still another writing in this group, the Epistle of Barnabas. A comparison shows the purely Jewish character of the basic text: in the Epistle of Barnabas the Christian passages of the Didache are lacking. Hence these are later additions.

It is not surprising that a Jewish teaching on morality is adopted by Christians. Jesus stands wholly within the tradition of the Jewish ethic, which he radicalizes. And primitive Christianity appropriates the forms and content of Jewish regulations.

The second part of the Didache (chaps. 7–15; Appendix II:11*a*) is a church manual with directions for worship services (baptism, fasting, the Supper, prayers). The Lord's Prayer also stands in this section (chap. 8). There follow then church rules about traveling apostles and prophets and about congregational officers, namely bishops and deacons. A brief apocalypse forms the conclusion of the book (chap. 16). Also important is a collection of sayings of Jesus which is inserted into the catechism (in chaps. 1 and 2) and is related to the Sermon on the Mount.

The conditions in the church which are reflected in this little book, when viewed from the perspective of later developments, give a quite ancient impression: free prophets, led by the Spirit, travel about in the church. The organization of the community, the definition of offices, is still not very highly developed. But one already detects the beginning construction of forms. Further, it has become necessary to erect safeguards against frauds, who represent themselves to be apostles and prophets in order to make a business of it.

Upon consideration of the various features of church life in relation to one another, we may place the emergence of the Didache in the first decades of the second century, probably in Syria. It had a strong influence on later books of church order.

b) The so-called *First Epistle of Clement.* This is a writing of considerable length from the church at Rome to the church at Corinth, probably during the reign of Domitian or shortly thereafter, and thus composed in the nineties of the first century. The occasion for it is this: in Corinth "young people" were rebelling against the elders (1.1, 3.3). The report of this has·reached not only Rome, but also the church generally (47.6-7). Now the Roman church reacts. She recalls Paul's First Epistle to the Corinthians which combats divisions, gives admonitions to repentance and love and to submission to the presbyters (57.1). The teaching, especially moral teaching, is developed far beyond the range of the occasion indicated. The Old Testament is extensively quoted and expounded; numerous examples are cited from the Bible, and occasionally also from the pagan world and from nature. Especially valuable are some prayers, probably taken from the Roman community's liturgy (Appendix II:11*b*).

The situation of the church in Rome is indicated: until recently it has been persecuted (1.1). This is one point of reference for a dating of the epistle. This cannot be the persecution under Nero. The epistle looks back on this persecution as already some distance removed. That is, as examples for encouragement, it cites the martyrdoms of Peter and Paul, then the deaths of many martyrs (chaps. 5 and 6). These can only be the victims of the Neronian persecution. This passage, incidentally, is a crucial point in the discussion about the end of Peter and of Paul.

The new persecution may well point to the time of Domitian, toward the end of his reign (A.D. 95/96). The epistle is sent by the "church of God which sojourns in Rome as an alien" (on this idea of alienness, cf. I Peter 1:1). A certain Clement was already regarded in the second century as the author. When the historical picture changed later and people traced the introduction of the office of bishop back to the apostles, he was made the second or third successor of Peter in the Roman bishop's chair. But the epistle shows that there still was no monarchical episcopal office in Rome around the year 100.

The significance of the epistle is independent of the question as to the author. It holds a key position for knowledge of the development of the organization, of the idea of tradition and succession, and of the attitude of the church toward the state. In spite of the persecution, the Christians pray for the well-being of the ruler. In doctrine the Old Testament plays a prominent role. It is the textbook of morality. The ceremonial law is without significance in practice. It is beyond question that the Christians are not bound to it. But it is the pattern for the liturgical and hierarchical order of the church.

Finally, the epistle is the document of Rome's early style of church politics.

c) Only a little later, during the reign of Trajan, around A.D. 110, the bishop *Ignatius of Antioch* writes his works. Extant is a collection of seven epistles in very solemn style. He writes them as a prisoner and one condemned to death, while being transported through Asia Minor to Rome, where the arena awaits him. The recipients are churches in Asia Minor: Ephesus, Magnesia, Tralles, Philadelphia, Smyrna; and the bishop Polycarp of Smyrna. A letter is also sent ahead to Rome. The first three and the letter to Rome are composed in Smyrna, the others in Troas. Polycarp collected them (cf. his letter to Philippi 13.2; see below). Their genuineness was earlier disputed; today it is almost universally acknowledged.

The language and religio-historical background show contact with the Johannine writings. Yet Ignatius probably did not know these writings themselves (but this is a disputed point).

These letters too are documents of the development of the structure of the church, especially of the hierarchy: at the head stands the monarchical bishop; under him he has presbyters and deacons. Of course at the time of Ignatius this is still to a large extent a program, not yet the general ecclesiastical reality. This order of things is theologically justified by Ignatius: it is a likeness of the heavenly hierarchy of God, Christ, and apostles. The sacrament is already understood in strongly mysterious terms. From Ignatius comes the famous definition of the Supper as a "medicine of (means of attaining) immortality" (*pharmakon athanasias*). It receives its power from Christ's death and resurrection. Hence Ignatius most strongly emphasizes the reality of Christ's incarnation. He fights against heretics who deny this. Ignatius sees the whole of salvation threatened by this denial. The sacrament unites the believers with Christ and unites the church. Out of his total understanding of salvation Ignatius develops the idea of martyrdom (especially in the epistle to Rome): it is the imitation of the sufferings of Christ. One can speak here of a connection of sacramental mysticism and passion mysticism. In the theological respect he is the most important writer among the Apostolic Fathers.

d) One of Ignatius' epistles was, as we have mentioned, directed to the bishop *Polycarp of Smyrna*. Already during his lifetime Polycarp was held in high regard and served as the spokesman for the churches of Asia Minor. Later he won the highest fame by his martyrdom (the date is disputed; it falls in the period between 155 and 177). After the death of their bishop, the church composed a gripping account of it which still exerts its influence today.

Thus Polycarp collected the epistles of Ignatius. He sent a copy to Philippi and wrote an accompanying letter, the *Epistle of Polycarp* (there perhaps are two epistles combined in the extant version). The content is primarily moralistic. It is worthy of note that Polycarp is the first author known to us who quotes writings which then are later included in the New Testament canon (letters of Paul, I Peter).

e) The so-called *Epistle of Barnabas* is really a tractate. The author is unknown. The writing consists of two parts. Chapters 1–17 develop, by means of examples, the view that the Old Testament must be interpreted not literally but allegorically. The Jews have misunderstood it. They have never received the covenant. God offered it to them, but they had already fallen into the worship of idols. In truth all the cultic prescriptions are allegorically coded moral instructions or predictions of Christ. In the second part, chapters 18–21, the same Two-Ways catechism is incorporated as is in the Didache.

Since the tractate lacks any allusions of a historical kind (except one reference to the destruction of the Jewish temple), a dating of it is not possible. The guesses range from about 70 down to 140. It enriches our knowledge of the efforts to define theoretically the relation between church and synagogue. The confrontation of the two produced a whole category of literature, into which this tractate is to be fitted.

f) *II Clement* likewise is not an epistle, but a sermon, the earliest Christian sermon extant. It contains a number of words of Jesus, which it draws not from the Gospels but from a collection of Jesus' sayings. The author and date are unknown.

g) The most curious creation of the entire group is the *"Shepherd"* of *Hermas*. The author Hermas identifies himself in the book. He is writing in Rome. According to a note from the second century (Canon Muratori), he was a brother of the Roman bishop Pius (to 155). The book contains three parts:

(1) Five Visions. Hermas imitates the literary form of apocalyptic: heavenly figures unveil secrets to the seer. The end is near. The church is not in condition to receive her Lord. The believers must repent. God is offering one last chance for them to do so.

(2) Twelve "Commandments."

(3) Ten Parables, likewise about the end of the world and repentance. The book is saturated with symbolism. An angel in the form of a shepherd instructs Hermas. The church appears as a celestial woman; it is constructed as a tower.

4. Further accounts

a) Before 150, bishop *Papias* of Hierapolis in Asia Minor zealously collected everything that he could bring together of ancient traditions. Of his five-volume work only a very few scanty fragments remain; they make it appear that the loss of his work is endurable. The historian Eusebius attests Papias' intellectual weakness. Down to the present his notes about the emergence of the Gospels are endlessly discussed. Both collectively and singly they are historically worthless.

The church historian *Eusebius* has gathered materials on the history of the Jerusalem church before and after the Jewish War. His most important source for these is Hegesippus (around 180; Appendix II: 3*b*).

b) There are hardly any *non-Christian sources*. The Jewish historian Josephus mentions the execution of James, the brother of Jesus (Appendix II: 3*a*). The persecution of Christians under Nero is known through the Roman historian Tacitus (Appendix II: 5). The question is whether archaeological material also may be adduced. Cross signs are found on ossuaries (caskets in which the bones of the deceased are preserved) from that period which have been discovered in Jerusalem. This is not the Christian symbol, however, but a Jewish protective mark. From time to time much dust is stirred up over an inscription which allegedly comes from Nazareth; it contains an imperial edict against the desecration of tombs. With some imagination it is connected with the empty tomb of Jesus.

CHAPTER II

Chronology

In general terms the setting in time is established: it is the time of the early Roman Empire. In the New Testament, three of the first four emperors are named: Augustus, Tiberius, and Claudius (Appendix II:2). The history of Paul extends into the time of Nero. Also named are Roman governors: Pilate, Felix, and Festus; rulers in Palestine: Herod the Great, his sons Archelaus, Philip, and Herod Antipas; of the later Herodians: Agrippa I (Acts 12:2: Herod; Appendix II:1), and Agrippa II.

But if one asks for more exact dates for the events in church history, the material is scanty. For the New Testament writings are concerned practically not at all about what is the indispensable scaffolding for the historian, an exact location in time. In this respect the early Christian writings distinguish themselves from the works of Greek and Roman history as well as of Jewish history. Of course this omission is a sign that people were pursuing other interests than those of objective history.

What is said above applies even to the writer who is counted as the historian among the authors of the New Testament, namely "Luke." In his two-volume work he gives only one single absolute date (it is the only one in the New Testament at all), in Luke 3:1: John the Baptist appeared in the fifteenth year of Tiberius' reign, about A.D. 28. Unfortunately, it cannot be ascertained how Luke arrives at this date: does he get it from a source, or did he himself calculate it? It is not to be doubted that with this date the time of the Baptist is, on the whole, correctly indicated. But a second "unfortunately" must be added: Luke says nothing about how long the Baptist was active, how long it was till Jesus came to him, or when and how long Jesus himself was active in public. In any case one may not uncritically transfer the dating of the Baptist to Jesus. Even the year of Jesus' birth is unknown. According to Matt. 2 and Luke 1, he was born during the reign of Herod the Great. Herod died in the year 4 *before* the Christian era. The contradiction between the year of his death and the Christian calculation is easily resolved, for the latter was first introduced in the sixth century. Thus an error in the calculation of the year of Jesus' birth could easily occur. And thus it is in itself entirely possible that Jesus was some years older than the figures familiar to us would indicate. Of course this is not certain. For the connection of his birth with Herod is found only in the setting of legends. For the same reason other constructions also fail:

If, after the birth of Jesus, Herod had the baby boys in Bethlehem up to the age of two years killed, one could figure out that Jesus possibly was born as early as 6 B.C. But this story is a legend. The narrator has no precise knowledge of Herod and his times.

The legend of the Magi (Matt. 2:1 ff.) is also used for establishing dates, even when this is regarded as legend: behind it may stand the recollection of a striking conjunction of planets in the year 7 B.C. Of course this latter is historical; it can be calculated astronomically. But it provides no date for Jesus. The legend does not tell us of a conjunction but of a miraculous moving star. And even if the legend was formed on the basis of that conjunction, it involved a late attempt at dating without historical value.

Fruitless also are the attempts to determine the birth year with the help of the census ("taxation") which Luke 2:1 mentions. Luke has thoroughly confused the facts. Actually the first Roman census took place in the year A.D. (!) 6/7; and it did not cover all Palestine, as Luke assumes, but only the region of Judea and Samaria (and the southerly situated Idumea), not Galilee. In the year 6, Augustus had deposed the ruler of this region, Archelaus, and had taken it under direct Roman rule. Hence the census. The ruler of Galilee, Herod Antipas, remained in power. Thus there also was no Roman tax assessment procedure there.

How long was Jesus active in public? The first three Gospels mention *one* Passover, the one when Jesus was executed. From this, one can conclude that his ministry lasted one year at the most. But this conclusion is not assured. The evangelists compress the events. In John, two (perhaps three) Passovers before that of the crucifixion are mentioned. But here, too, some doubts arise: this several-year outline does not come from early tradition, and it possibly has been confused at some points.

Can the year of Jesus' death be calculated? Again the broader context is not problematical. Pilate was governor of Judea from 26 to 36, and Caiaphas was high priest approximately from 18 to 37. But the exact year cannot be determined. The estimates range roughly from 27 to 34. The attempts at calculation begin with the fact that, according to all the Gospels (even John), Jesus was crucified on a Friday (i.e., on the day on which, according to our division of the days, the sabbath begins at six o'clock in the evening) and that this happened at the beginning of a Passover feast. Now on one point the fourth Gospel diverges from the first three. According to Mark, whom Matthew and Luke follow, this Friday was the first day of the week of the feast of unleavened bread, which according to the Jewish calendar begins on the fifteenth day of the spring month Nisan (the Passover lambs are killed on the fourteenth of Nisan; in the evening the Passover meal is celebrated). John, on the other hand, places Jesus' farewell meal one day earlier; in his account the day of the crucifixion was the fourteenth of Nisan.

So in what year was the fourteenth or the fifteenth of Nisan a Friday? This cannot be said for sure, since the beginning of the spring month was not calculated astronomically, but was determined according to the observation of the "new light," that is, the first discernible light after the new moon. In addition, leap years led to variations. If one takes these uncertainties into account, from the astronomical calculations there results at least a certain probability that the fourteenth of Nisan of the year 30 was a Friday (but possibly the fifteenth!); it is possible also that the fifteenth of Nisan, 31, was a Friday.

The primitive church: according to Acts 12:2, Agrippa I ("Herod") had James the son of Zebedee put to death, apparently not long before his own death. Agrippa I died in 44. He ruled over all Palestine (including Judea with Jerusalem) from 41 to 44. *Paul* met the couple Aquila and Prisc(ill)a in Corinth. They had been expelled from Rome by an edict of Claudius against the Jews. This edict, which is also attested elsewhere, was issued, according to one author—admittedly a late one—in the year 49. More important is a further point of reference: according to the book of Acts, Paul was brought before the governor Gallio (a brother of the philosopher Seneca) in Corinth. Gallio's administration can be dated by an inscription which was found at Delphi and is preserved. It lasted from 51 to 52. Nothing more precise can be determined, since Luke does not indicate how much Gallio's stay and that of Paul overlapped. Nevertheless, one can make further calculations from this starting point with a tolerable uncertainty of some two years. A handle for such further calculation is provided by the Galatian epistle in chapters 1 and 2. There Paul mentions his call; the date of this is at first unknown, so it may be put in the calculations as the year x. "After three years" (i.e., according to the way of counting time used then: after two full years; beginnings and ends of years were counted in), Paul travels to Jerusalem, i.e., in the year x+2. He goes a second time "after fourteen (= thirteen) years." Now does this mean in the year x+2+13 or x+13? This remains an open question.

This second trip takes Paul to the so-called apostolic council. This takes place before Paul comes to Greece, about 48/49 (on an earlier dating, in the year 43/44, see below, pp. 82-83). For Paul's call, then, one arrives at about the middle of the thirties or earlier (if one subtracts fifteen from 48 or proceeds from 43/44).

Uncertain also is the exact time of the rule of the two governors Felix and Festus (Acts 23–26). Felix took office in 52 (or 53?) and remained until about 55 or 60 (!). The accession of his successor Festus is correspondingly uncertain. The latter died in 62. In the interim before the arrival of his successor, the high priest Annas II had James the brother of Jesus executed (Appendix II: 3*a*).

The high priest Ananias (Acts 23:2) took office about the year 48. He was deposed under Felix.

There remains something like the following:
> Jesus: *ca.* 1-30;
> conversion of Paul: 32/35
> apostolic council: 48/49 (43/44);
> Paul in Corinth: 50/52.

By conjecture the following may also be added:
> Paul in Ephesus: between 52 and 56;
> trip to Jerusalem, and Paul's arrest: around 55/56;
> then two years' imprisonment in Caesarea, transport to Rome, two years' imprisonment in Rome. Thus his death perhaps should be put at about the year 60. To be sure, legend has it that he was put to death in the Neronian persecution (A.D. 64). But the likelihood is that he died some years earlier.

CHAPTER III

The Beginnings

1. The traditional picture of the primitive community

About the first years of the church there is only *one* source, the book of Acts. Its picture displays the main outlines. It gives an impression of coherence and therefore is persuasive. Even if one has doubts about the details, such as the healing power of Peter's shadow (Acts 5:12 ff.), there remains a strong impression of the life of the young fellowship. But the historian has to ask whether this coherence arises out of the historical actuality or out of the molding powers of the author of the book of Acts.

The study of this book leads to the conclusion that the history of the primitive church remains almost wholly unknown. It is true that there are individual events and—in bare outline—some persons to be recognized. But the course of the history of this church, its life form and constitution, must be reconstructed painstakingly and with only a few assured results.

If one first follows the author of Acts—according to tradition it was Luke, a companion of Paul—one gets this picture:

The resurrected Jesus appears to "disciples" in Jerusalem and its vicinity (Luke 24; Acts 1). He expressly commands them to stay in Jerusalem (Acts 1:4). Here the church is founded, here she receives the Spirit (Acts 2), and from here she grows (Luke 24:47; Acts 1:8).

With this the first problem is already posed: Mark and Matthew tell nothing of appearances of the resurrected One in Jerusalem, but (exclusively!) in Galilee (Mark 16:7; Matt. 28:16-20). This is the basis of the conjecture of many students that there was in Galilee a second "original congregation" or group of congregations. This has every likelihood in its favor. From the very outset the church was not limited to the city of Jerusalem. The only thing is, we know practically nothing about these communities in Galilee. One can only suspect their existence: in the Gospels a few Galilean localities, Capernaum above all, play a prominent role as places of Jesus' activity. This indicates that in these places the recollection of Jesus was cultivated, and thus that there was a congregation there. Thus the church was more widely distributed than Luke lets us see. His presentation follows a single line and has the historical development proceed in a straight line from Jerusalem.

According to Acts, even before the outpouring of the Spirit (Acts 2) the organizational foundation was laid. The spiritual and the outward leadership rests in the hands of the twelve apostles. But since the number is reduced to eleven by Judas' act of betrayal, a replacement for him must be chosen, so that the community will be in the form in which it must be to receive the Spirit and to be constituted in public (Acts 1:15-26).

Peter is the spokesman of the group, not as its head but as the man most highly regarded. There follows—ten days after the ascension—the outpouring of the Spirit, on the day of the Jewish Pentecost. The Spirit immediately exerts the marvelous power of the preaching which brings conversion: on this same day three thousand souls were "added" (Acts 2:41);

soon thereafter there were already five thousand (4:4). The Spirit creates in the community the ideal fellowship of love, which is expressed in worship, in the unity of doctrine, and in the sharing of possessions. He works miracles (Acts 3) and provides the strength to confess the faith under threat (Acts 4–5, then in the martyrdom of Stephen, Acts 6–7). He watches over the purity of the church; what is unholy is eliminated. When Ananias and Sapphira try to deceive the community—and this means the Holy Spirit himself—they die (Acts 5). The present-day reader will be offended by this story: why were they not enlightened instead? Why did they not get an opportunity for remorse and repentance? Why is forgiveness refused them? It cannot be denied that in this story there appears a religious idea of power and purity which contains elements of a magical conception: the church is a holy sphere, one loaded with power, so to speak; it is taboo. Anyone who touches something holy, without himself being holy, dies. An example of this in the Old Testament is the holiness of the ark of the covenant (I Sam. 5–6).

Therefore it cannot be a matter of attacking or of defending this way of thinking today. It has become foreign to us and cannot be transferred into our time. But it seeks to be understood in its place and in its own function: in the church no attack upon the foundations of her existence is possible. Anyone who attacks her is himself attacked.

Thus the church remains pure; she grows, and is received among the people with both favor and aversion (2:43; 2:47; 5:11). but keeping pace with the growth given her by God is the thickening of the shadows. This is —in Luke's mind—no accident. For to the community of the one who "had to suffer," the rule applies "that we through many tribulations must enter into the kingdom of God" (14:22). To suffer for the faith is a distinction (5:41). In an example it is shown how precisely through the persecution God guides the destiny of the church: the scattering of the persecuted ones leads to the expansion of the mission (Acts 8).

The first step in repelling the Christian preaching was taken by the highest Jewish authorities. They first tried Peter and John, and then all the apostles (Acts 4–5). The two accounts are alike to some degree. It could be that they are two versions of one and the same action. Against the peril the community is strengthened by prayer. She experiences a marvelous preservation.

On one occasion there emerges a problem of the inner life of the community; it does not, however, arise out of wickedness or out of differences of opinion over the essence of the faith. In Luke there are no differences of doctrine in the primitive church. Everyone follows the teaching of the apostles (2:42). It is only on the basis of the Gentile mission that debates later develop over the rightfulness of accepting Gentiles into the church (chap. 11) and over the validity of the law for Gentile Christians (chap. 15). But agreement was reached. Disturbance and division in matters of faith arose only after the death of Paul (20:29-30).

Thus the first tension arises simply through a defect of organization: part of the widows are neglected in the relief work (chap. 6). After the failure is discovered, it is quickly eliminated: a new agency is created, and the Twelve are relieved of the work of the diaconate. They continue to devote themselves to the teaching office. For the relief work a group of seven people is responsible, among whom is Stephen.

Then comes the first great persecution. It opens with the stroke against Stephen, who dies as the first Christian martyr.

Here, at the latest, some inconsistencies in the Lukan account become visible. Why are not the apostles, the bearers of the mission, persecuted (they are the very ones spared: 8:1!), but specifically those who care for the poor? The passage 6:8 ff. leads to the answer to this question. Here—contra the arrangement of 6:1-6—Stephen appears as a miracle-worker and Spirit-filled speaker. Thus it must be asked what is concealed behind the story of the Hellenists and the deacons.

The drama heightens. The great persecutor, Saul, enters the stage. At the same time the gaze of the reader is again directed to the divine protection: at the death of Stephen the heavens are opened. The existence of the church is assured: the apostles can remain in Jerusalem. And those who are driven out now spread the church across the country. Saul the persecutor is struck down by the Lord and is made into a chosen instrument (chap. 9; what significance Luke attributes to this scene is shown by the fact that he repeats the story twice more, in chaps. 22 and 26). Step by step the program sketched in Acts 1:8 is fulfilled: the church extends beyond orthodox Judaism and reaches the Samaritans (chap. 8). Soon there follows—at the direction of the Spirit—the baptism of the first Gentiles by Peter (chap. 10).

At this point the survey can first be interrupted. For now begins a new epoch, that of the Gentile mission, the emergence of the church composed of Jews and Gentiles together. The knot is tied by the mission of Barnabas and Paul (chaps. 13-14) and is untied by the apostolic council (chap. 15). Then the original congregation disappears (until a little episode in chap. 21) from the horizon of the book of Acts.

2. The testing of the picture

Individual inconsistencies and conjectures have already been noted. Hence the methodical testing must extend beyond the details to include the whole of this presentation.

Certainly historical is the circle of the Twelve (cf. also I Cor. 15:3-5). It organized the community (see below). But the equation of the Twelve with the apostles, and thus the conception of the "twelve apostles," is a relatively late idea. The role which the Twelve actually played after the founding of the church can hardly be detected. They do not appear acting as a group.

Certainly the church was stirred by its experiences of the Spirit. But the miracle of Pentecost, as it is told, is not at all conceivable. Diverse features are mixed. At one time the believers are in a house, at another they are in public. On the one hand one gets the impression of a mass experience of ecstasy in the presence of which the spectators grope helplessly for an explanation. On the other hand they understand in miraculous fashion, each in his own language, what the Spirit-filled people are saying.

What the book of Acts tells about the community of possessions ("primitive Christian communism") is in itself not a unity. It is represented as a general renunciation of private ownership (2:44-45; 4:32). But then it is told of one individual, Barnabas, that he gave his possessions to the church. This is set forth as a special achievement, and thus as an exception (4:36-37). It is clear that the portrait is idealized. That complete community of goods never existed thus. Of course, reference is made, in defense of the Lukan picture, to related phenomena in the ancient world. The Pythagoreans draw a similar picture of their original community. But this too is in fact an idealized, not a realistic, portrait. Most of all, now, there is in the immediate vicinity of the primitive community the Jewish communistic fellowship of the Essenes. Anyone who entered the cloister at Qumran surrendered his possessions to the community. But even this does not prove that the Christian community was organized along communal lines. Characteristically lacking in the book of Acts is the one necessary mark of any communistic community: such can exist only if not only consumption is communally regulated but, above all, production is organized. In the Jewish groups this is the case.

The relationship between church and Jewish authorities remains unclear in the book of Acts. The apostles are forbidden to engage in public activity. They do not heed this restriction and yet remain undisturbed in Jerusalem, while all the rest of the community must leave the city (8:1-4). And afterward the community is found there again, as though nothing had happened (9:26 ff. and elsewhere).

We have already mentioned the similarity of the reports in Acts 4 and 5. The attempt is often made, with the help of the Jewish penal law of that time, or, more precisely, the rules about trials, to reconstruct the actual course of events. But this is impossible for methodological reasons. For, in the first place, the exact stipulations of these rules are known only for a later time (after the destruction of Jerusalem and the dissolution of the "supreme council"). In the second place, even if they were known also for the primitive Christian era, one could at the most only arrive at some conjectures. A reconstruction presupposes that at least some points of the trial were faithfully noted down in the records. But this is not the case. Thus the point of accusation remains unknown, as does the legal procedure also.

The representation of the relationship of the Twelve to the "seven" (Acts 6) cannot be correct. We shall have to go into this in detail.

The report shows some gaps. Saul goes to Damascus to hunt out Christians there. That he wanted to combat Christianity there is historical. This comes out in his own letters (cf. Gal. 1:17 with II Cor. 11:32). The only question is whether he went there from Jerusalem (he himself says nothing about this). The incompleteness of the book of Acts is evident in the fact that we do not learn there how Christianity came to Damascus. After the reading of Acts 1–8 we do not suspect that there is a congregation there.

Many students assume that for the history of the primitive community Luke possessed one or more ancient sources, perhaps even one which came from Jerusalem itself. Recent literary-critical analyses have made this increasingly unlikely. It is Luke himself who shaped the individual reports which he was able then to assemble into the larger picture. Where and how he found them cannot be detected. Hints point to the Hellenists who came from Jerusalem to Antioch. But through how many hands did their stories pass before they reached Luke?

The conclusion of this testing of the picture appears essentially negative, as a summary of what we do *not* know. Now this applies above all to the external events. But the coin has another side, and there the imprint is more clearly preserved: norms of the faith were worked out in the primitive community which were recognized as valid also outside Jerusalem, e.g., by Paul, and which shape the later history: the outline of the teaching of faith about God's saving act in Jesus; on the basis of this belief, the orienting of man to the promised future of salvation; moral standards, basic forms of worship with teaching and prayer, baptism and the Supper, norms for commerce with the "world," which is defined by the confession of faith together with the consequences which the confession has for the one who makes it.

The first Christians are Jews, without exception. For them this is not simply a fact, but a part of their conscious conviction. For them their faith is not a new religion which leads them away from the Jewish religion, but the confirmation of the promise to Israel. It is precisely the Christians who are the genuine Jews. Hence, from the very beginning, a relation to the history of Israel belongs to the concept of the church. Even though at first this may still have lacked conceptual clarification, still on this point also, Jerusalem determined the future formation of ideas: Jesus is the Messiah; the church is his people, the true Israel. This historical self-consciousness was responsible for the fact that the new communities which arose outside Jerusalem knew themselves ideally to be joined with the founding of the church and with the mother congregation. For them this had more than sentimental value: it was an insight of faith, in which the historical connection of the faith was expressed. The church is *in principle* a unity, and this is visibly represented by the original community.

The traces of this outline are sketched in the epistles of Paul as well as in the Gospels.

3. The founding of the church

Information about the emergence of the church is given by the tradition of the appearances of the resurrected Jesus, partly in the form of concise formulas (Luke 24:34: "The Lord has truly risen and has appeared to Simon"; I Cor. 15:3 ff.), partly in the form of detailed narratives. The latter are of later origin and, evaluated historically, are legends. Thus we must take the formulas as our starting point.

We shall not treat the "nature" of the appearances here. It is not to be doubted that those who appear as eyewitnesses of these actually had these experiences. Their content—the transition of a deceased person into a supernatural mode of being and a heavenly role as Lord of the world— is not an event within objectively verifiable reality. It constitutes the nature of faith that it is not based on a fact which is accessible to general observation and evaluation. And it knows that this is not a deficiency, but rather justifies its assurance.

For a judgment about the appearances it is to be noted: there is no testimony of a neutral observer, that is, of one who was not convinced. By the very self-understanding of the Easter witnesses there cannot be such an observer. And further: unbelievers, indeed even opponents (Paul) were convinced.

The attempt has been made to explain, using the tools of psychology, how the spiritual state of Jesus' followers after his death solidified into such experiences. Thus: their despair over Jesus' downfall had been overcome by the continuing impact of his personality and turned into a new certainty about his mission. This certainty then generated the visions in which they beheld him as living and exalted in heaven. But all such attempts at explanation remain conjectures. Actually we know nothing about the inner frame of mind of Jesus' followers after his death. Only in a relatively late stage of the Easter narrative is there even any indication of a disappointment (Luke 24:21). But this is not a realistic description from the personal recollection of an eyewitness, but only serves as a foil for the certainty of the Easter faith. No psychological hypothesis can answer the essential question of substance: why did the appearances produce precisely *this* effect? Why did the disciples not withdraw into solitary meditation but go out into the public?

Thus: what did those involved tell about their experiences? What implications did they draw from them? What effects were produced? And how did these effects, on their own part, affect in return the self-understanding of the believers?

Characteristic first of all is the fact that the earliest documents are silent about the matters of spiritual experience in those involved. They only report the content: the crucified Jesus was disclosed to them in the existence form of the "resurrection," and they experienced this as their salvation. I Cor. 15:3-5 provides the firmest footing for us. Here Paul quotes a confessional formula which he found already in use in the church and which therefore belongs to the first years of the church:

"That Christ died for our sins according to the Scriptures, and that he was buried,
and that he was raised on the third day according to the Scriptures, and that he appeared to Cephas, and then to the twelve."

Paul then continues the series of appearances, down to himself. But the original extent of the confession is what is given above. Luke 24:34 confirms that Jesus appeared to Simon Peter/Cephas (as the first one; see above). On this appearance rests the prominent position of Peter in the first years of the church. It stands out against the background that before Jesus' death Peter had denied his master.

The position of Peter at the head of the group of the Twelve and thus of the community left its mark also in the Gospels: there he appears repeatedly as the spokesman for the disciples. His future position is predicted to him (Matt. 16:17-19).

The following statements are conjectures. They are offered as an attempt to give some clarification of the tradition at some points.

Perhaps Simon had first received his nickname Cepha (Aramaic; slightly graecized as Cephas) = Petros (Greek), "rock," on the basis of this appearance. The formulation of Luke 24:34, "He appeared to *Simon*," points in this direction. One can conjecture further. It is indeed striking that Jesus appeared to "the twelve." This surprises us: according to the account of the Gospels and the book of Acts, after Judas' betrayal there were only eleven remaining. Besides: why would just twelve people have been gathered somewhere when Jesus appeared? This is curious, especially since there are reasons for the assumption that this group was first assembled only after the death of Jesus. On the other hand, it did not first emerge in the course of the community's development. It is rather the original cell of the community. Perhaps we may conceive of the events thus: on the basis of "his" appearance (which indeed he could not keep to himself; this is ordained by the appearance itself), Peter gathered this group, of course from among his fellow disciples. Then his nickname, "rock" (the foundation), becomes understandable. And then from the gathering of this circle other insights may be gained. Twelve: this means that from the appearance Peter gained the awareness that the exalted One was calling together the people of God of the end-time, the true Israel. For of course the Twelve represent the twelve tribes of the people of Israel. Thus the appearance immediately determines the understanding and the form of the church. It is significant further that this group, which was composed at least mostly of Galileans, did not go back to Galilee, the home of Jesus and the region of his activity. By the fact that they settled in Jerusalem they document this belief that they represent the true Israel.

It is Peter who immediately draws the necessary conclusion from the fact that Jesus is alive: this must be proclaimed. The believers must go before the public—in Jerusalem, where Jesus was put to death.

What has been presented here as conjecture is morover all that can be said about the teaching of the historical Peter. It is true that the book of Acts reports some speeches from him. But these do not go back to Peter himself. And the two epistles which are handed down under his name likewise were not written by him (cf. further Appendix I, pp. 151 ff.).

In conjunction with the confession quoted above, Paul enumerates other appearances (I Cor. 15:6-8): one to more than five hundred brethren, of whom the majority were still alive when Paul wrote I Corinthians (around A.D. 55). The conjecture has occasionally been expressed that this appearance is identical with the Pentecost experience. This is unlikely: Jesus does not appear on Pentecost, and on the other hand, for the appearances it is characteristic that they appear to have no recognizable ecstatic character.

Further, Jesus appears to his brother James, who up to this time apparently was not his follower (cf. Mark 3:21, 31), but now is converted. He owes his later position in the church to both his kinship with Jesus and this appearance. He gradually rises to the leadership of the Jerusalem community. Finally, Jesus appears to "all the apostles." Are these the Twelve again? In view of the form of expression and the context, this is unlikely. This early period knew nothing of "the twelve apostles," but on the one hand "the twelve" and on the other hand "apostles" or "the apostles." From the texts it is not absolutely clear whether the apostles were an open group of missionaries or whether they formed a closed group. In the early period there was indeed no unequivocal definition at all of the concept of apostle. In I Cor. it becomes clear as the dominant feature only that for *Paul*, the apostle has his commission directly from the exalted Lord. He understands his own position in these terms. He himself is the last in the series which he enumerates.

The picture of the development which is to be drawn hypothetically from I Cor. is entirely different from the one offered by the book of Acts. But there is one fundamental agreement: the church knows herself to have been founded by the exalted Lord, and that not by way of inner impulses, but by a direct act of communication. And along with the founding the missionary commission is given. Since God is the creator and Lord of the world, the resurrection of Jesus affects the world. The church cannot withdraw (as the Jewish sects do), in order to live for her own inner edification. This connection of Jesus' resurrection, founding of the church, and mission was later set forth in the scenes with the "missionary commandment" (Matt. 28:16-20; Luke 24:46-49; Acts 1:8).

Some problems of the Easter *narratives* can only be indicated here. The tradition knows on the one hand of appearances in Galilee (Mark 16:7; Matt. 28:16-20; John 21), and on the other hand in Jerusalem (Luke 24; Acts 1; John 20). —Paul does not say anything about the place except in his own case, which was near Damascus.— The two traditions are at first separate; indeed, they are mutually exclusive. In Mark there is no place for appearances in Jerusalem; in Luke none for any in Galilee. The two strands are first combined only late, by allusion in Matt. 28:9-10, and clearly in the Gospel of John, where the "Galilean" chapter 21 stands alongside the "Jerusalem" chapter 20. Chapter 21 however does not belong to the original contents of the book, which is concluded with chapter 20. It is an appendix added by the editor (cf. 21:24).

In general it is assumed that the locating of appearances in Galilee is the earlier tradition. Thus the appearances later were understandably shifted to Jerusalem as the place of the resurrection and chief center of the church. Yet there are counter-arguments: why was Jerusalem and not Galilee chosen as a seat by the Galilean disciples? If they first saw the resurrected One in Galilee, they must have fled there after Jesus' arrest and—in spite of the appearances—returned to Jerusalem. This movement cannot be inferred from the sources. It is also psychologically improbable. As evident as it is in itself that they fled, why should they have returned? Through the appearances there, Galilee would have become the land of the salvation experience. Of course if one assumes that Jerusalem was the place at least of the first appearances, one must try to explain how the Galilean tradition later arose.

But since we know nothing about the congregations—certainly present—in this region, we cannot go beyond conjecture.

How are the stories of the empty tomb to be judged? There are in essence three hypotheses:

(1) It was actually discovered (on the third day after the death of Jesus) that the tomb was empty, however one may explain this. But then we see no line drawn from there to the emergence of faith (and, if one holds the Galilee hypothesis, no reason for the migration to Galilee).

(2) They are not actual ancient legends but apologetic constructions which are meant to support the Easter faith. This latter is correct. But they still are independent traditions apart from the appearance stories.

(3) They are originally rapture stories which presuppose that Jesus is already in heaven.

In concluding the subject "The founding of the church," we must deal with the famous saying of Jesus to Peter, Matt. 16:17-19: "Blessed are you, Simon, son of Jona! For flesh and blood has not revealed this to you, but my Father in heaven. And I say to you: you are Peter, and on this rock I will build my church, and the gates of hell will not prevail against it. I will give to you the keys of the kingdom of heaven, and all that you bind on earth is to be bound in heaven, and all that you loose on earth is also to be loosed in heaven."

The core of this, "you are Peter, and on this rock I will build my church," is written in letters of gold in the cupola of St. Peter's in Rome. It is the "fundamental" saying of the Roman church.

If Jesus himself spoke this word, all the conjectures expressed above about Simon as the "rock" are erroneous. For then he already possessed his new name when the resurrected One appeared to him, and he was already prepared for the founding of the church and his own role in it. But there are reasons to think that this saying first arose in the community and was subsequently put in the mouth of Jesus. For in reality it does not look forward to the church as a future entity, but interprets its nature as the already existing community of believers. Incidentally, this judgment is gaining ground even among Catholic theologians—an illustration of the fact that the Catholic Church is by no means "refuted" by such historical judgments.

CHAPTER IV
The Primitive Community

1. The faith

The total content of the faith is determined by the appearances of the resurrected One. But how? Of course not in the simple sense that the Christians only hammered on the one sentence, "Jesus has risen." Otherwise, for example, Jesus' teaching would not have been repeated orally or soon even written down. As Jesus had done earlier, the Christians called for repentance; they proclaimed the forgiveness of sins, salvation for the poor. They confronted their hearers, and themselves, with the imminent kingdom of God. If one evaluates their teaching only in formal terms, one can characterize it as doctrine of an eschatologically oriented Jewish sect insisting on radical obedience toward God. But this content, expectation of the end and obedience, is given a new imprint by the confession, "Christ is risen." This is not merely an addition to the traditional Jewish convictions and patterns of life, in which the Christians in fact remained even after their conversion. The new faith brings with it a new understanding of the traditions about doctrine and commandments as well as of its own position in God's plan of salvation and within Israel. If one wishes to grasp the relation of "old" and "new," one must inquire into this self-understanding. It is documented in the phrases in which the Christians expressly defined their faith.

Since the appearances of the resurrected One demand the confession of him before the world, the faith produces formulations of a particular style. Such are found scattered throughout primitive Christian literature. Since their content is concentrated on the person of Jesus (as the Messiah, Son of God, and so forth) and the work of salvation (death and resurrection), it is a simple matter to survey the primitive Christian doctrine of the faith. But the heart of the matter, namely the faith itself which is expressed in these phrases, still is not grasped thereby. They still are not explained when their wording is explained. For they are not only statements about Jesus but also reflections of the concrete situation of the believers.

The Christians do not understand their faith as a new religion or ideology nor their community as a religious fellowship which has seceded from Israel or at least, like the people of Qumran, has clearly kept its distance. They are Jews and remain Jews, and indeed together with their other comrades of religion and race. They do not propagate a new idea of God. They believe in the God of Israel, the "One" (Rom. 3:30; I Cor. 8:6; Mark 12:29), the Creator, who made a covenant with Israel and ordained the law for her. The Old Testament is their Holy Scripture. Their picture of the world and of history is Jewish. They share with apocalyptics the expectation of the end of the world and the resurrection of the dead, judgment of the world, and the kingdom of God (cf. Dan. 7:13-14; 12:2-3). They know—even as Jews—that they are sinful and need God's mercy. They have a picture of the heavenly world with the hosts of angels, of the underworld with Satan and the evil spirits, of the earth as the playground of the "powers." They appropriate the Jewish conception of hypostases, intermediate beings between God and world which are more or less personified: "Wisdom," "the Word." They interpret the nature of Jesus with the Jewish designations for the deliverer who brings redemption to Israel: "Messiah," "Son of Man."

But all this store of convictions is now sifted and newly interpreted: the interest in the apocalyptic images of the end of the world recedes. More important is the question of what the attitude of the judge will be. Because of the concentration of belief on the person of Jesus, the speculation about angels and demons also disappears. When one compares the New Testament with Jewish writings, one recognizes a sharp reduction in cosmological conceptions. Even the Jewish hypostases no longer have any value in themselves: they serve to help in the understanding of the person of Jesus. The same is true of the messianic concepts: they no longer take their meaning from the nationalistic (Messiah) and apocalyptic (Son of Man) interpretation of history; they are entirely oriented to the person of Jesus. Holy Scripture becomes the documentation of the prophecy of Christ: he died and rose again "according to the Scriptures" (I Cor. 15:3-5). God, the Lord of Israel and of the world, is experienced in a new way: as the Father of Jesus, who by means of the sacrifice of his Son has brought about the forgiveness of sins.

An essential instrument for the mastery of the theological problems is the tradition of the teaching of Jesus in the community. The confession of the exalted Lord forms the outline. But this outline is filled in by recollections of Jesus—his miracles (see the Gospel of Mark), his sayings (above all in a writing which is no longer extant, but can be reconstructed in its essence from Matthew and Luke and is officially labelled as the "Logiasource," abbreviated as Q, for "Quelle," "source." For more details see the introductions to the literature of the New Testament). These however are not repeated unaltered, but are related to current questions of faith and the life of the community. But there remains a positive, historical basic element of recollection.

Two currents are distinguished: one which is concentrated on the confession of the death and resurrection of Jesus (it was in this form that

Paul became acquainted with Christianity), and one which explained the same confession by means of the tradition about Jesus. Unfortunately we do not know where and how the two streams are to be combined historically. It will not do to identify them with the well-known groups of the primitive community, the "Hebrews" and the "Hellenists" (see pp. 56 ff.).

The relationship of "old" and "new" can now be read in the forms and contents of the confession. So long as the Christian mission was directed to Jews, that which today forms the content of the "first article of faith," that there is *one* God, the creator and Israel's shepherd, did not have to be expressly proclaimed at all. This is indeed the common "old" conviction. What is to be confessed by the Christians is the new: what this "old" God *now* has done, i.e., that he has raised Jesus from the dead. This clause also stems from the apocalyptic world image, as far as its conceptual material is concerned. But it will bring its own meaning into force.

This faith is summarized in short, easily remembered clauses. Two types of these emerge. In the first type, the faith is formulated personally, as an expression about the nature of Jesus: "Jesus is the Messiah" (in Mark 8:29 these words are put in the mouth of Peter). In the second type, the formulation is substantive in character, an expression about the work of salvation: "God has raised Jesus from the dead" (Rom. 10:9); expanded: "Christ died and rose again" or "was raised" (this is the basic form of the formula, cited above, in I Cor. 15:3-5, still further expanded there). Both expressions (about person and work) are joined, as in Rom. 1:3-4: before his resurrection Jesus was the Son of David, i.e., the Messiah; after the resurrection, the Son of God.

Thus the outward scope of the teaching of the faith was very limited. For a Jew, however, everything needed is clearly said, particularly since the proclamation is accompanied by the energies which the Spirit set in motion.

But both in the debate with the world around them and in the faith's own process of thought, there arose questions which demand further reflection and new expressions. For the clauses of the confession are not abstract and timeless definitions; they are historical discourse addressed to the world and to the community itself, from which something new is constantly to be brought to light. They do not have their definitive character by virtue of an unalterable wording. Such is not prescribed; and this is not accidental.

It is not the letter that blesses, but the saving event proclaimed in the confession. Hence the phrases point beyond themselves. They make hope possible. The Christians, like some of the Jews, expect the judgment of the world, in which God pronounces his judgment according to the good or the evil that has been done. But the attitude toward the judgment is qualitatively altered by faith. For the believers know the judge. He is the one who came to call sinners, not the righteous.

In Judaism there are no dogmatic prescriptions about the eschatological conceptions. One can reject them entirely, as do the Sadduccees. One can conceive of the beyond and the future thus or thus, and can expect a Messiah or not. In Christianity also no uniformity prevails. There are traces of the conviction that after death man goes immediately into Paradise or into hell (thus the story of the rich man and poor Lazarus in Luke 16:19 ff.). Others anticipate that only the elect will rise, and the damned will remain in death. The dominant expectation is that of a general resurrection of all the dead with judgment and the pronouncement of sentences.

More significant are the differences of opinion about the practical consequences drawn from the expectation of the end. Some infer from it the task of the world mission, and others, on the other hand, conclude that the mission is to be limited to Israel (Matt. 10:5-6). The justification of this view is the expectation that God himself will, at the end, gather the nations around Zion and the reconstituted Israel.

With the assertion that Jesus is the Messiah, it is made abundantly clear to the Jew what hour has struck and what is needed now to be saved. If this assertion is true, then one's eternal destiny depends upon how the exalted Jesus judges the individual. And this is determined by how the latter now, in this world, responds to Jesus, whether he confesses him or—there is no third possibility—denies him (Mark 8:38; Luke 9:26; 12:8-9; Matt. 10:32-33).

The approaching conflict is delineated in this point. The consequence of this conviction is that a rift must develop in Israel. The division does not come about through the assertion that a certain man is the Messiah. Such a conviction is entirely tolerable in Judaism. Rabbi Akiba is said to have proclaimed Simon bar Cochba, the leader of the Jewish rebellion of A.D. 132-135, as Messiah. Now of course things are different in the case of the Christians. They confess one who was put to death at the instigation of the Jewish leadership. Faith involves taking a position with reference to this death and hence with reference to the participants. It is true that not all the primitive Christian writings discuss this explicitly. The writing which can be reconstructed out of Matthew and Luke, and which gathered together mainly Jesus' teaching, contains no interpretation of Jesus' death. But this subject early becomes the object of reflection and is explained thus: this death was ordained in God's plan of salvation; it is a sacrifice which brings about the forgiveness of sins and establishes the New Covenant. This confession of the crucified Jesus as the founder of the New

Covenant, indeed, precisely of his death as the founding act, is bound to lead to the crisis.

The conflict also breaks out with regard to still another point, namely the law. If the confession of Jesus decides one's salvation or doom, the law must then be assessed entirely differently. For it is no longer that which mediates between God, nation, and individual and which alone can lead to salvation. It is true that people were not aware of this at first. The first Christians did not draw the conclusion of freeing themselves from the law. But at least one group would soon comprehend that on the basis of faith they were free from the law. Then the collision with orthodox Judaism was at hand.

When, where, and how the crisis would break out in the open would depend on how the community translated its faith into the practical shaping of its life. Several possibilities are inherently conceivable. One has already been indicated: the community could retreat to the edge of the cultural region, as did the Qumran group, and there gaze into the heavens in anticipation of the coming Son of Man. In this case it abandons the world to the evil powers. It only reserves for itself a protected place. It does not go into the world with its message, but issues an invitation for people to attend church.

If it behaves thus, it does not actually believe in God as the Lord of the world, or it does not do justice to his lordship. And the significance of Jesus is in essence reserved for an apocalyptic future.

On the basis of her faith the church had to choose another way. She remains in the world (and thus, seen from without, is more conservative than the Qumran group). Thereby she visibly sets forth the fact that she is not a sect (Luke later expresses it in just this way: no "sect" but a "way," Acts 24:14). She documents Jesus' claim upon Israel.

For the same reason she develops no ascetic regulation of life with regard to either sex or food or clothing. Peter, apostles, Jesus' brothers were married. Ascetic-sounding instructions such as Mark 6:8 are expedient arrangements for special commissions. Even the Jewish custom of fasting, which the community continues to practice, is not an ascetic but rather a cultic observance. Even possessions are not ascetically renounced. Jesus had warned against wealth. But he did not demand general surrender of property even of his closest followers. This holds true even in the community (on the alleged "community of goods" or "primitive Christian communism," cf. p. 36).

On the average, the community was poor. For her, this was a sign that she was chosen of God. With this conviction she was close to a type of Jewish piety which is usually labeled "the piety of poverty": God casts down the lofty and exalts the lowly and humble. It is the piety which is expressed in many psalms and finds its highest expression in the New Testament in the Beatitudes (Matt. 5:3-10) and in the song of Mary (the "Magnificat") in Luke 1:46-55.

When possessions and property are spoken of, the thoughts go far beyond material circumstances: what is involved is the whole of the attitude toward the world, whether man is lord over his possessions or is possessed by them. It is true that occasionally also possessions are regarded as bringing woe, and poverty as bringing blessedness (in the story of poor Lazarus), but this thought serves as illustration; it does not become a program.

About the attitude of primitive Christianity toward property, much has been written—part of it with contemporary reference to modern capitalism, modern social problems, and socialist movements. In this connection it must be observed that primitive Christian communism was never a social actuality. And Luke, who in the book of Acts draws this picture of the community of goods, does not make of this a program for the structuring of the church of his own time.

2. The forms of community life

a) We can hardly speak of fixed forms in the sense of a constitution and an order for worship in the early period. The common life was formed out of the self-awareness of the believers, the look backward to the resurrection of Christ and the founding of their fellowship, the forward look to his early "return" in judgment, and the experiencing of the Spirit.

How they understood their fellowship can be read from the self-designations which they assume. They are—not accidentally—such as were already used by eschatologically oriented Jewish groups: the "saints" (Rom. 15:25), the "elect" (Mark 13:22, 27). These words express the idea that Israel is indeed the chosen people, that the individual Jew, however, is not already among the blessed by virtue of his belonging to this people. Instead, God chooses from Israel the few pious ones who practice genuine obedience. The *Christians* believe that through the resurrection of Christ the last time has dawned, in which God calls together his chosen people. It is disputed whether they also called themselves "the poor" (on this, cf. Rom. 15:26; Gal. 2:10). This too is a motto of one Jewish type of piety: God bestows himself upon the oppressed; he casts down the proud (see above, p. 47). Further, the designation "ecclesia" appears early, a word which we translate as "congregation" or "church" (frequent in Paul; in the Gospels only in Matt. 16:18; 18:17); its meaning is the same: the community of God's chosen ones in the end-time. Expressed in the specialized language of the theologians: the Christian church understands itself to be the eschatological community.

This is not in contradiction to the fact that she remains in the "world." Quite the contrary. *Because* she is chosen by God, she can be sure of her holiness and yet continue in encounter with the world. From Jesus she has certain rules for the conduct of life. Since the Christians still know themselves to be Jews, they appear to have continued to participate in the Jewish worship in the temple and in the synagogue. But this participation now has acquired a new sense. It documents the fact that the Christians hold to their membership in the chosen people and confess the God of Israel. But it was precisely on the basis of this idea of God that Jesus criticized the Judaism of his day and the abuses of worship. And it was in their own gatherings that the believers had the actual, the new, experienced fellowship.

b) The new convert had already been introduced to the Christian self-consciousness by the rite of admission, *baptism.* By this means he received the forgiveness of previous sins and a share in the life of the people of the New Covenant. The power of the new life is the Holy Spirit, who is bestowed through baptism.

The Christians appropriated the rite of baptism from John the Baptist. Jesus himself had been baptized by him. It is not known how baptism then arose in the community after his death. In any case, so far as we can see, it is a fixed practice. The Christians, however, distinguish their baptism from that of John: he baptized merely "with water"; it was only Christian baptism that had the power to bestow the Spirit (Mark 1:8).

There are, to be sure, some scholars who hold that in the primitive community, too, baptism was at first only a rite of purification. Its connection with the bestowal of the Spirit is said to have been made first in the Hellenistic Church. There is no doubt that the Hellenistic communities were heavily affected by the works of the Spirit (prophecy, ecstatic experiences, healing of the sick). But such effects were prevalent also in the original community. The most important documentation of this is the Pentecost narrative in Acts 2. In its present form, of course, it bears features of Hellenistic Jewish Christianity. Hence it may be asked whether it was not a later generation that introduced the experience of the Spirit into the idealized picture of the primitive community. But even if the narrative is permeated in Hellenistic style with legendary motifs, still it remains as a probable historical kernel that the power of the Spirit was experienced in the primitive community. There are still other traces of this: Prophets appear in Jerusalem: Agabus (Acts 11:28, 21:10); Philip "the evangelist" has four daughters who possess this gift (Acts 21:8-9). It is true that Philip belonged to the "Hellenists" (see below). But in fact these at first lived in

Jerusalem as one group within the original community. The manifestations of the Spirit in the Hellenistic communities radiate from Jerusalem. Later, in the fifties, there appear in Corinth pneumatic persons who appeal to their tradition's connection with Jerusalem (II Cor. 10 ff.).

Thus it must be assumed that from the beginning onward, baptism was administered and experienced as baptism with the Spirit. Its effects (forgiveness of sins, incorporation into the New Covenant people, bestowal of the Spirit) presuppose the "confession" on the part of the one being baptized: the acknowledgment of his sins (Mark 1:5) and the positive confession of belief in Jesus. Baptism was performed "in the name" or "on the name" of Jesus. The utterance of this name is a fixed component part of the rite; the laying-on of hands belonged to it. By this act the one baptized is incorporated into the possession and protection of Jesus, and the saving effect of Jesus' death is transmitted to him. The earliest sources give no further prescriptions for the rite. Yet it is certain that, where possible, the "baptism" was an immersion. It may be asked whether the one baptized was immersed by a baptizer or immersed himself in the presence of the assembled community. The former is the more likely. For one "is baptized"; there is a "baptizer" present. Paul says of himself that he was baptized (I Cor. 1:14, 16), Later, the Didache (Teaching of the Apostles; see above, pp. 24-25; Appendix II:11a) gives more specific instructions: one is to baptize in "living" water. If none is available, then one can also baptize in other (i.e., standing) water. If there is no cold water, or if it is not suitable, then it may be warm water. If both are lacking, then it suffices to pour some over the head three times "in the name of the Father and the Son and the Holy Spirit." Here, as in Matt. 28:19, the later, three-part formula is already in effect. Originally, however, the one-part formula, "in the name" of Jesus, was dominant.

The sources say nothing about the baptism of children or even infants.

c) The ideal picture of the community and its *gathering* is sketched in Acts 2:42-47. Again one must attempt to discover the sober everyday reality behind the idealizing portrait. Perhaps already early the first day of the week (our "Sunday") became the favorite day for gathering together. At any rate Paul appears to know it as such (I Cor. 16:2). And in the Gospels this is the day of Jesus' resurrection: Jesus died on a Friday and was raised "on the third day" or "after three days." The two expressions mean the same thing and cover the period from Friday to Sunday (the first and last days are counted in).

Fixed forms of worship cannot yet be recognized, only individual customs. In principle the free rule of Matt. 18:20 applies: "Where two or three are gathered in my name, I am there among them." Herewith is named the decisive element which constitutes the service of worship. It is the same as in baptism: the name of Jesus, which stands for Jesus himself. Beyond this a great amount of freedom appears to have prevailed. There are indeed also phenomena which cannot be simply covered in prescriptions, for instance prophecy. When a prophet is moved by the Spirit, he takes over. Of course we must not conceive the picture of the assembled congregation as though it were entirely dominated by ecstatic experiences. Even prophecy was not necessarily expressed in ecstatic forms. It is, among other things, sober instruction, an authoritative establishing of binding regulations by the authority of the Spirit. A certain order, even if this is not yet fixed, is indicated by the presence of officers who are connected with the service of worship. In I Cor. 12:28, Paul lists three which apparently date back to the earliest period: apostles, prophets, and teachers. This is an indication of the essential content of the meeting. Of course it includes prayers, Scripture reading, and teaching, whether more in the form of preaching or more in catechetical form. In this the example of the Jewish synagogue worship, which in fact is a service for teaching (cf. the sketch in Luke 4:16 ff.), has its influence.

From the early period of the church, of course, come all the liturgical formulas which even in the Greek-speaking areas were kept in their Hebrew or Aramaic original language: Amen; Hallelujah; the address of God as "Father" ("abba," Rom. 8:15); the appeal to the exalted Lord "maranatha" (I Cor. 16:22). Unfortunately the meaning of this cry is not clear. It can be translated "Our Lord, come!" or "Our Lord has come." Its *Sitz-im-Leben* makes it likely that it is meant not as a statement but as a petition: "Come!" Arguing for this view also is Rev. 22:20, where it is translated into Greek: "Amen, come, Lord Jesus!" Still another disputed question is answered by this passage: what is meant by the petition that the Lord may "come"? Is he thereby invited to come *now* into the gathering of the community and to share in the meal, or is he being asked soon to make his final appearance and to bring in the kingdom of God? It is clear that the "maranatha" belongs together with the Supper. In I Cor. 16:20-22, Paul refers to various elements of the liturgy: the "holy kiss," the "anathema" (the threatening curse by which the unbelievers are sent away before the beginning of the meal), and the maranatha. Thus this latter apparently belongs to the beginning of the Supper, as its opening. But it is not to be inferred from this that the meaning is, "Be present in our midst!" Instead, the Supper turns the gaze toward the advent of the Lord; hence he is begged, "Come!"—i.e., "Come soon!"

d) It is difficult to determine the nature of the common *meals*. Apparently we must distinguish:

(1) The community celebrated actual meals; by these she set forth the

fact of her fellowship. The mood is dominated by joy over the imminent coming of the Lord. The book of Acts labels these meals as "the breaking of bread" (Acts 2:42, 46). This expression is derived from the Jewish table customs. The Jewish meal was opened by the head of the family's speaking the table prayer and breaking a loaf of bread.

(2) She celebrated the sacramental meal in remembrance of the death of Jesus. Through the dispensing of bread and wine, which by the recitation of the words of institution are offered as Christ's body and blood, the believers obtain a share in the salvation event. The questions, later so vigorously disputed, of how Christ or his body and the elements of bread and wine are related, are not yet brought up. In any case, what is constitutive is the action, the act as bestowal, not the character of the substance of the elements.

How are the two meals related to each other, the meal of the fellowship which served to satisfy hunger and the sacramental celebration? What is certain is only that originally the appeasing of hunger also was joined with the observance of the sacrament. With extreme caution one can infer from some suggestions of Paul in I Cor. 11 that the fellowship meal (the meal for appeasing hunger) originally was opened with the sacramental dispensing of the broken bread as the body of Christ. Thus the meal then followed. It was concluded with the "cup of blessing" (I Cor. 10:16); this expression is Jewish, and thus comes from the Jewish Christian church. Thus the two sacramental acts of dispensing bracketed the meal. It is not known whether the community also had meals without the observance of the sacrament.

Excursus. There is lively debate over whether the Christian idea of the sacramental meal and its structure are borrowed from non-Christian models. Judaism has no sacraments. To Judaism the idea is alien that eating and drinking of certain consecrated substances according to a certain ritual will establish communion with God. Yet among the Jews there are meals with a religious temper, preeminently the yearly Passover meal, in memory of the deliverance of the people from Egyptian bondage. The Christians early interpreted their Supper as a Passover meal: Christ had died as the true Passover lamb. Yet this is not the earliest interpretation of the death of Christ and the sacrament.

Another hypothesis is that the Christians took ceremonial meals of Jewish "societies" as their model. These societies did exist, but they did not have a kind of meal observance comparable to the Supper. In recent times reference is made to the Qumran sect, who twice daily had their meal with bread and "juice." But this too is only an external similarity.

What about non-Jewish models? Sacramental rites were widespread during those times. There were observances in which one sat at the table of the god (in his temple, of course) and was the guest of the god. People were also familiar with the idea of partaking of the deity by eating the sacrificial food. Between these ideas and the Christian sacrament there was a general conceptual connection. But for the understanding of the content of the Supper this connection is not fruitful. For the meaning of the Supper was not determined by the substances eaten, but by the exposition of Christ's saving deed.

e) There is much discussion over how the service of the Word and the service of the Supper were related. Of course there was also teaching during the meals; but in what form? Apparently there were no rules governing this. And it may be doubted whether it is historically accurate to make an abstract distinction between the service of the Word and the sacramental service. Apparently there were both types. The meeting for teaching was also open to non-Christians. Indeed, it served not only for edification but also for missionary work. The Supper could be observed only by believers. But one can hardly assert that every meeting turned into an observance of the Supper.

As to the material of the teaching, only a few conclusions are possible. In a certain way, prayer also belonged to the teaching. For the content of prayer was not oriented to mystical experience. It presupposes clear conceptions about the relationship to God. The model is the Lord's Prayer, which is handed down in a short version and a long one (Luke 11:2-4; Matt. 6:9-13). Its style exhibits similarities to the main Jewish prayer, the prayer of the Eighteen Benedictions. The Gospels offer further indications of the teaching. They contain collections of the sayings of Jesus which are gathered together in the form of catechetical pieces; thus, especially, the "discourse on the plain" in Luke 6:20 ff., which is expanded by Matthew into the "Sermon on the Mount." The main parts of the teaching were early arranged according to a definite pattern: the doctrine of last things formed the conclusion.

The best witness for the intellectual level of the primitive community is the work of thought and tradition whose results were later found in the Gospels. This poses the biggest riddle in the primitive Christian literary tradition. As stated above (pp. 43 ff.), the gaze of the believers was directed at the exalted One, whose "coming" they expected, and the hope of this coming was based on their confidence in the historical saving work, Jesus' death and his resurrection. Thus in fact the ancient formulas summarize the faith. But what significance did the recollection of Jesus' person, his way of life, his miracles, his encounters with friends and enemies, his teaching, his critical debates with the scribes, have? For Paul and almost all the theology that followed him, none whatsoever! Here the entire significance of Jesus lies in his death and resurrection. But alongside this there stand the Gospels. In them, too, the saving work forms the core of the faith. This is shown by the external scope of the passion and Easter narratives. But in the saving work the Gospels include the deeds and teachings of Jesus. Where was this tradition collected, sifted, cultivated, and intellectually appropriated? We do not know. But with methodological caution we can attempt to bring out what shows traces of reflective reworking in the community. There are hints in the fact that Jesus' sayings refer to problems of the community, e.g., there is interest in the debate with the rules of the Jewish law (the Sabbath) and of piety (fasting). At any rate, the achievement of these nameless mediators of the tradition is obvious. The historian Eduard Meyer judges that, measured by its outward success, Paul's impact reaches much further; but in intellectual significance, in spite of, or rather because of, his theological training, he does not approach the primitive community. One will not want simply to echo this liberal scholar in his judgment about Paul; it is affected by the liberal antipathy toward theology. But it is correct as far as the primitive community is concerned. Meyer rightly points to the quality of such creations as the temptation narrative and the passion narrative.

If one assembles the elements of the liturgy and compares them with the worship of later times, the forms appear very simple. But the primitive community not only had other concerns than the construction of a liturgy. It concealed within itself tremendous energies which could not be fettered in fixed forms (the model for such would indeed have been available in the Jewish liturgy).

Its vitality is documented outwardly in the expansion of the church. A few years after Jesus' death there are congregations not only in Jerusalem and Judea, Galilee, and Syria (Damascus), but also in Samaria; that is to say, the church early overcame the barriers which existed between Jewish orthodoxy and Samaritan heresy. Beyond here it rapidly spread along the Mediterranean coast as far as Antioch. But this development already takes us into a second phase of the history.

f) In one particular area the usual picture of the primitive community is especially clearly drawn—and precisely here everything is an open question: *how was the church organized?* The traditional conception is: at the head there stand the twelve apostles (twelve! the traitor Judas was eliminated from the circle; but Acts 1 tells that a replacement for him was determined by casting lots). Beneath them stand the elders (Acts 11:30; 15:6; 16:4); then come the deacons (Acts 6). Finally, there is—as the democratic element—the congregational assembly. It is the picture in Acts 1:15-26; 6:1-6, that the assembly makes the decision—on the suffrage of an apostle (or of more than one). The threefold grouping of apostles, elders, and congregation is cited in Acts 15:22. This picture is complete—but again, it is only a picture. Even within the book of Acts there are some discrepancies. It is indeed rather certain that there were elders in Jerusalem—but beginning when? How does James, the brother of Jesus, who does not belong to the circle of the Twelve, fit into this picture? How are the three "pillars," two of whom are also members of the circle of the Twelve—Peter, John, and then James (Gal. 2:9)—related to the Twelve? It is also worthy of note that in the Gospels a group of Jesus' three closest confidants emerged: Peter, and the brothers James and John, the sons of Zebedee. In the picture given in the book of Acts, this group in the community does not come into view. And yet James the son of Zebedee must have played a part for at least a decade, for he was arrested and put to death in the year 43.

The main problem, however, is presented by the group of the "twelve apostles." It must be remembered, first, that a distinction is to be made between the Twelve and the apostles. Their identification is a later idea. But even the historical role of the Twelve cannot be discerned. Not even the names are completely certain (on this, see Appendix I, p. 149). About their activity hardly anything tangible is told. According to Acts 6:1 ff., their task was that of proclamation and teaching. But this is a later construction. Except for Peter, they disappear from history without leaving a trace. Only Peter (and John? Acts 8:14 ff.) appears to have left Jerusalem, to do missionary work (or to supervise): I Cor. 9:5; Gal. 2:11 ff.; esp. Gal. 2:7-8. At least we know nothing of any other of the Twelve. And finally even Peter disappears from view.

Especially striking is this: in his rather detailed account of the apostolic council (Gal. 2), where Paul dealt with the representatives of the original community on fundamental questions, he does not mention the Twelve at all, but only the three "pillars." They are his partners in negotiations and apparently represent the community. From this it is to be inferred that by the year 48 (or 44? on the chronology, see p. 32), that circle no longer existed. But where did it go? How did it happen that in its place the smaller circle of the three appeared? It is, by the way, too fine a distinction to make a gradation in rank out of the order in which Paul names the three. He names James first, not, however, because he was the one presiding, but because, as the representative of the strict Jewish-Christian tendency, he was the most important partner in the negotiations when the Gentile Christians' freedom from the law was the issue. Indeed, the attempt was made in Galatia also to play off James against Paul. Hence Paul emphasizes that James has recognized that freedom. Thus there is no longer any doubt that the agreement is universally valid.

At a still later time, then, only James is still there. He has become the recognized leader of the community. In Acts 21:15 ff., together with the elders he represents the community. But again, all details are obscured. May we assume that it was he who organized the collegium of the elders?

Wide-ranging hypotheses are connected with the person and career of James: in contrast to the Twelve, he is said to represent a dynastic principle, the leading position of Jesus' family. Now it is true that after the death of James, members of this family had the leadership of the community. But how did things stand during James's lifetime? One single note in the New Testament suggests that, like the "apostles" and Cephas, the brothers of Jesus were engaged in missionary work, and thus were not pursuing family politics in Jerusalem. From a later time, the church historian Eusebius hands down some reports which are to be discussed in connection with the death of James and the further fate of the original community (in the time of the Jewish War). The sources are lacking for the assertion of a dynastic idea on James's part, and the little that is known about him argues against any such.

Can we draw inferences about the primitive Christian community from the organization of the Qumran community, which is well known through its documents? There, for example, it is prescribed ("Manual of Discipline," col. 8): "In the council of the community shall sit twelve men and three priests." But this sheds no light on the Christian community. If the latter had had the Qumran community in mind, then a circle of twelve men would have had to continue to exist. But it does disappear. Groups of twelve and three members are simply typical. In the primitive Christian community there was lacking what is foundational for Qumran: a strict division of members into classes by rank, the definition of the obligations and rights within these, e.g., the painfully precise regulation of the order of seating at meetings and at meals. It is no accident that the sources relate so little of the organization of the primitive community. It finds its essence represented not in the outward form, but in the fulfillment of its task, in the mission. Thus even the Twelve are not so much a governing body as the symbolic representation of the nature of the church as God's people of the end-time.

3. Groups and currents

The community is held together by the common faith. But within this context there is a certain amount of room for difference. In the book of Acts one special group, that of the Hellenists, stands out (Acts 6). Later there are differences of opinion at the apostolic council: one group demands that the former pagans must also let themselves be circumcised (Gal. 2:4; Acts 15:5). Even after the council the attitude toward the Gentile Christians is not unitary. Followers of James fight in Antioch for a rigorist position, to be sure no longer for the Gentile Christians but for the Jewish Christians: the latter may not practice table fellowship with the Gentile Christians.

Who are these "Hellenists"? What role do they play? Once again one must attempt to lay bare the historical state of affairs beneath a layer that has been painted over it.

The Hellenists are *Jewish* Christians whose native language is Greek. They apparently stem from the Diaspora and they (if not even their ancestors) have moved to Jerusalem. This frequently happened, and in view of the mobility of the population common at that time, need not surprise us, especially since with Jews, religious motivations played a part. There were synagogues of such Diaspora Jews in Jerusalem; this appears from Acts 6:9 and from reports in the Talmud. A Greek inscription has been found in Jerusalem which belonged to a synagogue.

Arguments now arise between the Hellenists and the rest of the community. According to the book of Acts, of course, they are rather harmless: in the care of the widows by the community, the Hellenist widows were being neglected (incidentally, this picture of the care of the poor does not harmonize with a community of goods, but shows an organized charitable undertaking). The Hellenists protested, and the matter was speedily settled. The disturbance arose simply because the Twelve were overburdened with their double task, preaching and ministry. Hence the organization is expanded. The Twelve concentrate on the "ministry of the word." The "table ministry," i.e., the relief work, is transferred to a group of seven men. The wrong is eliminated, unity is restored, and the model of the later office of deacon is created.

Thus the book of Acts. At first glance this appears to be a plain report. On a second look, one discovers that it is not consistent within itself. Even if the Twelve were overburdened, how did it happen that only the Hellenist widows—and all these—were neglected? One must assume that the Hellenists to some extent lived apart from the rest of the community. Further, it is striking that all seven of those who cared for the poor have Greek names (Acts 6:5); one is a proselyte from Antioch. Thus are they all Hellenists? It is true that even in Palestine Greek names are common (cf. Andrew and Philip from the circle of the Twelve), but still it is remarkable that in an entire group not a single non-Greek appears. This state of affairs leads to the next question: why were only Hellenists chosen for this purpose and not, as would have been appropriate in the matter, a mixed group? This question cannot be answered if one simply takes Acts 6:1-6 as a faithful historical account. In that case, then, particularly the continuation of the narrative becomes incomprehensible. For now it turns to the most prominent member of the group, Stephen. There is nothing at all by way of extraordinary charitable activity told of him, as would be expected. He is represented as a miracle-worker and, above all, as a missionary and debater powerful in word and Spirit. Thus he is performing the "ministry of the word" which has just been assigned to the Twelve. Here the historical reality evidently appears: the persecution does strike Stephen and his group—not, of course, because they cared for the widows, but because through their missionary activity and the peculiar contours of their teaching they caught the public fancy. This is confirmed by yet another fact: *after* the persecution of the Hellenists, another member of the group of seven, Philip, is one of the most significant missionaries (Acts 8). He distinguishes himself in such a way that he is called "the evangelist" (Acts 21:8). His daughters possess the gift of prophecy (Acts 21:9).

It is clear that the seven are not people who look after the needy, but the leading body of a special group in the community; they do not stand *beneath* the Twelve, but *alongside* them. When they cause offense in public, this must be related to particular points in their teaching. Unfortunately, we probably do not have any original documents of this teaching still extant. It is true that Stephen delivers a long speech before the court (Acts 7). But this can be used as a source for the views of the Hellenists only with considerable restrictions. It is indeed likely that it is not a free composition by Luke, but that he used an earlier source which in some way stems from the Hellenistic tradition. But even then we do not have a firm footing. This earlier speech is not a thematic presentation of Christian doctrine but a summary of parts of Israel's history under particular, limited perspectives. One may regard it as a trustworthy kernel of the tradition that the Hellenists criticized the Mosaic law and the temple cult in a way different from that of the Twelve (Acts 6:13-14). Perhaps for this purpose they appealed to Jesus' criticism of the Jewish ordinances and the perversion of the cult into ritualism. Thus they became aware more clearly and more quickly than the rest of the community that the faith brought with it certain consequences for the law. These beginnings of reflection on the law are confirmed by their conduct after their expulsion from Jerusalem: now they accept Gentiles into the church without making the observance of the Jewish law an obligation for them.

Once again the presentation of the book of Acts must be corrected. According to that account, it was Peter who was the first one to admit Gentiles to the church (Acts 10). It is true that Luke does not say explicitly that these remained free of the law. But he suggests it: before Peter enters the Gentile house, he is instructed by means of a vision that the Jewish regulations about clean and unclean are not valid, indeed, that they contradict the nature of God as the Creator of all living things. And Peter baptizes the Gentiles—again on a direction from heaven—without circumcising them. This is the presupposition of the related argument in Jerusalem.

This account corresponds to the historical picture given in the book of Acts, according to which all initiative, even that for the non-law-observing mission, must issue from, and be sanctioned by, Jerusalem. But in other passages there are traces indicating that in actuality, members of the Hellenists' group took the first steps toward the Gentile mission: before Peter, Philip does mission work on the Mediterranean coast (Acts 8:40). In the passage Acts 11:19-30 are contained some valuable early accounts from which it appears that it was in Antioch that the first large mixed community of Jews and Gentiles arose. This community is no longer bound to the law. And indeed, evidently not only the Gentile Christians are free from it; the Jewish Christians also detach themselves from its obligations, not only in Antioch. This can be deduced from the biography of Paul. He explains in the Galatian epistle (1:14) that he has persecuted the Christians (Jewish Christians!) out of zeal for the traditions of the fathers. Thus the Christians with whom he had to do had been emancipated from these traditions; of course not from Israel's God and not from the ethical commandments, but apparently from the cultic prescriptions and casuistic ordinances. It will be seen that the content of Paul's conversion becomes comprehensible only from the assumption that already before him there was a non-law-observing Jewish Christianity.

Back to the situation in Jerusalem! The Hellenists had no long-lasting influence on the thinking of the community there. They were soon driven out of the city and stayed away for good. But on their side they preserved the connection with the mother church, an external relation as well as an ideal one. The external connection is shown by the close ties between Jerusalem and the most important establishment of the Hellenists, Antioch. The ideal relation may well have continued to function in Luke's idea of the church: Jerusalem, as the place of Christ's resurrection, is not only the historical place of origin, but the ideal leading place of the church. Barnabas appears to have played an important role as mediator of the unity of the new with the old community, for the recognition of the Gentile mission and freedom from the law. He was a Hellenistic Jew from Cyprus, but is not named as a member of the Hellenists' circle. His significance must have been far greater than the few extant notices about him would indicate.

4. The church's position in the public eye

"The public" is first the Jewish public in Jerusalem. Although southern Palestine was a Roman province and Jesus was condemned by the Roman governor, the Roman authorities appear not to have troubled themselves with the Christian movement after the execution of Jesus. This is not surprising. Pilate hardly saw in Jesus any political danger. He condemned him out of opportunism, not out of conviction, and he must have regarded the matter as closed therewith. The Romans had no interest in religious arguments, so long as the public peace was not disturbed to an extent that the local authorities could no longer control it.

What was the attitude of the Jewish authorities? The impression is this: apparently, except for the blow directed at the Hellenists, the Christians could not only stay in the city but even expand, and this remained true up until the Jewish War (A.D. 66). Isolated actions against them occur, and danger constantly hovers over them. It is reflected in the words of the Gospels (Mark 13:9). Some years after Stephen, James the son of Zebedee suffered martyrdom. Peter disappears from the city; is it because he is threatened? But in spite of these blows the community is able to remain until the death of James the Lord's brother and the chaos of the Jewish War. Any consistency in the attitude of the Jewish authorities can hardly be recognized. The execution of James the son of Zebedee comes during the brief reign of Agrippa I, who emphatically represented himself as a Jewish zealot.

According to Acts 9:1-2, the Sanhedrin also intervened outside Palestine. It sent Saul with authority to Damascus. In reality it possessed no official powers in this city, and Saul probably did not even go there from Jerusalem. But of course it is possible that the supreme Jewish authority also used in the Diaspora the recognition which it enjoyed throughout Judaism and that it prompted disciplinary measures in the synagogues, such as whipping (the thirty-nine lashes). Paul was beaten at least five times (II Cor. 11:24).

Acts 4 and 5 tell of the first actions against the Christians. The details can no longer be determined. Legendary features (of a miraculous liberation of the imprisoned "apostles") have entered into the narrative. The two accounts in Acts 4 and 5 are so similar that one can surmise that they treat—in two versions—the same event, once as a trial of Peter and James, and once of all the "apostles."

The *Pharisees* repeatedly appear as kindly disposed toward the Christians. In Acts 5:34 they are represented by the scholar Gamaliel (I); according to Acts 22:3 he had been the teacher of Saul. Of course then the conduct of teacher and pupil would be difficult to harmonize. Luke's picture is influenced by the fact that for him, the Pharisees and the Christians are bound together by their common belief in the resurrection of the dead (Acts 23:6 ff.). That there was this agreement is correct. But it is another question whether this agreement determined the attitude of the Pharisees toward the Christians. The attitude toward the law was a decisive matter for the Pharisees. This is why the Pharisee Saul became a persecutor. It is true that the community that stayed in Jerusalem had not yet detached itself from the Jewish ordinances. But the Jewish public must have noticed that even on this point, new developments were in the making. It is no accident that Agrippa I, who made a show of piety of a Pharisaic style, acted especially harshly, and had James executed and Peter arrested (Acts 12). It is equally obvious that the *Sadducees* were hostile to the Christians. They rejected the belief in the resurrection and tended toward rigorous maintenance of the penal law. Later a Sadducean high priest had James the Lord's brother put to death (see below, p. 156).

The next blow that the book of Acts reports after the hearings of chaps. 4–5 affects, according to this account, the entire community, but in actuality it struck only the group of the Hellenists. The time cannot be ascertained. The *terminus ante quem* is the conversion of Paul, *ca.* 32-35. For this already presupposes the Hellenistic mission outside Jerusalem. The book of Acts concentrates the persecution on the person of Stephen, the first martyr, and then on Saul as the chief persecutor. If one reads the story of the martyrdom of Stephen, one gets the impression on the one hand of a popular tumult with a lynching, and on the other hand of an official legal proceeding with death sentence and execution: witnesses are present at the stoning of Stephen. This corresponds to the stipulations of the penal code. Stoning is the usual Jewish penalty for blasphemy. Efforts are now being made to probe into the actual course of events with the help of the regulations concerning Jewish penal procedures which are set forth in the Mishna, in the tractate "Sanhedrin." Yet a clarification is not being achieved. For the fluctuations in the Lukan account are intentional: the Sanhedrin behaves like a gang, and holds true justice in contempt.

That Saul/Paul was present at the execution (thus Acts 7:58) may well be a later construction. Because of Gal. 1:22, one may question whether he was in Jerusalem at all before his conversion.

After the expulsion of the Hellenists, peace appears to have come at first. The Twelve (subsequently the three "pillars") and most of the community still live in the city. This too appears from the Galatian epistle: two years after his conversion Paul visits Peter there and on that occasion also meets James (the brother of Jesus).

In the years 41-44, Judea was not a Roman province. The Emperor Claudius had handed this territory over to the Herodian Agrippa I (in the book of Acts: "Herod"), who earlier had received parts of Palestine from Caligula. His action against James the son of Zebedee has already been mentioned. Acts 12:3 explains it by saying that he wanted to make himself popular with the Jews. This fits in with the rest of the picture of his policies. The Jews did not regard the dynasty of the Herodians as genuinely Jewish. Herod the Great came from Idumea, the ancient Edom. Besides, he had left a bad reputation. His son Archelaus, who inherited Judea, was so hated that the Jews sought and secured his deposition by Augustus. Agrippa I now attempted to improve his prestige, among other things by the promotion of the Jewish religion. Abroad he represented himself as a Hellenistic man of the world.

Soon after the execution of James, Agrippa died (A.D. 44). According to Acts 12:23 he was smitten by God because of his *hybris*: he had allowed himself to be venerated as a god. The Jewish historian Josephus also gives a similar report (Appendix II:1).

Once again quiet returned. A few years later the "apostolic council" (Gal. 2; Acts 15) could take place. Of course many students assume that this had already occurred during Agrippa's lifetime (before the actions taken against James and Peter). This assumption is occasionally supplemented by another one: at that time, along with James, his brother John also died. This would be a further proof that the council took place at this earlier time; for John was present at the council (Gal. 2:9). The thesis of John's martyrdom at this time is based on Mark 10:39. There Jesus prophesies the death of the two sons of Zebedee. This is certainly a back-dated prediction (*vaticinium ex eventu*). But it is not said that the two brothers will die *at the same time*. And the silence of the book of Acts about the death of John could hardly be explained. The date of the (martyr's) death of John remains unknown.

The martyrdom of the other James belongs already to the preludes to the Jewish War. Here and there in the Gospels it seems that, in spite of the periods of quiet, the church was aware that the sword was suspended over her head. In this threat and the outbreaks of violence she sees the woes of the end-time (Mark 13).

CHAPTER V

Expansion Prior to the Apostolic Council

About the number of Christians in Jerusalem, the book of Acts gives some figures which are not realistic: the community is said to have grown at one stroke by three thousand members (at Pentecost: Acts 2:41), then by five thousand, and is said to have grown further without ceasing (5:14; 6:7). According to Acts 21:20, in the fifties there were already many tens of thousands. These data must not be taken statistically. They are meant to render impressive the marvel that here the Lord himself is at work. At that time Jerusalem had some twenty thousand inhabitants!

For the external history of the church, the book of Acts remains the major source. In addition to this, there are a few passages in Paul's letters and some geographical notes in the Gospels in which the expansion of Christianity apparently is reflected, e.g., Mark 3:7-8: the people come to Jesus from Galilee, Judea, Jerusalem, Idumea, Perea, and Phoenicia. With this the evangelist indicates that in his own time there are Christians in these areas. It is interesting to see how the other evangelists change the geographical horizon. Matthew (4:24-25) omits Idumea and Phoenicia, thus the extreme south of Palestine and the region on the Mediterranean coast. Instead he inserts the Decapolis, the region of a league of Hellenistic cities; it lies for the most part east of the Jordan. Thus he establishes a bridge between Galilee and Perea. At the time of Jesus (not at the time of Matthew), Galilee and Perea belonged to Herod Antipas. The Decapolis separated them. Matthew also lists Syria. Thus he has in view the communities in the northeast inland area. Luke, on the other hand, shifts the field of vision to the coast (Luke 6:17). For the time in which the evangelists are writing, one can simply add up these data and one then has a certain picture of the dissemination of Christian communities in Palestine and its environs.

From the Gospels something may also be learned about the form of the mission. The "commissioning discourses" in Matt. 10 and Luke 9 and 10 contain instructions for missionaries in the form of Jesus' directions. In this way Luke lets us see that the conditions that prevailed in the church of his day were different from those during the lifetime of Jesus. Striking is one saying which is found only in Matthew (10:5-6): here the missionaries are restricted as a matter of principle to the territory of Israel. Has Matthew here preserved the program of a strictly Jewish Christian group who denied the salvation of the Gentiles? Another explanation is that this group did not exclude the Gentiles from salvation. But they, like Jesus, expected that God himself would gather in the Gentiles at the end of the world. First Israel—and only Israel—must be called to obedience. With both explanations, of course, one asks why Matthew admitted this program into his book. For he himself does not share it in either form. Indeed, he closes his book with the missionary command of the resurrected One: "Go and make disciples of all nations." Thus there remains one further attempt at explanation: this command only to seek out Israelites represents Matthew's view of history. Israel is in fact the chosen people. Jesus turns to them. If they reject him, then after his death the "vineyard" will be handed over to "another people" (Matt. 21:41, 43). This saying then would not be a document of a special group of Jewish Christians, but precisely of Matthew's universalism. It serves to show the reader the way of the gospel from Israel into the world. The missionaries have the right to support by the congregations (I Cor. 9). Later, in the second century, the "Didache" (chap. 11) gives detailed instructions against people who abuse this right (Appendix II:11*a*).

Quite early there were congregations in Judea even outside Jerusalem. I Thessalonians (written around 50) mentions such (2:14). The book of Acts mentions them summarily (1:8; 8:1). It also knows of communities in the coastal region: Lydda, Joppa, and Ashdod (Azotus; 8:40); the most significant one apparently was in Caesarea, the residence of the Roman governor. A constant exchange appears to have prevailed between Jerusalem and the new foundations. Of course there was not yet an overarching organization. The presuppositions for such were lacking. There were authorities. But the rights and obligations of the communities in relation to one another were not yet defined in terms of law. There was no place for a leadership which would have embraced all the communities.

The bearers of the mission outside Jerusalem were chiefly the Hellenists who had been expelled. The mission in the coastal plain and in Samaria is connected with the name of Philip. Then, according to the book of Acts, Peter also appears there. It is undoubtedly true that he came only after Philip. For if he had founded these communities, his name would not have been obscured by that of Philip.

A certain generosity prevailed in the practical attitude toward the law. This is shown by the fact that not only were Samaritans, according to strict Jewish opinion heretics, individually and occasionally admitted,' but in Samaria communities arose and were recognized. Certainly opinion was not united everywhere and from the outset about the Samaritan mission. Various voices must have been raised. They can still be heard in part in the tradition. Acts 8 is difficult to evaluate in this regard: Philip baptizes the new converts in Samaria; but the Spirit is withheld from those baptized. They receive the Spirit only when Peter and John come, thus when the work of Philip is sanctioned by Jerusalem. This is first a consequence of Luke's idea of the church, according to which Jerusalem is the leading place of the church. However, there could be concealed here an indication that the advance of the mission from the orthodox to the heretics set off discussions in Jerusalem until it was given recognition there. Such discussions are also reflected in the passages in Luke's Gospel in which (the) Samaritans are defended, in the parable of the good Samaritan (Luke 10:30 ff.) and in the story of the grateful Samaritan (Luke 17:16). Curiously, both take place in the vicinity of Jerusalem, and thus point to the debates there. John 4 also explicitly justifies the mission in Samaria, by telling that Jesus himself converted Samaritans. Whether Jesus actually had followers in this area can be left undecided. In any case, John 4 presupposes the existence of Samaritan congregations and shows that a compulsion was felt to justify these against attacks within the Christian community.

Damascus appears quite suddenly. If in the early or mid-thirties, a few years after Jesus' death, Paul seeks out this city as the place of his battle against Christianity, it must have been rather prominent here. This congregation too must have been founded by the Hellenists, for Paul sees the law threatened.

Other than these—except for the allusions in the Gospels already mentioned—one hears only a few place names, also in the Gospels: some localities are emphasized as places of Jesus' activity: Capernaum, Cana, etc. Some narratives about Jesus have stuck to them as "local traditions," i.e., they were handed down here. This presupposes the existence of a community.

After his conversion, Paul went for approximately two years to "Arabia," i.e., according to the language of that time to the kingdom of the Nabataeans, east of Palestine. He hardly spent the time there, as some think, in solitary meditation on his experience, but, in keeping with the commission he had received, in missionary efforts. We learn nothing of any success he may have had.

The expansion moves rapidly along the coast northward, through Phoenicia (Tyre, Acts 21:3, 7; Sidon, Acts 27:3; both together, Mark 3:8; Luke 6:17; Ptolemais, Acts 21:7) to Antioch (Acts 11:19 ff.); across the sea, Cyprus was reached.

Antioch becomes the most important center of the expansion. It maintained a prominent position for centuries. Its significance is far greater than the book of Acts indicates. It not only extends to the position of Christianity in the public eye, though of course to this also: here the designation "Christians" (*christianoi,* Acts 11:26) first appears. It is given to them by outsiders. For it presupposes that one takes "Christ" to be a name (not a title, "the Messiah"), and thus is not correctly informed about the person of Jesus. Thus the Christians now are recognized by the non-Jewish public as an independent group. That they are now so clearly distinguished from the Jews of course is related to the fact that now Gentiles are becoming Christians in greater numbers.

According to Acts 10, even before the founding of the community in Antioch, Peter accepted into the church a group of Gentiles, the centurion Cornelius in Caesarea, together with relatives and friends. The book of Acts shapes this conversion into a programmatic act: the Spirit himself gives the decisive impetus. The instrument, Peter, must be a representative of the original community, since in fact he too must give account of this event.

In reality there was no such single act which solved the problem once and for all. Evidently the Christian missionaries also met with acceptance here and there in the immediate vicinity of the Jewish communities in which they appeared.

What moved a Gentile to become a Christian? The primitive Christian sources provide little psychological information about this. For them, conversion is a work of the Lord himself. It is rendered comprehensible from the content of the saving message, not from the psychological state of the one converted. Yet motivations can be discerned. For one thing, the Christian mission could have an impact on people who had already attached themselves to Judaism. There were "proselytes" who had wholly gone over to Judaism; there was one such—from Antioch (Acts 6:5)—among the "Hellenists" in Jerusalem. In addition, there were sympathizers, "God-fearers." These acknowledged the basic views of the Jewish religion, the belief in one God, the chief moral commandments. But they did not officially join; they did not have themselves circumcised and did not take upon themselves the law in its full scope. Of course the community life as such also exerted its influence. The community in Antioch appears to have displayed vitality created by manifestations of the Spirit. Prophets appeared (Acts 11:27-28; 13:1). In the primitive Christian view, "prophecy" is indeed also prediction, announcement of the future event; but it is primarily convicting discourse, which lays bare the interior of man (I Cor. 14:24). Also among the gifts of the Spirit are miraculous powers and the gift of healing (I Cor. 12:9-10; Rom. 15:19). Paul received his decisive impulses in this milieu.

Joseph *Barnabas,* a Jew of the Diaspora who had earned a place of high regard in Jerusalem (Acts 4:36-37), appears as the chief mediator between the two great centers. According to Acts 11:22, he came to Antioch as an official investigator. Once again this is the Lukan scheme. In any case, in the new place he became the leading man; in Acts 13:1 he is named in first place. At the apostolic council, together with Paul he represented the community.

In this early period with its intense hope, the living together of Jews and Gentiles in the new fellowship apparently caused no difficulty of any significance. The two groups did not separate. The Hellenistic Jewish Christians had no scruples against table fellowship with the Gentile Christians. It is shown by Gal. 2:11 ff. that this fellowship first was observed in Antioch quite naturally.

The Pharisaic zealot Saul/Paul collided with this kind of Christianity— new in relation to Jerusalem—in which even the Jewish Christians had cast off the restrictions of the Jewish ceremonial law. And after his conversion he grew up in this way of life. Here he formed his theological ideas about faith, law, and liberty of the faith. It was not he who detached Christianity from the law. Some Christians had already become aware that faith abrogated the law's way of salvation. Paul now grasps this as the fundamental problem for the understanding of faith.

With this already practiced but not yet theoretically explained freedom, the problems ripen which are then treated at the apostolic council. Yet the problem of the law does not form the only line of development. In order to understand the course of things, it is necessary to take into account the profound process of transformation which befell the Christian forms of life and thought on Hellenistic soil and which reached much further than only the questions of Jewish law. Only against the background of this process does the theology of Paul become historically understandable. Before our account turns to this process, the picture of the expansion must be completed.

Up to the point in time from which the mission can be followed with the help of Paul's letters, the book of Acts again is full of gaps. Communities arose in Syria and Cilicia, part of them through Paul's efforts in these areas (Gal. 1:21). The book of Acts compresses this work into a first "missionary journey" of Paul and Barnabas (Acts 13–14): communities are founded in the southern part of the interior of Asia Minor. What looks here, in Acts, like a short, successful undertaking, in fact embraced more than a decade, the details of which—except for those related in the two chapters in Acts— remain unknown. In conclusion, it must be mentioned that Christianity came to Rome early. But this is only to be inferred; it is nowhere told. Perhaps a solitary recollection is still preserved in the writer Suetonius, the biographer of the Roman rulers from Caesar to the end of the first century: the Emperor Claudius had expelled the Jews from Rome because at the instigation of a certain Chrestus disorders had broken out among them (Appendix II:2a). This is the edict which has already been mentioned above in the chapter on chronology. Is this agitator Chrestus really "Christus"? If so, Suetonius has mistakenly assumed that he had personally appeared in Rome. Nevertheless there could be here an echo of disputes among the Roman Jews which were set in motion by the incursion of Christianity.

CHAPTER VI
Hellenistic Christianity Before Paul

1. Problems

"Before Paul" does not mean that the early form of Christian life and thought to be presented here ceased with Paul, but that it developed before he entered the church, was determinative for him, and even further developed alongside him and after him. Paul was one missionary and thinker alongside others, albeit the most significant of them. In his lifetime his influence extended essentially only to the communities which he himself (either directly or through his pupils) founded. And even in them he frequently had to fight hard battles to repel agitation from without (Galatians; Philippians; II Cor. 10–13). In the second center of the church, Antioch, he appears no longer to have possessed any influence after the conflict with Peter and Barnabas (Gal. 2).

There are no independent documents from the time before Paul still extant. Perhaps one can still reconstruct from the book of Acts some fragments which pertain to the community in Antioch. For the rest, one must, by means of analysis of Paul's letters and later writings, hypothetically deduce the ideas and life patterns of the early period. This is possible to a certain extent, since these writings are deliberately set into the tradition; occasionally they explicitly quote phrases that have been handed down; they discuss traditional patterns of life and worship.

There is no break between the original community in Jerusalem and the Hellenistic church. The connection is provided in part by persons. As mentioned earlier, the Hellenists still clung to an ideal connection with the original community. Barnabas maintains the connection between the two places. The church knows itself to be a unity. It expresses the common faith in formulations which are the fixed property of the tradition and which join Christians of all places in a unity. The connection with the mother church is not only one of feeling. It is rather established by doctrine itself: the faith is historically founded by the appearances of the resurrected One. It continues to be related to the testimony of the historical eyewitnesses. The Lord himself is the ground and guarantor of unity.

A development now can also be discerned in the forms and contents of the confession formulated in phrases. So long as the mission was directed only to Jews, the Christians were not obliged explicitly to confess their monotheistic faith. For this was not at all a point of dispute, and it formed the self-evident presupposition: the Christians are Jews and, from the very outset, monotheists. They rather are confessing a new act of this God: that he has sent Jesus as the promised Messiah. But to Gentiles one must also explain the presupposition: that there is *one* God; hence there is also only *one* "Lord" (I Cor. 8:6). The confession now, formally speaking, has two "articles." Substantively speaking, this is nothing new. It is only the explicit unfolding in the new situation. In this, for the first "article of faith" one held to the Israelite tradition; the formulation "one God" is the basic confession of Israel (Deut. 6:4).

Also in the christological part of the confession the form of expression is changed. The Jewish title "Messiah" is meaningless and incomprehensible for non-Jews, even if one translates the Hebrew or Aramaic word "Messiah," "the Anointed," into Greek (*christos*). For the Greeks, "anointing" is not a religious act of consecration, but an aspect of care of the body. In the Greek-speaking area "Christ" becomes a part of the name "Jesus Christ." This happens before Paul's time, for he uses this double name as a matter of course, although as a Jew he knows the meaning of "Christ." Incidentally, later on, when even in the Gentile Christian territory the Old Testament was more extensively used in theological labors, occasionally the original, titular sense was re-established (see Luke in Acts 2:36; 4:26).

The title which now emerges in a dominant position is "the Lord" (*kyrios*). The way in which Paul uses it shows that he found it already in regular use. The question as to where and when it arose and became widespread is disputed and cannot be answered with the material now available. The earliest documentation is the Aramaic exclamation discussed above, which Paul introduces into the Greek communities also: "Maranatha!" the prayer for the parousia of the exalted Jesus. Here the meaning of "Lord" is determined by the imminent expectation that marked this early period. In Hellenistic Christianity the word then absorbs new elements of meaning and expresses the believers' total understanding of redemption.

These could identify themselves in brief as "those who call upon the name of the Lord" (I Cor. 1:2). Thus in the "calling upon," i.e., venerating of the Lord, one sees the nature of the new faith. This expression comes from the Greek translation of the Old Testament; thus it arose in the Greek-speaking territory (Joel 3:5; cf. Acts 2:21). Three motifs in the meaning of "Lord" stand out. As earlier, it still points to the parousia: "The Lord is near" (Phil. 4:5; cf. Phil. 3:20). The Lord sits at the right hand of God and subjects the powers to him. To the church he demonstrates his position as "Lord" in the power of the Spirit and in the effect of the sacraments: people are baptized in his name. The power of the Supper is based upon his death and resurrection: "The Lord Jesus, on the night when he was betrayed . . . (I Cor. 11:23 ff.). Reverence is due him, and the appropriate form of this is the acclamation in worship: "Jesus is Lord" (I Cor. 12:3; Phil. 2:11). It is this invocation which gives its character to the gathering of the community. It is itself the working of the Spirit (I Cor. 12:3).

If the veneration of the "Lord," that is, of a heavenly being, and the experience of the Spirit, which produces ecstasies, are so closely connected, it is quite natural for that faith to turn into a fanatical experience of the ascent of the soul into the upper world. This indeed corresponds to tendencies in the Hellenistic environment in which the Christians live and out of which they come. Of course one can ask, "Why should Christianity not be the cultivation of the ascent of the soul to higher worlds? Could not profound religious insights be opened up thus? Is not the mystical cultivation of the inner life, the spiritual connection of soul to soul, rendered possible thus? Is not mysticism, absorption and ascent, among the finest flowers in the garden of religions, even in the Christian religion?" On the other hand, as a regulative force for all potential developments in the church, this question must remain on guard: what is truth, namely, in accordance with the historical founding of the church, with the norm "in Christ"? At this point now we must go into the religio-historical and psychological problematic of the Hellenistic form of Christianity.

2. Christianity and Hellenistic religious history

The form which Christianity assumes in the Hellenistic milieu is determined not only by doctrine but also by how the hearer receives this doctrine. He is in fact already stamped by religious ideas and by general ideas of his world as well. Only in a sense do these ideas invade the church from without. They are brought in by the new converts and form a component part of their thought formation in the church. Here a fundamental question emerges. The Christian faith is exclusive. Anyone who serves this Lord can no longer participate in the worship of any other God, neither outwardly cultically nor inwardly. Anyone who sits at the Lord's table cannot also sit at the table of the "demons" (i.e., of the pagan gods: I Cor. 10:21-22). How then could a blending with alien religious forms arise?

To pose the question thus is to overlook both the reality of the world and the nature of faith. One must attempt to hear the Christian teaching through the ears of a hearer of that time and to see the Christian way of life with his eyes. He hears of a divine being who appeared as man, died, and ascended again into the upper world (Phil. 2:6 ff.). He sees that rites are performed by which heavenly powers are supposed to flow into the initiate. He will view Christianity as one of the oriental cults—offensive to the Greek—which are beginning to move out of the Orient to the West. These form communities of a new style. In them are no longer gathered the whole populace to worship an official deity, so to speak, whose cult is supported by the city. Instead, now believers are gathered, often from all strata of the population, in closed rooms for esoteric rites. Christianity also offers this very same picture. Perhaps (the meaning is not certain) Acts 17:18 gives an indication of how Greeks could misunderstand the Christian teaching. The Greek hearers of Paul understand that the theme of Paul's teaching is "Jesus and the resurrection." It is possible that Luke intends this to be understood thus: that this teaching is so utterly strange to them that they misunderstand him to be speaking of a divine pair, Jesus and his female companion "Resurrection" (Greek "*Anastasis*"). At that time such a misunderstanding was not farfetched. There is a parallel that is close in time and place:

In this very period, Simon Magus, who appears in Acts 8, is traveling through the countries with his teaching. He comes from Samaria but moves to the West. He proclaims that he is the earthly manifestation of the most high God (see below, p. 126 and Appendix II:10).

On the other hand, of course the observant contemporary noted the connection of Christianity with Judaism: the redeemer who had died and had been exalted was, as man, a Jew. Neither of the two religions had any images of God.

Whether he now rejects Christianity or is converted, he is affected by such impressions. The question then is: what net weight do these continue to have or even first acquire in the church? What is the valid criterion for the appropriation, rejection, or reshaping of religious ideas? Must the church resign itself to an unavoidable process of amalgamation, with the danger of losing its own nature? What is the valid, the abiding?

An attempt to find an answer must be aware of the historical character of faith: it is not a timeless synthesis of certain metaphysical ideas. It is the response to the proclaimed saving act of God and thus can, in its very existence, be grasped anew in each new situation. It is not timeless "being" but ever new understanding. Christianity is not exclusive by virtue of its introducing religious ideas which had not existed earlier. Indeed, according to primitive Christian interpretation, historically new is precisely what the basic Christian ideas are not. The church knows itself to be the true Israel; its book of religion is the Jewish Holy Scripture. There the outline of the idea of redemption is prefigured, the idea of the covenant and its renewal, of atoning and vicarious sacrifice, and so on. What is *new* is God's saving act itself. The message of this saving act applies to the Jew as Jew, and to the Gentile as Gentile. Here and there existing ideas are appropriated in order to expound this saving act:

Jewish Christianity interprets it not only with the help of the Old Testament covenant and sacrifice, but also by means of incorporating it into the apocalyptic frame of reference, with its outlook on the final world crisis, the collapse, the resurrection of the dead, the judgment, and the new world. In Gentile territory, mythological conceptions serve for explanation, thus the schema of the descent of a redeemer from heaven, his appearance as man, and his return into the upper world (Phil. 2:6 ff.). Thus it is historically correct if one characterizes early Christianity as a "syncretistic" construction (by "syncretism" we mean the mutual interpenetration of religions; in the narrower sense the religious blending process in late antiquity). But with the statement that Christianity participated in the religious movement of its time, the substantive question still is not broached. It reads thus: is that still Christian or not?

Any utterance about the faith is historical and is expressed in historical forms, and thus in forms conditioned by the times; this was true then as it is today. Christianity is never a so-to-speak pure distillate. It always bears human-historical form. The same is true of the ideas and phrases in which it is represented and sets forth its substance. For the essence of Christianity it is not crucial whether it bears features of a given time, but rather what is proclaimed—in historical form—as salvation. The absoluteness lies in the connection of salvation with the person of Jesus. The pattern of the appropriate question is afforded by I Cor. 8:6, where Paul formulates it in terms of the world of that time: In the world there are many gods and "lords," but for "us," *one* God and *one* Lord. Of the two beings the definition is given: God is the Father and Creator; we are from him and to him. The Lord is the mediator of creation, and thus of our relationship to God; we are through him.

Now the question posed above can be taken up once more: why may faith not become a movement of spiritual ascent to higher worlds? The counter-question is: In this case is the Lord still really the Lord? Or is the one who ascends, who has the vision, who cultivates ecstatic experiences, himself identified with him, so that in essence "Lord" becomes a codeword for the experiencing "I" and its self-redemption? Dogmatically formulated: if faith loses its connection with its historical fixed point, the death of the man Jesus, then its object, the exalted One, becomes a mythical figure. The redeemer is separated from the creator. The locus of faith then is no longer the world, but a fantasy world which is a product of the subjective mind. The life together of the believers becomes the common song in heavenly choirs or is dissolved into a medley of the individual voices of the inspired. These are not merely theoretically constructed developments. In Corinth they are present in massive form. They delineate tendencies of the religious soul of all ages, and thereby I Corinthians, which critically illumines them and positively surpasses them by "the word of the cross," maintains its value through the ages.

3. The patterns of life

a) The Hellenistic Christians, like the original community, call themselves the "saints," "elect," the "church" (ekklesia: this self-designation perhaps first arose in the Hellenistic area). Thus they share the original self-understanding: they are consecrated to God, separated from the world, ready for the coming of the Lord. But what does it mean in practice, as a pattern of life, that one is separated from the world?

In the world of that time there were available, above all, two forms of withdrawal from the world:

The church could outwardly, as a group, retreat from the world, as, for example, the Qumran sect did. It could practice its holiness, as it were on the borderland of civilization, in isolation: Can this possibility exist in the presence of the norm of God's historical saving act? It would be a make-believe possibility, withdrawal into a non-historical make-believe holiness; "make-believe" not in the sense of subjective hypocrisy—the severe earnestness for righteousness on the part of the Qumran people cannot be denied—but "make-believe" in the sense of an objective illusion: even such a group, regardless of how rigorously it lives its religious ideal, is still world. Not only that it must maintain its material existence through the organization of production and distribution; not only that it must regulate the relationships of its members to one another by means of laws, and thus by worldly power. The problem goes still deeper: by the provision for the needs of its members, the group relieves them of material cares. Thereby it spares them the necessity of individual decision. The deed of love which is demanded again and again of the "ordinary" man in the world and which means the forgoing of something is replaced at one stroke, as it were, by a general renunciation of private possessions.

The second possibility is this: The community remains outwardly in its world, but detaches itself from the world by practicing asceticism, that is, by choosing poverty, refraining from certain foods, and practicing sexual continence. Even in this pattern of life it would have been existing in an illusion. Asceticism is first of all withdrawal of the individual into a concern for his own salvation, not concern for one's "brother"; it too is legalism and thus is worldliness.

But if the church is not to set forth its detachment from the world in any legalistic form, how then can it structure its life at all, and that in such a way that it is in harmony with the faith? This is possible only if the—

absolutely indispensable—regulations of the common life are essentially free and thus do not function as having saving power. They must be worldly-human and must not acquire any religious sanction.

b) Hence it is only a neutral and historical question, and not a crucial and substantive one, whether forms of *worship* were adopted from the synagogue or from the mysteries. The point that matters is whether the criterion of the faith becomes effective and insures that worship does not become the action of the pious man but rather gains a hearing for God's action. This rule applies to preaching, prayer, song, and sacrament. On the basis of this freedom, one is not much concerned about a uniform liturgical regulation. The Spirit blows where he wills. Of course forms were used that were already at hand: prayers, praise, blessings, songs, and formulas for the opening and close. Col. 3:16 and Eph. 5:19 mention songs. Christian psalms are found in Luke 1:46 ff. (the "Magnificat") and 1:68 ff. (the "Benedictus"); in these a pre-Christian original form still shows through. In any case they show the style-tradition of the poetry of the psalms. The songs of praise from Qumran offer splendid contemporary examples of these. In the hymns of the book of Revelation, the characteristic Jewish style appears in so intensive a fashion that some have assumed that here Jewish prayer poetry has simply been taken over. In and of itself this is conceivable. Ultimately the Christians knew themselves to be in harmony with the Old Testament-Jewish heritage. But in the case of Revelation we probably have to do with the author's own compositions. Even as such, these hymns are documents of the Jewish style-tradition. In the writings of the "Apostolic Fathers" there may be preserved some Jewish prayers—in Christian use. "Doxologies" such as Rom. 11:36 and 16:27 exhibit Jewish style; so also do the formulas of blessing such as Paul uses at the beginning and close of his letters.

But there are also non-Jewish parallels in style. Even these belong throughout not to the classical Greek but to the oriental history of style. An especially fine non-Christian example is the concluding prayer of the "Poimandres," a Gnostic tractate.

c) The forms of *mission* are free. In the world of that time, religious and popular philosophical propaganda was lively. Judaism courted "proselytes" and sympathizers (Matt. 23:15). The mysteries spread and (like Judaism) recommended themselves by means of literary propaganda. The wandering Cynic philosophers assume the features of religious proclaimers of salvation, e.g., in a famous picture by the philosopher Epictetus of the true Cynic as the herald and watchman of God. Outwardly the Christian missionaries resemble these preachers, and Paul feels obliged to distinguish himself from them (I Thess. 2:1 ff.). Of course the Christian mission—in comparison with all the then current rival movements—was intensified by virtue of the fact that it was an absolute necessity of life for the church. Judaism, for example, could in principle refrain from mission work. For its religious fellowship was also a physical and political national society. It could not at all become a universal fellowship. The wandering Cynic preachers primarily engage in self-edification; they do not found a community. They are spiritual aristocrats who wish to raise only a few above the rude masses. Their "mission" is "recruitment." This is true also of the esoteric mystery clubs. The church, on the other hand, *is* the people of God, *in that* it proclaims the Lordship of God in Christ over the whole world. If it were to refrain from doing so, it would be abandoning its very self.

d) The free and the traditional are mixed in the forms of *preaching*. The book of Acts appears to offer the most abundant material for the reconstruction of it. This book contains quite a number of "speeches": missionary addresses to Jews (the "Pentecost sermon" by Peter in Acts 2), and Stephen's discussion of Israel (Acts 7); a detailed discourse to Gentiles (Paul's "Areopagus speech," Acts 17); and an address to Christians (Paul's farewell address, Acts 20). But we must not at once infer the form of actual congregational preaching from the "speeches," for they are deliberate literary constructions. Nevertheless they provide certain hints. It must be assumed that (after the fashion of Stephen's discourse) people assembled and explained examples from the Bible, partly for warning and partly for positive edification: Heb. 11 strings together examples of faith. Further, they contrasted the experienced deliverance with the former lost condition. "Formerly—now" is a fixed form of presentation. The best example is Rom. 7:5-6; for here Paul writes the extended exposition in Rom. 7:7 ff. on the "formerly," and in Rom. 8 on the "now." Instruction about the new "walk" (Col. 3:5 ff.) belongs to the description of the Christian existence ("now"). The old and the new way of life can be contrasted in lists of virtues and vices. These lists are a form of ethical teaching which originally stems from Greek philosophy, then was adopted and modified by Hellenistic Judaism (the Wisdom of Solomon, Philo), and from there entered into Hellenistic Christianity. The *content* of the morality coincides to a large extent with the general ordinary Jewish and Greek ethical teaching. The new element is found in the *justification* of the ethical demand by means of the salvation event in Christ: the world is passing away; this conviction opens up the freedom with regard to the world which is realized positively in love. For Christ has died for the world.

e) In the Hellenistic church, the *sacraments* undergo a change in style.

The basic meaning is retained. This is given by the consistency in the rite and the cultic formulas. Baptism is performed "in the name" of Jesus Christ. The words of institution of the Supper are handed down, and they constitute the effectiveness of the action. But the understanding of the rite is expanded in the sense of the worship of the "Lord" and the experiencing of the Spirit.

Baptism removes sins, applies the salvation event to the recipient and at the same time commits him to the Lord, for obedience toward him and protection by him; it bestows the Spirit and therewith also the power to lead a new life. The commitment to the Lord is also the incorporation into his community. The Christian sacrament is distinguished from the non-Christian mystery by the fact that it does not have effect as a rite (*ex opere operato*) and is not an individualistically understood transfer of saving powers in which the individual would concentrate upon concern for himself. The new life is fellowship of the "saints," which has its norm in the fact that Christ has died for one's brother (I Cor. 8:11).

The *Supper* bestows participation in the body (and blood) of Christ (I Cor. 10:16-17). In it "spiritual food" and "spiritual drink" are proffered (I Cor. 10:3-4). As with baptism so also here, the enumeration of its effects is complex: the death of Christ is an atoning or a vicarious sacrifice; here atonement and substitution are not sharply distinguished. Both can be expressed by the same preposition "for." The Supper also introduces one into the community of the new covenant and repeatedly creates the fellowship. The rite of the Supper shows the forms to be somewhat fluid. Apparently in the Hellenistic region also, the Supper (the sacramental celebration, the dispensing of Christ's body and blood) was held in the context of an actual meal. I Corinthians contains some indications about where in the meal the dispensing of the sacrament was fitted in. We cannot say for sure, however, whether the practice was uniform throughout the church. In I Cor. 11:23 ff. the establishing of the original Supper by Jesus is pictured thus: before the common meal he gave the bread, and after the meal the cup. Apparently the meal was thus framed by the two sacramental acts. Yet at the time when Paul wrote I Corinthians this rite appears already to have been altered. From the liturgical hints in I Cor. 16:20-23 we may infer that the dispensing of both elements had been compressed into a single act: after the public worship, the unbelievers were dismissed with the solemn "Anathema"; with the "Maranatha" the community opens the esoteric meal.

Herewith another problem is broached: how is the "service of the Word," with prayer, song, Scripture reading, and preaching, related to the sacramental observance? About this we cannot postulate a general rule. To the Supper belongs the "proclamation of the Lord's death" (I Cor. 11:26), and thus the

Word. But we cannot assert conversely that the observance of the sacrament belonged to every occasion when the Word was proclaimed.

f) Finally, the *organization* is free. Above we have sketched the little that can be said about this in the original community. Its structure—insofar as we can speak of such at all—cannot be transferred without further ado to other localities. For the institution of the Twelve, and later that of the three "pillars," cannot be transplanted. Nowhere is the demand evident that the leadership of the community—outside Jerusalem also—must be organized as a collegium of twelve men. It is noteworthy that in the undoubtedly genuine epistles (it is a different matter in the disputed ones), Paul is *not* acquainted with the office of the *elders*. He apparently had not met it in Antioch (or elsewhere). In fact, even the book of Acts reports that in Antioch, prophets and teachers are the leaders of the community (Acts 13:1-3); nothing is said of elders (although the book of Acts does already know this office and presupposes it even for the Pauline communities, Acts 14:23 —thus historically incorrectly). The characteristic form is determined by the triad of chief offices which Paul enumerates in I Cor. 12:28: apostles, prophets, and teachers. These are not yet strictly separated one from another. Everyone has the position which the Spirit assigns to him by virtue of his gift; it is possible for one person to combine within himself several gifts. Since the Spirit works freely, of course there are also prophetesses; thus the daughters of Philip the "evangelist" (Acts 21:8-9). Women come to the fore in the worship services (I Cor. 11:2 ff.). The famous passage in I Cor. 14:33-36, which in contradiction to I Cor. 11 forbids them to speak in public, may not come from Paul, but may be a later addition from about the time of I Tim. (cf. 2:11-12), with the advanced kind of regulation characteristic of the Pastoral Epistles.

In summary: the organization does not yet, as in later times, possess control over salvation, nor does the individual office. There still are no sacred persons, no hierarchy. All have received the Spirit and are saints, as long as they are in the church.

CHAPTER VII

Paul (Before the Apostolic Council)

(on chronology, see Chapter II)

The *sources* are, above all, Paul's own letters, then also scattered allusions from those of his pupils (Colossians; Pastoral Epistles). In addition there is the presentation of the book of Acts. In some places the latter can be checked and corrected by the epistles, e.g., on the apostolic council (see below). Obviously, in Acts the events appear with a certain abbreviation. Indeed, the book does not even purport to give a biography of Paul, but a goal-oriented history of the course of Christianity; geographically speaking, it is the road from Jerusalem to Rome. What gaps there are in our knowledge may at least be intimated from the autobiographical sketch in II Cor. 11:22 ff.

There is difference of opinion about Paul, not only between his friends and his enemies, but also among his friends.

Between friends and enemies: to the former, he is the thinker who put Christianity in the position to become a world religion; to the others, he is the corrupter who turned the simple human religion of Jesus, the belief in God as Father and the ethic of love, into a complicated theological system, who concealed the immediacy of the relationship with God, as Jesus had displayed it, with his rabbinic-juridical doctrine of justification. The criticism of this doctrine as either incomprehensible or repugnant to the religious man is not a modern invention.

Among friends: some treasure him as the thinker who put the faith into conceptual terms and who thus helps it to come to a self-understanding. Others see precisely in his theology only the outer shell which must be shattered in order to press through to the glowing core of his mystical experience. Thus: here the religious thinker, there the prototype of the religious enthusiast.

Who then is Paul? First we must inquire about the historical circumstances of his theology, and then about the connection of this presupposition with his life story.

The conditioning milieu is first of all that of Hellenistic Judaism and its theology. Paul had studied this theology. Here he acquired concepts, ideas, and conceptions which he later used as vehicles of thought for making a comprehending exploration of the faith.

The year of his birth is unknown. In Philem. 9 he calls himself an old man. But this is a rather vague expression. According to Acts 7:58, at the time of the stoning of Stephen, in the early thirties, he was a young man.

This too leaves a good bit of leeway. Besides, this note is historically value-
less, because it does not come from primary tradition.

As the place of his origin, of his citizenship, and of a later sojourn, the
book of Acts names Tarsus in Cilicia, which is fittingly characterized in an
expression common in that time as "no mean city" (Acts 21:39). It was
then a famous center of education in which especially the Stoic philosophy
was cultivated, praised as such by Strabo and Dio Chrysostom, Paul's famous
contemporary and fellow countryman (he came from Prusa) who gave two
of his famous discourses in Tarsus. Now it is generally clear that Paul is an
avowed townsman. But his education is not Greek-philosophical; it is de-
cidedly and one-sidedly Jewish. Where elements of the contemporary popular philosophy appear (e.g., Rom. 1 and 2), they show up with a Jewish
refraction. Hellenistic Judaism had made ideas of Greek philosophy serve
its purposes in its debate with paganism. Here and there it amounted to a
comprehensive adaptation; this is true especially in the case of the philosopher Philo. The scope of Greek ideas in Paul as compared with those of
Philo appears as practically nonexistent.

The book of Acts also knows that besides the Roman-Greek name of
Paulus/Paulos, Paul also bore the Jewish name Saul/Saulos. Paul himself
does not mention this latter name. It was not uncommon among the Jews
at that time to have two names. Here is shown a certain striving for a
similar sound in the two names; cf. Jesus Justus, in Col. 4:11. In addition,
there were Semitic names which needed to be only lightly retouched in order
to become identical with genuinely Greek names: the Hebrew Simeon easily
became the Greek Simon.

Paul's family belonged to the tribe of Benjamin (Phil. 3:5). Paul himself joined the party of the Pharisees; when, where, and whether from family
tradition is unknown. His trade (again according to Acts) is that of "tentmaker." This is a business which flourished in and around Tarsus. Yet a
leatherworker or textile worker in the broader sense can also be meant.
The fact that he learned a manual trade says nothing about his social
position; this was customary for the Jewish students of the law. In its
estimate of manual labor, Judaism differed from the upper stratum of the
Greeks.

Jerome, in his commentary on Philem. 23, knows still more about the
family: Paul's parents are said to have lived first in Gischala (in Galilee)
and to have been driven to Tarsus by the chaos of war. One will hardly build
on this assertion which appears so late. For if it were correct, it would be
hard to conceive that Paul was born as the son of a Roman citizen. According
to the book of Acts, he possessed not only citizenship in Tarsus but also
Roman citizenship, and in fact had inherited the latter (Acts 22:28). Of

course some doubts may be raised about the accuracy of this statement: Paul himself never appeals to his rights as citizen. Legally speaking, the representation of the book of Acts is possible: many Jews had become citizens by virtue of the fact that as prisoners of war (e.g., under Pompey) they were taken into Roman slavery and later were freed. Freedmen acquired the rights of citizenship, though with some limitations in the first generation. Double citizenship in Rome and in a city of the empire was also possible.

According to Acts 22:3 and 26:4, Paul received his education in Jerusalem, with the famed Gamaliel. This is uncertain. From Gal. 1:22 one will rather infer that before his conversion Paul did not spend any time in Jerusalem, or at least not long. Incidentally, the dispute (on the basis of II Cor. 5:16) about whether Paul had seen Jesus in Jerusalem is a fruitless one.

Even if he had studied in Jerusalem, his education still was not that of the Palestinian rabbinate, but rather that which was determined by Hellenistic Judaism. Passages like II Cor. 3 show this.

A picture of his character can be gained from his letters only in limited measure. His temper could flare up sharply (Phil. 3:2 ff.). But only where it is required by the subject at hand does he speak about his own person. He has experiences of ecstasy (II Cor. 12:1 ff.). Even about these, however, he expresses himself only under compulsion. Thus we do not even learn whether this capacity was first awakened in his vision at the time of his conversion.

It is reliably known—he himself confirms it—that he took active measures against the Christians. But where? According to Acts, at first in Jerusalem; from there he was sent with authority to Damascus; but before he reached the city, the Lord met him in the way. Yet such behavior in Jerusalem may be ruled out by Gal. 1:22. He must rather have traveled through the country from (Cilicia-) Syria. He himself indicates the reason: zeal for the traditions of his fathers. This is properly Pharisaic and also shows that those Christians whom he was opposing had already dissociated themselves from the law; thus they were the Hellenists. When the Lord now checks him in this zeal for law and tradition, by means of this vision as such, his attitude toward the law is established, though it still must first be thought out theologically. Difficult to evaluate historically is his statement, emphatically made, that after this vision he had not conferred with "flesh and blood," i.e., had not received any Christian religious instruction; even items of doctrine like that of the Supper he had received from the Lord himself (I Cor. 11:23). The difficulty does not lie in the fact that according to Acts 9 he was introduced into the community by a Damascene Christian. On this point, as always when it conflicts with Paul, the book of Acts must be corrected. But how are we to conceive this independence of any Christian instruction? First of all, connected with this is an often observed and substantively disputed state of affairs in his epistles: that he appears to know practically nothing of the life of Jesus—except for his death and a few of his sayings. Only long after his conversion did Paul get in contact with Jerusalem (Gal. 1:15 ff.). Is his conversion then in essence the assimilation of his visionary experience? But again, how is this related to the fact that he refuses to make his visions the subject of his teaching (II Cor. 11–12)?

We must be clear on this: when Paul was fighting Christianity, the substance of Christian teaching was familiar to him. This indeed is the basis of his actions. And further: at that time the outward scope of this teaching was very small. The doctrine of God, of creation, the basic concepts of the doctrine of salvation such as sin, righteousness, and God's mercy, are the Jewish concepts. One can summarize what is new in a single sentence, the confession (see above) that "Jesus is the Messiah," or, hellenistically expressed, "Jesus is Lord." Obviously Paul understood that this sentence not merely accidentally but rather necessarily annulled the law as a way of salvation. And when the crucified Jesus, i.e., the one who had fallen under the curse of the law (Gal. 3:13), is revealed to him as alive, it is proved thereby that salvation does not depend on the law, indeed, that salvation and the Jewish maintaining of the law are in conflict. This awareness must now be put into practice by means of the mission among the Gentiles, as well as thought out, hand in hand with the mission.

Paul's first steps on this road, that of the mission and of theological understanding, are hidden from us. Epistles are preserved only from his last years, from the period after the apostolic council. About the first years after his conversion he remarks only that he went to Arabia. He went there to do mission work; this is shown by the connection of Gal. 1:16 and 17. "Arabia" is not the desert, but the land of the Nabataeans, who then follow him to Damascus (II Cor. 11:32-33). They do this surely because he was active in their region. The book of Acts is silent about this sojourn. According to this book, Paul begins in Damascus itself. He is obliged to flee from a plot against him. This agrees with II Cor. 11; only in the book of Acts the time appears foreshortened. It has Paul going then to Jerusalem, being introduced there to the community by Barnabas, and immediately appearing in public again. He is forced to withdraw, and goes first to his home in Tarsus. This picture must be replaced by Paul's own statements: some years after his call he makes a brief visit with Cephas. He passes over the content of their conversations, because it apparently was not of substantive importance for his own theology. Then he goes for at least a decade to Syria/Cilicia. There too he must have worked as a missionary. The book of Acts appears to have summed up some things from this period in the first missionary journey in Acts 13–14. Of course many scholars assume that the events of these two chapters take place only after the apostolic council. In that case this earliest period would be entirely left in darkness. Yet Paul must have remained in contact with Antioch (Acts 11:25-26, 30; 13:1-3). When the question of the Gentile Christians' freedom from the law becomes a burning issue, he, together with Barnabas, represents the community at the apostolic council.

CHAPTER VIII

The Apostolic Council

1. The presuppositions

The first problem has to do with the date (on chronology, see Chapter II). The basis for the calculation is Gal. 1–2: it takes place either 13/14 years or 16/17 years after Paul's call, the date of which again depends on the placing of the council. The book of Acts places it after the first missionary journey (Acts 15); but we were able to determine above that an extended stay of Paul in Syria/Cilicia is to be substituted for this journey. Further, a date cannot immediately be deduced from the book of Acts. There are, however, some reference points. The death of Agrippa I in the year 44 apparently precedes the council, and the latter is followed by the mission in Greece with the fixed point of about A.D. 50 in Corinth. These dates lead us to the time around 48/49. There are those, of course, who advocate an earlier date: the author of the book of Acts may have confused the order of events. A trace of this confusion appears to be evident in Acts 11: 27-30: Paul and Barnabas travel from Antioch to Jerusalem, in order to bring a gift in view of an impending famine. This occurs—so it would appear—shortly before the death of James the son of Zebedee, the imprisonment of Peter, and the death of Agrippa (Acts 12). According to the book of Acts, this was a worldwide famine. The other sources on this period know nothing of any such, though they do know of local food crises, e.g., in Palestine during the time of the governor Tiberius Alexander, A.D. 46/48. For confirmation of this date, it can be pointed out that the year 47/48 was a sabbatical year, in which the fields lay fallow, which was bound to intensify the catastrophe. Of course there remains the element of contradiction in the fact that this date does not agree with the book of Acts. Efforts have been made to resolve the difficulty, frequently as follows: Luke has confused two things. That earlier journey did not serve to deliver a collection, but was the journey to the council, which actually took place in the year 43/44. It is in fact true that in the outline of Gal. 1 there is no place for a journey of Paul and Barnabas together before the council. However: Acts 11:27-30 is not an ancient source account, but a later composition of the author out of various recollections; it cannot be used in determining dates.

Independent of the dating there is the substantive question: there is now a large number of Gentile Christians who are not bound by the Jewish law. Their position must be fundamentally clarified. Was the failure to subject them to the law merely a matter of tactics in adaptation, in order to render their entrance into the church easier? Was there not herein a culpable neglect of the fact that the church is the true Israel, and that therefore the way into the church at the same time leads—by way of circumcision—into the law? On the other hand, the demand for the circumcision of the Gentiles also would mean that the salvation event was not the only condition of salvation, that for the reception of grace a human achievement was to be brought forward. And it would depend on this achievement whether God would fulfill his offer. Christianity would then be a radical Jewish sect. Thus the alternative is posed: salvation through God's act or through the fulfillment of certain rules. In this connection it is no longer important whether it is the fulfilling of the whole law or only of its most important parts that is demanded of the Gentiles.

The matter has other aspects as well. It was not the Gentiles who first detached themselves from the law, but Jewish Christians. Indeed, the emancipation of the Jews had prompted Paul to a counter-action. Thus the fact that the Gentile Christians were not brought under the law was not based on any refusal of theirs; this had not even been demanded of them from the outset, although the missionaries were Jews. Jews and Gentiles lived together without strain. Thus Paul could even, without further ado, make Titus, a Gentile, his co-worker (even before the council, Gal. 2:3). The practical problem of the mission and the theological problem were intertwined, and were even identical.

As to the concrete *occasion,* Paul betrays nothing but the indication that he had traveled to Jerusalem on the basis of a "revelation." That is to say, the problem had already, through some occasion, become a burning issue. Then a fundamental solution was no longer to be evaded. And it was clear to Paul what this solution had to be.

Acts 15 has something more to tell us. Here the impetus stems from members of the Jerusalem community who are agitating in Antioch and are interpreting the circumcision of the Gentiles as a condition of salvation. Thereupon Barnabas and Paul go to Jerusalem. *Paul* avoids saying that they went as delegates of the community. For himself, at least, he emphasizes that he received the commission from the Lord himself. It is his concern to avoid giving the Galatians any suggestion that he is dependent upon human agencies. He meets the Jerusalemites as equal with equals, while in the book of Acts he appears as representative of a community that is dependent upon Jerusalem, one who is seeking instruction.

Although in Galatians Paul is speaking *pro domo,* his own explanation of things is the closer of the two to the historical realities. This is evident from the results of the discussion. The two parties concur that an agreement must be found, for the unity of the church must not be lost. It may be asked who had the greater interest at stake, tactically speaking. This was obviously the side of the new communities and their representative. Indeed, Paul above all finds himself in a new situation in church history. For him, not only outward recognition is at stake, but his very "call" itself: he was called to the Gentiles by means of a revelation. If the Gentiles must come under the law, his commission is frustrated (Gal. 2:2;)—and he will have to give account to the Lord.

2. The course of events

The substantive position of Paul is clear from the first, for it is theologically grounded. On the other hand, it is understandable that among the Jewish Christians the opinions were divergent. Prominent Jewish Christians like Barnabas had already long been at work, with success. The new congregations were not to be overlooked. In addition, there were Jewish Christians for whom the law was still in effect. It would be an oversimplification to describe them as narrow-minded. In their favor they had the salvation history: the church is Israel. Jesus, the Messiah, had established the New Covenant through his sacrifice. The sign of the covenant and of the promise is the law, along with circumcision. Whether circumcision was *replaced* by baptism or was rather sealed by it was not a simple question for a Jewish Christian.

As to the details of the discussions, Paul indicates that there were vigorous debates (Gal. 2:4): "false brethren" are at work; that is, they are demanding general circumcision in the church. "False brethren" must not be taken to mean that they were consciously malicious. It is an objective judgment: their behavior was working against the essence of the act of salvation. For Paul, a compromise position in the center was impossible, because freedom is the direct consequence of the cross, which has broken the curse of the law.

According to Acts 15, those who represented the standpoint of the law were Pharisees, and thus former comrades of Paul. This is probable anyway, apart from this report, and can even be deduced without reports in the sources. The book of Acts gives more details about the further course of events. According to it, the discussion was completely dominated by Peter and James. Both give their judgment—in substance coming out to the same thing: it would be too great a burden for the Gentiles to have to endure the law. The assembly agreed with them. Barnabas and Paul are only recipients of the decision. John, who according to Gal. 2 was one of the leading figures in the negotiations, is passed over, as is the presence of the Gentile Christian Titus, whom Paul uses as an example: circumcision was not imposed upon him. In general, Acts 15 is again one-sidedly engaged in favor of the leading role of Jerusalem. But in reality Paul was a partner in the proceedings, not merely one who received orders. Where the book of Acts and Galatians diverge from each other, Galatians always deserves to be preferred. Luke apparently did not possess a coherent source on the council but attempted to form a picture from scattered reports.

The conclusion: agreement is reached between Paul and the Jerusalem "authorities," among whom the three "pillars" are especially prominent (Gal. 2:6-10; enigmatic is the casual remark that it was of no concern to him what these authorities once had been). No "tax" is levied on Paul, i.e., the Gentile Christians are free without reservation. We are also unable to be entirely certain in explaining the statement that with respect to the circumcision of Titus he had not yielded even for an instant. Why does he emphasize this? Were there rumors circulating in Galatia to the effect that he had indeed yielded in part? Of course this assumption is not necessary. One can also interpret the statement to mean that Paul is simply citing with emphasis this especially clear proof.

The agreement also affects the Jewish Christians: they continue to keep the law, and thus remain what they are. Is this now a compromise between two positions? No, for Paul's demand for liberty is not an abstract principle but the setting forth of the "by grace alone." This is actualized for the Gentiles so that they do not need to produce any human achievements through the adoption of the law's stipulations. For the Jewish Christians the same point of view means that neither is any achievement—in their case, by shaking off the law—imposed on them. "By grace alone" means that each one is called as what he is, the Jew as Jew, the Gentile as Gentile; in I Cor. 7 Paul formulates it as "each one in his own calling." The Jew is no more obliged to give up his Jewishness than is the Gentile to become a Jew. Of course the keeping of the law has now taken on a new meaning for him: it now is no longer a means of gaining salvation but precisely a sign that salvation is bestowed without condition.

With this agreement the foundation for all the future mission is laid. This does not mean that the specific problems for all times were solved. Even this solution is a historical one; this will soon be evident. In the obligation of the Jewish Christians to the law, a conflict is set in motion, but of course at the same time the possibility of settling it is afforded. An open question is: how, on the basis of this decision, was the life together in the same community of Jewish and Gentile Christians formed? Was this not a step backward? Previously they had lived together without strain. But now must not the Jewish Christians, because of their ritual prescriptions of purity, withdraw? In Paul's view, certainly not, since for him the tie to the law is not a "legal" one; I Cor. 9:20-21! But apart from him conflicts could break out.

For the establishing of the mission, two additional arguments served, which did not limit the agreement achieved but concretized it:

1) The areas of labor were marked off: Peter and Paul stand over against each other as the exemplary apostle to the Jews and to the Gentiles respectively. Both are legitimized for their office by the Lord himself. From this the inference is now drawn that the Jerusalemites from now on are responsible for the Jews, and "we" (i.e., Paul and Barnabas) for the Gentiles. This delimitation is understood by many expositors as a geographical one: the one concentrates on Palestine, inhabited predominantly by Jews, and the rest of the world falls the lot of the others. But one cannot well imagine such a division as a practicable work program. Besides, this explanation would not correspond to the intent of the whole agreement. What it means is rather the Jews and the Gentiles in general. This is evident already from the fact that after the council Peter appears outside Palestine. Again one suspects a germ of future conflicts: when Paul comes into a city where Jews reside—and this is the case in every larger city—must he then refrain from addressing himself to the Jews? He did not do so: I Cor. 9:20! And his theology made it impossible for him to do so: Rom. 9–11! But this means that conflicts become almost unavoidable—and they do break out.

2) Paul and Barnabas obligate themselves to gather in their missionary territory a collection for the poor, specifically for those in Jerusalem (cf. Rom. 15:25-26). Paul gives assurance that he has immediately applied himself to the work. The collection is more than a charitable action. From this point on it runs like a red thread through the life of Paul. Therefore we shall have to return to it repeatedly in later passages. But since it gave and

still gives rise to many discussions, the fundamental matter should be treated here. Incidentally, it is striking that the book of Acts is practically silent about this agreement. It mentions it neither in chap. 15, nor later in the portrayal of Paul's mission, nor, where its mention appears unavoidable, in connection with Paul's last journey to Jerusalem, which in fact had as its only aim the delivery of the collection (Rom. 15:25-26). Only once is it mentioned, casually and belatedly (Acts 24:17), and then in such an obscure way that a reader unfamiliar with Paul's letters can hardly understand the allusion.

Now this collection has been explained thus: in reality it was a regular church assessment which was imposed upon Paul. By it he had been compelled to recognize that he, together with his congregations, was subordinate to the original community as the legitimate chief place of the whole church. Here Jerusalem is already playing a role like that of Rome at a later time. "The poor" does not mean needy ones in a social sense but is a religious designation for the original community. In support of this interpretation, reference is made to Judaism: every adult Jew in the entire world must pay a tax yearly to the temple in Jerusalem. From this it is inferred that following this example the collection had been established as the tax of the "true Israel." In actuality this alleged parallel is an argument *against* this hypothesis:

(a) *All* Jews, even those residing in Palestine, had to pay the temple tax. This would then accordingly have to mean for the Christians a tax on all, not on the Gentile Christians only.

(b) The temple tax is a regular, yearly assessment, the collection a one-time occasion.

(c) The collection is, as Rom. 15:25-26 and II Cor. 8:9 explain, a charitable action for actually poor people.

But of course the meaning of it is not exhausted in *caritas* as such. This collection is the visible demonstration that the church is a unity; that with its founding the Gentile church—in different life forms—is not detached from the historical setting; that precisely when the church now is composed of two groups not only of different life styles but also of diverse *heilsgeschichtlich* stance, she is the *one* church of Jews and Gentiles. The collection demonstrates the historicality of the church and the universality of salvation: the two are a unity.

In summary: a foundation is laid, but there are still gaps. Some Jewish Christians did not acquiesce in the decision (Galatians!). The life of Jewish and Gentile Christians together is more problematical than previously. The separation of responsibilities between Jerusalem and Paul is unclear and will lead to conflicts.

3. The problem of the "apostolic decree"

At one point there is an open contradiction between Paul's account and
that of the book of Acts. It is true that even according to Acts 15:10, 19,
the "yoke" of the law was not imposed on the Gentiles. But there is an
additional point here: instead of the law, the Gentiles are obligated to
observe a minimum of ritual prescriptions; this additional decision is usually
called the "apostolic decree." The book of Acts presents it no less than
three times (15:20, 29; 21:25). Its content: the Gentiles are to abstain,
first, from meat sacrificed to idols, second, from fornication, third, from
eating "things strangled" (i.e., meat from animals which are not slaughtered
according to the Jewish ritual prescriptions), and fourth, from blood (foods
which are prepared with blood, e.g., blood sausage). These are the four
prescriptions which according to Lev. 17–18 apply also to the non-Jews
who live in Israel.

That this decree was issued at the council is ruled out by Paul's definite
assertion that no additional stipulations were made (Gal. 2:6, with the
already discussed exception, which is not a rule at all: "only that we should
remember the poor," vs. 10).

Can the contradiction between Acts and Paul be explained? Of course
any attempt remains a conjecture. One hypothesis is: Paul did know about
the decree. This is evident from various traces in his epistles, above all in
I Cor. 8–10. These chapters show that in Corinth two subjects of the decree
have become acute issues: sexual immorality and the attitude toward meat
sacrificed to idols. Paul deals with them in detail, but does not mention
the decree. Did he not *know* it, or did he not *want* to know anything of it?
Is not the latter probable? Why then has just this problematic arisen? Must
we not assume that the decree has become known in Corinth and has now
kindled these disputes? One can conjecture still further: since Peter is mentioned in I Corinthians, it could be indicated that he has been in Corinth
personally and has been contending for the decree, while Paul has rejected
it and therefore passes over it in silence in his epistle. Yet with this
hypothesis, inferences are too confidently drawn from the silence. Besides,
even if the decree had come to Corinth in this way, it would be proved
precisely thereby that it was *not* decided on at the council, but by some
other group on another occasion and, in any case, *after* the council.

On behalf of the same assumption—that Paul was acquainted with the
decree—appeal is also made to the Galatian epistle. It is striking to note
how heavily Paul emphasizes that there was no additional requirement. His
presentation is polemical, one-sided. In the time between the council and
the composition of Galatians, the decree is supposed to have been published

in Galatia. Now Paul explains (thus the stress is to be placed in the sentence): "To *me* (to me alone, personally) this demand was not made."

Paul certainly is waging a personal apologetic in this passage; but for this very reason he could not have argued *thus* if the decree had actually been issued by the council. Otherwise he would have played trump cards right into the hands of his opponents. Thus it remains likely that he did not know the decree at all. If he did know it, he is in any case denying that it is a part of the agreement at Jerusalem, and he disputes its validity (not with respect to the contents, fornication, etc., but with respect to its legal character).

But how does the book of Acts come to connect the decree with the council? In order at least to arrive at some reasonable conjectures, we must ask: where are these definitions meaningful? Thus where must they have been produced? Obviously they are meant to make it possible for Jewish and Gentile Christians to live together: the Gentiles are to hold to the Jewish prescriptions enough that the Jews will not be contaminated by their association with them: i.e., the decrees arose in a mixed community. This fits in with the fact that the question as to the structure of the common life of the two groups had not been answered at the council; indeed, that the council could even lead to a worsening of the situation.

Again, one can allow the conjecture—it is no more than this—to range still further: in Antioch—apparently not long after the council—there comes the famous collision between Paul and Peter (together with Barnabas: Gal. 2:11 ff.). Peter comes to Antioch and associates with the Gentiles in the old free style. But then some of James's followers come—and Peter and Barnabas withdraw from association with the Gentile Christians. Here is portrayed a possible negative effect of the council: that the existing mixed communities are divided, since the Jewish Christians now are brought back under the law again. In this the letter of the council's decision is being followed—but what about its spirit? In any case, Paul contests such a conclusion. He argues: through his actual table fellowship with the Gentile Christians, Peter has documented the fact that the division was not the intention of the council. The agreement of the council is not a law which can be so formalized that it can be employed against the council's own presuppositions and intentions—the unity of the church. Peter and his comrades had understood this and practiced it quite correctly. When they now retreat to the letter, away from the spirit, they do so not out of subjective conviction or objective substance, but out of subjective fear of pressure from without, that is, out of irrelevant and improper reasons to which they are sacrificing the unity of the church. They are playing the hypocrite, that is, their conduct and the truth of the gospel are poles apart. With the report of this incident in the Galatian epistle, Paul appropriately introduces the extensive, fundamental exposition of the doctrine of justification.

One would like to know how the affair turned out. In Antioch the majority appears to have chosen the side of Peter and Barnabas. Paul's connection with this community appears to be broken off from this time on. He also no longer works with Barnabas. The separation is noted in Acts 15:36-39, though it is given the innocent interpretation of a purely personal difference. From this time on, Antioch disappears from the field of vision until the period after the year 100, the time of bishop Ignatius. In the latter's epistles, the community appears to be essentially Gentile Christian (Ign. Phld. 5.2; Magn. 8.1; 9.1). For him Paul is an authority. Perhaps one may infer from this either that that break was not total (Paul does later mention Cephas and Barnabas without rancor; cf., e.g., I Cor. 9!) or that relations were later reestablished (cf. Acts 18:22).

Now it is possible to picture the relationship between this dispute and the decree conjecturally thus: this collision rendered the gaps in the council's decisions evident, namely the lack of a rule for living together in a mixed community. In order to close these gaps, someone drew up and issued the decree, of course without Paul's knowledge and agreement, but covered with the authority of Peter. According to another hypothesis, the decree had already been decided on in Jerusalem and sent to Antioch *before* the council. This became then the specific impetus for the council: the conflict broke out in Antioch; now it was to be eliminated. But there are weighty considerations arguing against this placing of the decree: could Paul then have been silent about it? Could he in this way blame Peter—and not James—for the initiative in this dispute?

The decree has a later history. It prevailed, to a large extent. In a later time, when the church consisted predominantly of Gentile Christians and the battles over the law had ceased to resound, people no longer understood it as a cultic regulation but as a moral commandment, namely as a prohibition of idol worship, bloodshed, and fornication. Therein the distinction between mortal sins and lesser sins is portrayed. On the positive side, the prohibitions were expanded with the "Golden Rule." The decree was incorporated into some manuscripts of the New Testament in this new version.

CHAPTER IX

Paul and His Communities

1. Overview

Here we come into the only epoch and the only area of primitive Christian history which can be perceived directly. For here primary sources, the (genuine) epistles of Paul, are available; all that are extant come from the time after the council. They give a picture of Paul's mission after the council, the progress of his labors, the founding and formation of communities, and of their inner life. Added to the epistles as a secondary source, there is the book of Acts, which makes it possible to some extent to follow the outward course of things. It is true that this book oversimplifies this course of events; but it relates Paul's route through the various areas and the sequence of the founding of the communities, on the whole, reliably.

This is true in spite of the fact that through a comparison of the book of Acts with the epistles, some gaps become evident: e.g., in Acts, the mission in Galatia, where a number of communities existed (Gal. 1:2), is actually passed over. Galatia is mentioned only twice in passing: according to Acts 16:6 Paul travels through Phrygia and Galatia, but without preaching there; the Holy Spirit prevents him from doing so. He is to travel at once to the coast and from there to cross over to Macedonia. Then in Acts 18:23 one learns, surprisingly, of a second trip through the same countries, when Paul "strengthens all the disciples." The discrepancy between the two notes is so striking that by way of explanation of the former it has been suggested that we translate it to read: "They went through Phrygia and the Galatian region since they had been hindered by the Spirit from preaching in (the province of) Asia." This would indicate that in Phrygia and Galatia—as contrasted with Asia—they did preach. The Greek wording does allow this interpretation; but then the geographical data no longer fit. For Paul's way then would lead from the west coast of Asia Minor to the east or northeast into the interior of the country. But the book of Acts intends to indicate precisely the reverse of this, that Paul is surely and steadily led from inland Asia Minor to Macedonia.

Another possibility of explanation is this: the communities to which the Galatian epistle is addressed do not at all lie in Galatia proper (Galatia: the abode of the Celts of Asia Minor, around the present-day Ankara, at that time Ancyra). It refers instead to communities south of the country of Galatia, whose founding is told in Acts 13–14 ("first missionary journey"). The cities there indeed were not inhabited by Galatians, but they belonged to the same province in the political structure. If one assumes this, then one no longer needs to seek for the "communities of Galatia" in unnamed places. But could Paul thus, without further ado, address others as "Galatians," a name which at that time was not exactly highly regarded?

Another lack in the book of Acts concerns the inner life of the communities: for it, there are no internal struggles such as become visible in Galatians and I and II Corinthians. The church appears as a firm, fixed block. In it the pure doctrine is preached and accepted. This picture still has its impact today. In the book of Acts there are only a few apparent exceptions to the rule of unity: in Ephesus there appears a strange group of Christians who know nothing of the Holy Spirit (Acts 19:1 ff.). And Apollos preaches there, filled with the Spirit, but at first only inadequately informed about the teaching of the Christian faith (Acts 18:24 ff.). But these episodes only contribute to the total picture; such outsiders are quickly and smoothly incorporated into the church. It is only for the time after Paul's death that the emergence of internal crises is foreseen. The prediction of such at least is indicated as part of Paul's testament (Acts 20:29-30).

The book of Acts tailors the whole expansion of the church after the council to the person of Paul. This is done in two ways:

a) The work of other missionaries is no longer considered; if they are even mentioned, it is only with a bare indication, such as that Barnabas and John Mark worked on Cyprus (15:39). They are, so to speak, dismissed from view with this note. Passed over also are Peter's activity, the branching out of the original community (again except for one allusion, in 21:20), and the mission of Jesus' brothers (I Cor. 9:5).

b) Paul's colleagues appear as mere traveling companions. Thus important people like Titus are not even mentioned. In actuality the colleagues Timothy, Silas, Titus, etc., fulfilled independent tasks. In critical situations they were entrusted with important missions, thus Timothy according to I Cor. 4:17, and Titus according to II Cor. 7:6. The organization of the collection (see above) demanded a certain ability at organization and in independent co-operative labor (II Cor. 8–9). Even after Paul has moved on to another place, the communities remain centers of the mission, which is led by Paul's pupils. This can be discovered from the Epistle to the Colossians. This epistle is perhaps (or rather: probably) not composed by Paul himself. It reflects conditions in Asia Minor, in the vicinity of Ephesus: in the Lycus valley there exist Christian communities which were not founded by Paul personally, in Colossae, Hierapolis, and Laodicea (on this, cf. also the undoubtedly genuine Epistle to Philemon). The founder of the community in

Colossae is Epaphras (Col. 1:7; 4:12; Philem. 23; not named in the book of Acts).

One of the questions completely neglected by the book of Acts is that of the financing of this mission. The traditional notion, which of course is based on Acts and some passages in Paul's letters, is too idyllic: Paul is a craftsman (Acts 18:3: "tentmaker") and as such earns his living. This is in fact confirmed by Paul himself, in I Thess. 2:9; I Cor. 4:12; 9:1 ff. Of course this is not to be doubted. But with his pay he probably could not even finance his own costs (unless he was a small businessman): travel costs, books, writing materials, pay for stenographers. And it would not have sufficed at all to pay his colleagues (again, for their travel costs, etc.). An indication of the activity in its organizational center is found in II Cor. 11:28.

Paul gives some indications: throughout the church the rule applies that the missionaries are supported by the communities in which they are staying: I Cor. 9. Now Paul and Barnabas voluntarily renounce this support without making a rule of the renunciation. Paul gives a twofold justification of his action. First, with his special position: he is not a missionary of his own free will; he has been taken into service by the Lord; he cannot do otherwise; a constraint is laid upon him. From this he draws the conclusion not to accept any remuneration. Second, thereby he preserves his independence. When this is not at stake or is not put in a doubtful light, he can accept support, and he does so, for example, from the community in Philippi: Phil. 4:10 ff.; clearest is II Cor. 11:7-10. Perhaps Acts 18:5 also indicates something of this: first Paul works in Corinth as a craftsman; then Silas and Timothy arrive from Macedonia; from this point on, Paul devotes himself wholly to the Word. This probably means that they brought the needed money, so that Paul is no longer dependent on his earnings. Incidentally, he keeps these funds for support separate in principle from the collection for Jerusalem. He places emphasis on the fact that the latter is checked by representatives of the communities: II Cor. 8:18 ff.; 9:3 ff.

Theology and missionary methods are most intimately connected. The foundation is Paul's consciousness of being sent as an "apostle."

The concept of the self-consciousness has fallen into discredit in modern theology: Paul's life and work cannot be understood in terms of the subjective and psychological, and thus of the self-conscious, but from the objective character of his commission and the theological interpretation of it, and thus in terms of his self-"understanding." Now for him his call certainly was not only a subjective experience, but also a call that occurred objectively. He had not—according to his own consciousness—created his commission out of himself. And in the theological exposition of his work, he does not trouble himself with the psychical side of his experience. But this very fact can be labeled as his self-consciousness.

The content of his consciousness of mission is that he is sent to the *Gentiles*. This presupposes liberty. He can be a Jew to the Jews, a Gentile to the Gentiles (I Cor. 9:19 ff.). The sphere of his labor is the whole world (i.e., in fact, the Roman Empire), with one limitation: so long as others are not already doing missionary work in a given place. He does not encroach on another's territory (Rom. 15:20). His method results from this principle:

The principle cited does not mean that he avoids places where there are already Christians, but those where an actual community already exists. When he came to Corinth, some Christians were indeed already there, such as the couple Aquila and Prisc(ill)a; the same was true in Ephesus, according to Acts. Paul now builds a community. He goes into the centers, such as the provincial capitals: Thessalonica, Corinth, Ephesus. When the community here is firmly established—after some two or three years—he shifts the place of his activity. The community carries on the mission. At the time of II Corinthians there were already several communities in Achaia (1:1). When Paul has finished gathering the collection and is about to deliver it to Jerusalem, he sees his task in the eastern half of the Roman Empire as completed (Rom. 15:19). Therefore after his trip to Jerusalem he intends to go to the west—not to Rome, for a community already exists there, but to Spain (Rom. 15:24, 28). In preparation for this journey, which will take him by way of Rome, he writes the letter to the Romans.

Incidentally, a warning must be uttered against a cliché that occasionally appears in the literature. Frequently this missionary procedure is traced directly to Paul's eschatology. He did expect the end of the world in the near future. On the other hand, he saw his task as a worldwide one. Now one can combine these and say that he felt himself under an immense pressure of time; that he was aware that before the return of the Lord he had to reach the ends of the earth; that therefore he hastened without rest from city to city.

That he hoped for the early coming of the Lord is just as true as that he understood his mission as "ecumenical." But he did not draw this conclusion therefrom. Nothing shows any feverish haste; on the contrary, he gives himself time. He is neither an apocalypticist nor a technician in making converts. His main point of view and his conclusion from his eschatology and his concept of the church did not read "everywhere," but rather "building up of the church." He knows that others are working beside him. He counts on factors which are overlooked in modern interpretation; for example, that Satan is casting hindrances in his path (I Thess. 2:18).

According to the book of Acts, the usual way leading to the founding of a community is this: in a new place Paul first goes into the synagogue and attempts to win the Jews. These, however, refuse, either altogether or for the most part. Paul must leave the synagogue, and now he turns to the Gentiles. He is able to find a point of contact with the "God-fearers," that is, those who are sympathetic toward Judaism.

That Paul sought a point of contact in the synagogues may not be ruled out by the agreement of the apostolic council. There are Jews among his co-workers. According to II Cor. 11:24, he had five times suffered the synagogal punishment of thirty-nine lashes. This presupposes that he appeared before the synagogue and submitted to the disciplinary authority of the Jewish community. There he could also most readily gain contact with the Gentiles. Yet the presentation given by the book of Acts is too schematic; it betrays a certain tendentious character: according to the order of the *Heilsgeschichte* as Luke sees it, Paul must first seek to win the Jews (13:46). Only when they refuse to believe is the way to the Gentiles indicated. In this form, this does not correspond—at least not entirely—to the Pauline understanding of the *Heilsgeschichte*. He sketches this out in Rom. 9–11: Certainly salvation appeared in Israel, but Israel rejected it. It is for just this reason that he is sent to the *Gentiles*. Through their acceptance of it, Israel was to be made jealous. God's aim is also Israel's salvation.

2. The outward course of the mission

It is customary, following the book of Acts, to divide this part of Paul's mission into the second and third missionary journeys. In fact, there is in Acts 18:18 ff. a certain division indicated by a journey of Paul to Palestine. But it has no objective significance in the shaping of the mission.

Apart from the deficiencies mentioned above, the book of Acts reliably presents the course of events. It heavily underscores the transition from Asia Minor to Europe (Macedonia: 16:6-10). From this point on, the history of Paul stands in full light; from here on, it is also documented by his letters. Of course these are concentrated on those happenings in the communities which are immediately connected with questions of the faith and problems of the ordering of life. Only in exceptional cases do they go into the personal fate of Paul: the Corinthian epistles mention an instance of extreme peril in Ephesus (I Cor. 15:32; II Cor. 1:8); II Corinthians contains a catalog of sufferings which suggests what he encountered at the various mission stations as well as on the journeys between them (11:22 ff.).

Incidentally, even the book of Acts does not give any travel experiences, though it does tell of things that befell him in the cities.

The first station in Europe is *Philippi* (inland from Neapolis, the present Kawalla), correctly presented in Acts as a Roman colony. To be sure, that account must be corrected in several other points; in this passage it is heavily obscured with legends. The name of the first convert, Lydia, is lacking in the Philippian epistle, and conversely, the people named there are missing in the book of Acts. In reading the latter, one gets the impression (in spite of 16:18) that Paul's stay was relatively brief. But this does not fit in with the picture of the community which the epistle affords: it is outwardly and inwardly strengthened, and stands on its own feet. This probably presupposes a longer period of building-up. Paul and Acts agree in saying that he had to endure hardship there (I Thess. 2:2). The sharp attack on the Jews in Phil. 3:2 makes us suspect Jewish participation in this. In the book of Acts, on the other hand, the occasion for it is given in some measure in anecdotal form: Paul drives the spirit of soothsaying out of a fortune-telling slave girl. This means a loss to her owners, who previously had made their livelihood from the slave girl. They drag the missionaries before the authorities.

In any case, when Paul left the city (or, rather, was compelled to leave), the community was firmly established. Paul is and remains affectionately and personally related to the community as to no other. Even after his departure he receives support from Philippi, and from this community he accepts it (Phil. 4:10 ff.). No other epistle has such a warm tone as that to the Philippians. Of course even on the horizon of this community there arises the fanaticism which gave Paul so much trouble in Corinth (see below); but the community as such appears intact.

The next station is *Thessalonica* (Acts 17:1 ff., confirmed by I Thess. 2:2-3; cf. Phil. 4:16), the present Saloniki, at that time capital of the province of Macedonia. In the book of Acts we get the familiar picture: Paul enters the synagogue. Some Jews and many sympathizers are won. The counter-action begins. Paul and Silas (in this passage Timothy is passed over) must leave the city; they go to the provincial city of Berea. According to Acts 17:2 the entire stay in Thessalonica lasted only some three weeks. This is improbably brief. For here too there subsequently existed a sturdy community, as I Thessalonians, written soon afterward (in Corinth), shows: the community has proved true in suffering (2:14); its moral state is praised (4:1; cf. the general praise in 1:8, then in 3:6 ff.). Paul emphasizes that here he accepted no support from the community; he worked, and he also received help from Philippi. Later he did accept help from the communities in Macedonia (II Cor. 11:9). The flourishing of Christianity in this area is illumined by II Cor. 8:1 ff.; in spite of their suffering and their deep poverty, the communities there give joyously for the Jerusalem community.

About *Berea* we know only what the book of Acts tells (17:10 ff.). Paul himself does not mention this community in the extant epistles. It may be included in the collective designation "Macedonia" (II Cor. 8–9; 11:9). Among Paul's companions on his last trip to Jerusalem, there is a Sopater from Berea (Acts 20:4); these companions, as representatives of their communities, deliver their contribution to the collection.

Although at first things in Berea went more favorably than in Thessalonica, Paul finally had to leave here too. The book of Acts simplifies the events. According to it, Paul himself goes to *Athens*. At first he leaves Silas and Timothy behind; but they are to follow him soon. In Athens he waits—in vain—for them. During this stay he delivers his famous speech on the Areopagus, but wins only a few people for Christianity (Acts 17:34). The two fellow workers then reach him only at the next station, in Corinth (Acts 18:5). I Thessalonians shows, however, that Timothy was with Paul in Athens; but he was sent back to Thessalonica to strengthen the community in their sufferings (I Thess. 3:1 ff.). It is correct that he then joined Paul again in Corinth. On the strength of his report, Paul wrote I Thessalonians.

Paul's visit in Athens is especially famed—thanks to an artistic piece of Luke's, a portrayal in which local Athenian color is guardedly and successfully introduced and which opens into the "Areopagus speech," which exerts its fascination even until today. Of course it is a masterpiece not of Paul but of Luke. Apparently it did not succeed in establishing a community in Athens. The book of Acts knows only two names of converts. In I Cor. 2:3 Paul makes an allusion, for us all too brief, about his condition at that time.

In *Corinth* it was quite a different matter; there he succeeded in getting a foothold. At that time Corinth was the capital of the province of Achaia (central and southern Greece) and at the same time, thanks to its prominent location "between two seas," an important commercial spot on one of the main lines of East-West trade. Its alleged immorality was proverbial. But it will hardly have been different from other large and port cities.

The chronology in Chapter II has indicated that Paul's sojourn in Corinth forms the pivotal point for the dating of his career.

Here he meets the couple Aquila and Prisca (thus Paul; Priscilla, according to Acts 18:2). They had been expelled from Rome by the edict of Claudius mentioned earlier. It must be assumed that they were already Christians when Paul became acquainted with them. In I Corinthians he lists the people whom he baptized in Corinth, only a few, it is true, but still the first (1:14 ff.; 16:15). Aquila and Prisca are not among them. Besides, he does not indicate elsewhere that he had converted these two, nor does the book of Acts. But if they were already Christians, we see here a trace of the earliest emergence of Christianity in Rome—already before the year 50—and in Corinth: Paul was not the first Christian in the city. Nevertheless he asserts, with justification, that he had founded the community and baptized the "firstfruits" of Achaia. For we cannot speak of a community there before his appearance on the scene. This course of events, incidentally, was to be repeated in Ephesus.

According to Acts 18:11, his sojourn lasted about one and a half years. More clearly than elsewhere the detachment of the Christian community from the synagogue and its becoming organizationally independent is underscored (Acts 18:6-7). Gentile Christians form the majority in the community (I Cor. 12:2). But there are also Jewish Christians (Paul indicates this in I Cor. 9:19 ff.). The book of Acts knows, *inter alia*, of the conversion of Crispus, one of the leaders of the synagogue. In the list of greetings in Rom. 16:21 ff., three are singled out explicitly as Jewish Christians: Lucius, Jason, and Sosipater. If one combines the names in I Corinthians, Acts, and Rom. 16:21 ff., the large number of Latin names is noticeable. This is not surprising: Corinth had been destroyed in 146 B.C. by the Romans. It was not until 44 B.C. that Caesar refounded the city, this time as a Roman colony (cf. Philippi; see above), that is, as a settlement which served chiefly to accommodate the veterans of the army. From that time on the city bears a strong Roman stamp; the excavations (Latin inscriptions!) provide a picture of this.

This Christian community quickly flourished. Its significance at the end of the first century is reflected in the prophecy in Acts 18:9-10 and in I Clement, the writing of the Roman church to the Corinthian one (see above). Of all the Pauline communities it is also the most intellectually active, and therefore especially vulnerable also. Paul is obliged to write several long letters to this community (see below).

The time between the departure from Corinth and the beginning in *Ephesus* is obscure. The account in the book of Acts can hardly be understood. Did Luke for some reason put together a detailed account in such a way that it became unclear, or did he do just the opposite, gather scattered reports and painstakingly try to set them in a certain sequence? One should read Acts 18:18–19:7! Paul goes to Ephesus; however, he does not remain there, but travels to Palestine—we do not learn why and for what purpose. He returns to Ephesus by way of Syria and inland Asia Minor. One episode, which is related in this passage (19:1-7), cannot be utilized because it is so obscure. More important is the note about Apollos, who began the work in Ephesus independent of Paul. He quickly developed into a highly regarded teacher who also extended his activity to Corinth; I Corinthians (1:12; 3:4 ff., 16:12) shows with what success. Aquila and Prisca moved from Corinth to Ephesus—probably in order to give support to Paul's work. This is confirmed by Paul's letters (I Cor. 16:19—greetings from Ephesus to Corinth; Rom. 16:3? if Rom. 16 is, as many assume, a fragment of an epistle to Ephesus, not to Rome!).

The new center, Ephesus, was at that time the seat of the governor of the province of Asia, one of the largest and most famous cities of the empire, a commercial center and seat of the widely esteemed cult of the "Ephesian Artemis," whose temple was one of the seven wonders of the world. No less famous, of course, was the "Ephesian literature," that is to say, magical literature, which flourished behind the religion. The book of Acts gives fascinating episodes with lively local color. Paul appears as one of the itinerant teachers of that time. He rents an auditorium (19:9). His success is documented in typically Ephesian scenes: the occult arts are brought to grief—not without a touch of the burlesque—and books of magic go up in flames. The name of the "great Artemis" must be invoked in order to defend business interests against the Christian danger. The book of Acts seeks to avoid the suggestion that Paul was forcibly driven out (Acts 20:1). Yet this may well have happened. His allusions in I Cor. 15:32 and II Cor. 1:8 can hardly be understood in any other sense. As compared with Paul's own allusions, the episode of the tumult caused by Demetrius the silversmith (Acts 19) gives a somewhat idyllic impression. Yet the indication that certain businesses suffered because of the spread of Christianity is instructive, at least for Luke's time. The famous letter of Pliny the Younger to Trajan about the treatment of Christians, which was written only a little later, discloses something of the same sort (Appendix II:7a).

Was Paul temporarily imprisoned in Ephesus? Of course the book of Acts says nothing about it; but this is no proof. Paul was in prison several times: II Cor. 11:23. The question is of some significance for the time of the composition of the "prison epistles." This is the name given to Ephesians, Colossians, Philippians, and Philemon. If one excludes Ephesians and Colossians, because their authenticity is doubtful, Philippians and Philemon remain. When and where were they written? The traditional opinion is: in Rome. But in several passages one gets the impression that Paul is not very far away from those to whom he is writing. In that case there remains as the possible place of writing either Caesarea (Acts 24:27) or Ephesus. In the latter case, these letters then would not be documents from the last period of Paul's life, but would have been written at about the same time as Galatians and the Corinthian epistles. This opinion is widely held at the present (on the details, see the volume entitled *Einleitung in das Neue Testament* in the series *Grundrisse zum Neuen Testament*).

In spite of Paul's expulsion from Ephesus, the community there continued to exist and to be actively missionary. The communities in the Lycus valley were established from Ephesus; their existence is known through the Colossian epistle (4:13). Already in I Corinthians (16:19) "the churches of Asia" send greetings to Corinth. Ephesus soon becomes one of the centers of the church. One of the seven letters of the book of Revelation is addressed to her, as well as one of the letters of Ignatius of Antioch.

At this point the narration of events must cease for the time being. For Ephesus is Paul's last missionary center. As Rom. 15 shows, he now concludes his work for the entire eastern part of the Roman Empire and gathers together the results of his labors up to this point. The visible sign of it is the gathering of the collection in Macedonia and Achaia. The particulars can be reconstructed with some effort from II Corinthians. Thus Paul apparently had to leave Ephesus and did not venture to return there: on his trip to Jerusalem he passes the city by and summons the representatives of the community to Miletus (Acts 20:16-17). This is an involved and time-consuming arrangement and can be explained only by his having been banished from Ephesus. But first he goes back to Greece by way of Troas. In Troas there again appeared a great opportunity for the mission (II Cor. 2:12). But Paul has something else in mind, not only the long-range plan for delivering the collection in Jerusalem and for transferring his field of labors to Spain. First there is a grave crisis to eliminate, which had broken out in Corinth.

3. Crises

In the book of Acts the conditions within the communities appear harmonious. Crises are created only from without. The picture offered by the epistles is a different one.

It is not yet a crisis when some disputations arise somewhere over questions of doctrine, as in Thessalonica (cf. I Thess. 4:13 ff.): do those believers who die before Christ's parousia also attain eternal bliss? Paul makes no accusation out of the fact that there is doubt on the matter, but seriously deals with the substance of the question. The community appears to have accepted his statement. At any rate, we hear nothing more of further debates on this point. Paul's authority was not called into question. It is a different story in the two crises which Paul himself treated as such: in Galatia and in Corinth. If we wish to understand the style of the discussion, we must remember Paul's self-awareness: he is the spiritual father of his communities.

Just as he does not intrude into alien territory, so also he fights off any alien intrusion. This goes beyond a matter of personal jealousy; he knows that he is free of such: Phil. 1:14 ff. But when the substance of his work is in danger, when the cause which the Lord entrusted to him is being undermined, then for the sake of the cause he must also bring his own person into the matter and must defend his authority as an apostle, for the sake of the freedom of the communities. For he has his authority precisely as that of service (I Cor. 3:4 ff.), while his rivals exercise their own pneumatic power and subject the communities to human lordship, to the *hybris* of the "spiritual ones" (i.e., "Pneumatics").

Struggles appear to have arisen elsewhere as well as in Galatia and Corinth. At least some allusions appear in Phil. 3:2 ff. and Rom. 16:17-20 (from a letter to Ephesus? see above, p. 99). If the Philippian epistle was written in Ephesus (see above, p. 99), these movements all fall within the same period, and one could surmise that this is not accidental. On the other hand, the positions of the opponents in Galatians and in the Corinthian epistles are basically different, and the allusions in Phillippians and Romans are not sufficient to allow us to make a certain identification.

The background of the Galatian crisis is formed by the apostolic council, the declaration of the Gentile Christians' freedom from the law. The official representatives had reached an agreement. But before the council, during it (Gal. 2:4), and thereafter, still other currents were swirling about among the church people. Determined Jewish Christians still declared the keeping of the law to be a condition of salvation for everyone, and they appear to have found a hearing even among Gentiles. This may be surprising. The specific arguments, the way in which the agitation was carried on, and the thinking of the receptive hearers have not been handed down to us. But we may imagine: first there is the model of the original community. Further, Jesus was a Jew. If salvation had appeared in Israel, if the Father of Jesus is identical with the God of Israel and of the Old Testament, if the Old Testament is recognized as Holy Scripture—even by Paul!—with what right then is its most important content declared to be invalid? And how far should freedom from the law go? Is perhaps even the moral law to be abolished, and therewith the very foundation of the conduct which is pleasing to God? Is the consequence of Paul's teaching plain immorality, "libertinism"? It is possible that the demand of the "Judaizers" (i.e., those who postulate the law for the entire church) was made still more profound by means of cosmological wisdom and cultic practices: Gal. 4:3, 9-10 appears to indicate this; the Colossian epistle later offers a similar picture.

The sources are silent as to how this Judaizing movement spread and how it penetrated remote Galatia, of all places (Luke mentions nothing at all of this). The Galatian epistle is the only source through which we know anything at all of the whole matter. It certainly was not inspired from Jerusalem, by James or even by Peter, as has been supposed. In his defense Paul appeals to the apostolic council (Gal. 2), and in doing so of course he takes for granted that Jerusalem is still holding to the agreements. But for him the issue is far more than the formal fulfilling of an agreement. In his highly agitated epistle to Galatia the recollection of the council is only the introduction, not the main chapter of the argument. And when people deny him the rank of apostle, he is fighting for far more than personal prestige. When people introduce the law into his communities, they are destroying his work (2:2) which the Lord himself committed to him and for which he must someday give account to God. Whether the law should be in force or not is not left up to the discretion of men. This has been decided by the crucifixion of Christ. To press the demands of the law means to set the cross and grace at nought (2:21; 5:4). Paul goes far beyond polemics: he meets the opposing propaganda with the positive development of the doctrine of justification through faith alone. This gained for the Galatian epistle its high regard in the Reformation. It is the first draft of Paul's major work, the Epistle to the Romans.

The period in Ephesus is the climactic point in Paul's life. It is the period in which we can trace the internal movements in the young communities, above all in that of Corinth, which was pulled this way and that. The two Corinthian epistles, to which we owe the most significant insights into these things, make us aware again—and more clearly here than elsewhere—of how much the book of Acts has abridged the story. It puts the mission stations in sequence and in each case leaves the earlier ones out of the account until Paul travels there again. In reality there was a constant lively interchange between Ephesus and Corinth, through letters and delegations and by Paul himself. We must make the best of the fact that there are some points of obscurity in details. For the main outlines of the course of events can be discerned. Uncertainty arises primarily because of the question as to whether the two Corinthian epistles were composed by Paul as they now stand in the New Testament. For details on this, we must refer again to the volume on "Introduction" (*Einleitung* . . .). Here we shall draw the inferences for the reconstruction of events.

We know of at least four letters of Paul to Corinth: first of all, two letters are extant. And in each of these another is mentioned: in I Cor. 5:9 Paul refers to an earlier letter. Then comes a letter from Corinth to Paul (I Cor. 7:1). In response to this, Paul writes the letter which we call I Corinthians. The scholars have searched for that earlier letter. Many think that it is to be found within I Corinthians, which is thought to have been constructed subsequently out of the earlier letter and the one that answered the Corinthians.

Similarly, we learn in II Cor. 2:4 of a letter which Paul wrote with many tears; it must have been composed after I Corinthians (whether this letter is a unity or a subsequent compilation). In this case also the question is raised whether the sorrowful letter has not been fitted into the present II Corinthians.

We confine ourselves to the main features of the course of events: The reports fly back and forth between Ephesus and Corinth. Paul is most recently given information by Chloe's people (I Cor. 1:11). This Chloe is otherwise unknown; we cannot even determine whether she lived in Corinth and sent her people to Paul at Ephesus, or whether she lived at Ephesus and for some reason had her people visit Corinth. At the time when I Cor. 16:17 was being written, there was a Corinthian delegation with Paul.

The situation is characterized by the key word "divisions" (I Cor. 1:11). Names of missionaries are being used as party slogans: Paul, Cephas, Apollos. A fourth group appears to be outbidding them by putting the name of Christ on their banner. To be sure, one must not overdramatize this: the community has not yet gone separate ways. The letter is directed to the entire community and presupposes that they still are gathering together as a company. But the group slogans are a symptom of a deep-seated ill. In this respect it does not so much depend on the role which Peter and Apollos played. Did Peter himself occasionally put in an appearance in Corinth? The way in which Paul speaks of him makes this unlikely. It is more likely that his reputation made its way into the city and that people were playing him—as the superior, the recipient of the first appearance of the resurrected Lord (I Cor. 15:3 ff.)—off against Paul. Apollos made an impression by his appearance. Apparently he understood how to represent a well-defined position even over against Paul. But he did not occasion a division. Paul emphasizes collaboration with him (I Cor. 3) and urges him to go to Corinth (16:12). More important is the fundamental thing: for the first time we can recognize, by allusions, the first steps toward a Christian heresy, on Paul's part the dawning awareness of this phenomenon, and the first working out of criteria for evaluating and opposing it.

Paul attests the community's wealth of knowledge (1:5). But Christianity is on the way to being transformed into a mystery religion of the ancient style. Faith is oriented not to the death of Christ but to his heavenly glory. In the sway of the Spirit the believer experiences his own participation in this glory and hovers above the world. The sacrament bestows the power for this. The Pauline doctrine of the freedom of the faith becomes a stimulant of the spiritual man, who by meditation rises to higher worlds: "knowledge" liberates (cf. 6:12; 10:23 with 8:1 ff.). The spiritual man is elevated above the rules which have to do with the flesh. He possesses sexual freedom and freedom with respect to the phenomena of pagan religion. For example, he can accept an invitation to a pagan temple for a meal. In fact, he cannot be defiled by the pagan cult, for he knows that the gods do not exist.

Ideas of Paul, freedom slogans of popular Greek philosophy (Cynics, Stoics, Epicureans), ideas of the imparting of saving powers by means of rites and sacraments, all are mingled here. Now Paul does not discuss the detailed convictions as such. He traces them back to the heart of the matter. For him this is the reversal of the direction of thought: the Corinthians understand faith as the ascending movement of the enlightened person. In contrast to this, Paul places faith as the grasping and acknowledging of grace. The direction is from above downward, not the other way around. Faith is bound to the historical work of salvation, the death of Christ. This is not annulled by the resurrection, but on the contrary is confirmed. Thus the cross remains the constant determinant of the believer. It is what makes the church what it is. The Corinthian enthusiasts tend to let each one be responsible for his own salvation—though the others may see how he attains it. Paul shows that one has his salvation in the community, in the knowledge that Christ has died for his brother. Further, the sacrament does not infuse tangible, mysterious saving powers, but rather incorporates one into the church as the body of Christ. Faith does not soar above the world, after the fashion of a fanatic, but knows itself to be firmly set in the world, not yet translated into sight. The Spirit is the guarantee of the coming salvation, not yet the transformation into a celestial mode of existence. We still find ourselves this side of the resurrection.

This is roughly the state of the discussion in the first Corinthian epistle, or, if one prefers, in Paul's first two epistles to Corinth. The development appears so serious to Paul that, even before the epistle is finished, he sends Timothy (I Cor. 4:17). The epistle itself is delivered by the Corinthian delegation which is with Paul at the time (16:17). Paul anticipates the return of Timothy (16:10). From II Corinthians it appears that the latter's mission failed. The situation must have worsened. Paul himself hastened to Corinth. There matters came to a grave confrontation (II Cor. 2:1; cf. 12:14; 13:1). He journeyed back to Ephesus, but did not give the community up for lost; he now wrote a letter "with many tears" (it perhaps is preserved in II Cor. 10–13) and sent Titus. The agitation against him appears to have reached a climax: in Corinth a group pushes in from without, claiming for itself the authority of those in Jerusalem and denying Paul the right to the title of apostle. They say that he is not legitimated by the tradition. The sign of this defect is that he lacks the Spirit. Among other things, one of the effects of the Spirit is the gift of overpowering free discourse. But just look at Paul! (II Cor. 10:10).

The lowest point in Paul's life appears to be reached here: the climactic point of the crisis in Corinth coincides with the deadly peril in Ephesus (II Cor. 1). Paul leaves Ephesus and travels to Troas on the coast, where he hopes to meet Titus. In the meantime he engages in missionary work here too (II Cor. 2:12). When Titus does not arrive, he travels to Macedonia to meet him. Here Titus reaches him: he has been successful, and everything is going well again. Paul can write the joyful epistle which probably has been woven into "II Corinthians" (1:1–2:13, 7:5-16). Further events disclose that the success was enduring. Now Paul himself comes to Corinth again. Here he spends a winter. During this stay he writes an epistle to Rome, in preparation for his move to Spain. This epistle became the most important document Paul left behind him. In it the fruit of his thinking— together with the thinking-through of the crises—is summed up. During the winter he also concludes the collection (on this, cf. Gal. 2:10; I Cor. 16:1 ff.; II Cor. 8–9). Then he travels with the representatives of the communities through Macedonia, by way of Troas and Miletus to Jerusalem (Acts 20: 1 ff.). There he delivers the collection. Soon afterward he is arrested. His premonitions expressed in Rom. 15 are fulfilled. The book of Acts tells at length of his arrest, hearings before various authorities (the Sanhedrin, the governors Felix and Festus, once in the presence of King Agrippa II), his transfer to the imperial court at Rome with the dramatic voyage and the shipwreck on Malta. This account remarks that Paul was held in mild arrest for two years—and then it breaks off the narrative. If Philippians and Philemon were written in Rome (but cf. p. 99), they cast a little more light on these last years. This is especially true of Phil. 1:12 ff.: The imprisoned Paul continues to work, with success, but under hostile attacks by Christian rivals.

The end of Paul's life is unknown. The only certain thing is that he suffered martyrdom: this is assured by documents from the end of the first century. Luke suggests it in the farewell discourse which he puts in Paul's mouth on his way to Jerusalem (Acts 20). The deutero-Pauline Pastoral Epistles presuppose it. I Clement mentions it (Appendix II:4), as does Ignatius' epistle to the Romans (4.3). But it cannot be true that Paul did not die until the Neronian persecution (in the year 64); actually he must have died some years earlier.

4. The Pauline communities

a) It is no accident that about the *organization* only incidental notes are available, not detailed congregational orders or thematic treatments (a generation after Paul this will have changed). The loose external form of the Hellenistic communities prevails also in those founded by Paul. The most important source is I Corinthians with its occasional suggestions for an order. They are not systematic, but are occasioned by grievances which grew out of the exuberant manifestations of the Spirit.

The point of view for the structure, insofar as such appears required, simply results from the aim, i.e., from the idea of the church: over the entire world the church is *one*. But this does not mean that there is an overarching organization with fixed authorities and agencies. The unity is given "in Christ." The church is not the sum of all the congregations. Rather, the whole church is represented from place to place in the individual congregations.

The visible bond of unity is the common confession of the one Lord Jesus Christ. There are authorities who are recognized everywhere, the apostles. But their rights are not defined. In the individual congregations also there exists only a minimum of organization. In the Pauline communities there are not even elders; this holds true, incidentally, also for areas outside his mission field and on into a later time: the elders are lacking in the Epistle to the Hebrews, in the Didache (a church order!), and in the Epistle of Barnabas. The leadership of the community is determined by the sway of the Spirit. Of course if one sees this realized primarily in the experience of ecstasy, no ordered common life at all can come into being. But Paul makes it clear to the Corinthians who are being moved by the Spirit that the Spirit himself creates order (I Cor. 14; cf. vs. 40): God is not a God of confusion but of peace (vs. 33); his Spirit works accordingly. Paul expands the understanding of the gifts of the Spirit by defining them by the idea of the church: every gift which is employed for the building-up of the community, every "ministry" (I Cor. 12:4 ff.), is a gift of the Spirit. Hence there are indeed special positions and commissions, but not clergy and laity. One can speak of a general priesthood in the communities, if one does not fill the "priestly" with cultic ideas but understands it in this simple sense: everything "that edifies" is ministry. Everyone performs his *own* contribution. The Spirit does not do away with individuality. "The saints" are placed on an equal footing "in Christ," and precisely thereby are set free so that each can make his contribution with his own gift.

As persons of special position Paul names bishops and deacons (Phil. 1:1). Of course the bishop is not yet the monarchical priestly church leader of a later time; this is already shown by the plurality of the "bishops" in a congregation. We do not even know how they were distinguished from the deacons. The latter provide some kind of "services." But the area of their activity hardly was strictly circumscribed. It must have resulted from the existing needs. Among these were the service at the community's meals and the care of the poor. Two characteristic passages which express the nature of ministry and authority show how open everything is. I Thess. 5:12: one should acknowledge the people who work for the community, care for it, and encourage it with exhortation. The word which is translated here as "care for" can also mean "to govern," "to manage." But precisely this indefiniteness shows that there was not yet any authority of office, but only the authority of service. In I Cor. 16:16 Paul says something similar: one should subject oneself to the people who have distinguished themselves through the performance of a ministry.

One detail shows how little they went beyond what was demanded at the moment and how little organizational preplanning there was: in I Cor. 16 Paul gives some directions for the collection. Each one is regularly to put something aside, according to his ability, so that all will be ready when Paul comes. Thus there was no administrator of this collection and no treasury.

The most important co-laborers are the teachers in the broader sense: apostles, prophets, and teachers (I Cor. 12:28). The dominant point of view is that of the proclamation. In this sense Paul defines his own position. He does not see the gift of the prophets in the unveiling of the future but in laying bare the secrets of a man and thereby convicting him (I Cor. 14:24). The teaching office has its prototype in the synagogue; but it receives a new imprint through the belief in Christ and through the Spirit.

I Cor. 1:26 ff. throws some light on the average social composition of the community: "not many educated ones, not many from the upper social level." In II Cor. 8:2 he mentions the "deep poverty" of the Macedonian communities. The widows (I Cor. 7:8) of that time were in a particularly oppressed position. The slaves may very well have been numerous; cf. I Cor. 7:21 ff. In Rom. 16 there is a long list of persons to whom Paul sends greetings. The names can almost all be documented elsewhere as slaves' names; part of them are even characteristic slave names. On the other hand, there are also slaveowners in the church: I Cor. 7:21 ff. When a "household" was converted, the slaves also will have become Christians. Are Chloe's people (I Cor. 1:11) of this kind? The Epistle to Philemon preserves an interesting glimpse for us. The pagan slave of this Christian has run away from him—to Paul. He was converted by Paul and sent back to his master. The epistle also shows that the social orders remain: when master and slave become Christians, this does not eo ipso mean that the slave is set free.

The people gathered in private homes (Philem. 2). Large meeting places indeed would hardly have been available.

b) There is no fixed order of *worship*. There is a basic set of forms for prayers, songs, preaching, and so forth, the same as in the Hellenistic communities in general (see above). But above all, the Spirit blows where he wills. The regulations in I Cor. 14 show how lively the assembly could become as a result: the ecstatic persons all talk at once. Thus the Spirit begets confusion. Is he therefore to be quenched? No! (I Thess. 5:19), but as Spirit he is to produce order. There is a criterion by which even the ecstasies are tested, the confession of the Lord (I Cor. 12:3). This is held up before the community as a rule for its problems and life forms, and above all for the questions of eschatology. Indeed, Paul himself leads the communities into a heightened expectation of the imminent Parousia (I Cor. 7:29, 31; Phil. 4:5). What is to be inferred from this? In view of the imminent end of the world, should one nevertheless marry? Paul advises against it (I Cor. 7); but he does not make a law out of his counsel. The Christians do not give up their everyday work in order to hold themselves in fanatical readiness to receive the Lord. One is ready simply by virtue of the fact that he believes and does his work. Paul's ethical instructions, precisely because they are eschatologically grounded, are civil as far as contents are concerned. The most impressive example is the famous passage on "the powers that be" in Rom. 13:1 ff. No ascetic ideal is developed. Asceticism can occasionally even be practiced as a means to an end (I Cor. 7:5), but it is not a means to salvation.

It lies in the very nature of the sources that the civil side of the life of the Christians does not come to light in any significant measure. Nevertheless some indications, particularly in I Corinthians, provide material for a sketch. What problems arose for those who entered the church can be gathered from the exclusivist claims of the faith. At that time all public and private life was permeated with religious customs and cultic practices. For the mystery communities—outwardly similar to Christianity—there was no problem: initiation into the mystery of Isis, for example, did not rule out participation in other cults. For the existence of the mystery community is set forth only in the service of worship. Even though personal ties of sympathy might exist between individual members, still the mystery community outside the cultic setting is not a community of life. Even for conversion to Judaism the conditions are incomparably more favorable than for conversion to Christianity. For Judaism is protected by certain Roman privileges. But if one is converted to Christianity, one is not only torn loose from all previous religious connections. The Christian is rather compelled actively to deny these. May he, for example, remain a member of the societies to which he belongs? The societies of that time all have a religious element. May he participate in family celebrations in which reverence is shown to the gods? May he accept an invitation to a meal at a temple? Conversion must have led to upheavals in the family and in the social milieu. I Cor. 7:10 ff. points to divorces as a result of the conversion of one marriage partner to Christianity. The counsel which Paul gives in this case is characteristic. Jesus' direction that divorce is forbidden serves as a principle. In this respect Christianity is distinguished from all its environment. But this prohibition is no "law." The Christian may not seek the divorce. But if the non-Christian partner obtains a divorce, the Christian is no longer bound. He or she may remarry. No non-Christian can restrict the freedom of the Christian life.

CHAPTER X
The Original Community from the Apostolic Council down to the Jewish War

An almost unbroken obscurity lies over the history of the original community from the apostolic council onward. Primary sources are totally lacking. It is true that one of the "catholic" epistles is attributed to the Lord's brother James. But quite apart from the fact that he hardly is the author, the epistle gives no historical data of any kind. After the council, the book of Acts turns away from Jerusalem and follows Paul's mission. Only once more (apart from the reference in Acts 18:22 to a visit) does the road lead to Jerusalem: when Paul comes (Acts 21:15 ff.) to Jerusalem with his collection (which Acts, however, does not mention at this point but only later and incidentally: 24:17!). Here James once more briefly appears as the highest authority in the community. Peter is not mentioned. This corresponds to the facts: at this time (in the latter fifties) he was no longer living in the city. Gal. 2:11 ff. shows him in Antioch; I Cor. 9 as a traveling missionary. This also coincides with the agreement reached at the council. Was he compelled to leave the city by a danger from without? This question would be answered if the council came before the persecution of Acts 12. Arguing for this is the fact that in Acts 12:17 James suddenly appears as the leader of the community (the book of Acts had not even mentioned him before this!).

But, as we said earlier, it is no longer possible to reach a certain conclusion. The stages of James's ascent cannot be traced out. It is certain, however, that from this point until his death (A.D. 62) he stands at the head of the community, surrounded by a college of elders. Later the tradition defined his position as that of the first bishop of Jerusalem. Of course this is an anachronism. If one seeks to investigate how the college of the three pillars was dissolved and how he gained his position, one gets into the difficult analysis of post-biblical texts which have a later historical picture and are overgrown with legends. The most important documents are treated in Appendix II.

The *elders* appear for the first time in Acts in 11:30, as representatives of the community: here still as the only ones, and then at the council alongside the "apostles." If one should date the council on the journey of Barnabas and Paul in Acts 11:27-30, then Acts 11 and 15 would give a double indication that at the council the body of elders already played a decisive role. Of course it then would be strange that in Gal. 2 Paul says nothing of this group. The most likely inference from the remarks in the book of Acts is that the circle of the elders was formed after the departure of Peter (and John?), about the same time as James's rise to prominence.

The Jerusalem community maintained its authority in the church in relation to those elsewhere. James watched out for the formal and correct observance of the council's decisions (Gal. 2:11 ff.). Did he fear a fraternizing of Jewish and Gentile Christians and the possible aftereffects of this fraternizing on the church in Judea? Such fears are voiced in Acts 21:15 ff. This agrees, moreover, with the suspicions of Paul before his last journey, in Rom. 15. Down to the very last, Paul—by means of the collection which he gathered—recognized the position of Jerusalem. In Galatia people played off the authority of Jerusalem against Paul (see above), as they did in Corinth. The agitators there appealed to the argument that they had the tradition of the original community behind them. Scholars disagree over what validity, if any, this claim had: did these people actually have the support of James, or was their appeal to him unjustified? The answer depends on the disputed evaluation of two passages: in II Cor. 11:5 and 12:11 Paul fights with vehemence and irony against "super-apostles" who are working their way into the community of Corinth. Does he mean by this term the apostles in Jerusalem? This is unlikely. In this connection it must be remembered that the Twelve and the apostles are not identical and that at this time the Twelve as a group no longer existed. It is true that in II Corinthians Paul energetically asserts his position, but he just as vigorously affirms the connection of his communities with Jerusalem.

The "super-apostles" are the agitators themselves, who are unmasked by Paul as *false* apostles.

From the internal history, only one event is reported: the meeting of Paul and James at the delivery (not mentioned by the book of Acts) of the collection (Acts 21:15 ff.). James and the elders fear a conflict with the Jews, since among the latter Paul's position with reference to the law has been under discussion. His fate, his arrest, attests the fact that this conflict, which indeed Paul foresaw, actually broke out.

May one infer from the silence of the sources that the community in Jerusalem which was faithful to the law was able to live virtually unmolested down until the blow against James in the year 62? This assumption would be too simple. In I Thess. (2:14-15) Paul launches a vigorous attack against the Jews because they are persecuting the communities in Judea. This epistle was admittedly written after the council and after Paul's collision with Peter. A second indication is found in the passage Rom. 15:31, mentioned above: the liberty of the Gentile Christians from the law makes the Jews suspicious of all Christianity. On the other hand, the Jerusalem community appears not to have suffered any further effects from Paul's arrest. It apparently was constantly protected by the high regard which James enjoyed because of his piety, even among the non-Christian Jews. Yet in the years preceding the Jewish revolt the situation apparently came to a head. When a vacancy occurred because of the death of the governor Festus, who also appears in the book of Acts, the Sadducean high priest Ananos (Annas II, a son of the earlier Annas who is known to us from the passion narrative) used it to put to death James and some others for transgression of the law. The historian Josephus, who otherwise carefully remains silent about the Christian movement, preserved the event in his *Antiquities of the Jews* (Appendix II:3a); this is one of the rare cases in which the writing of the church's history can lean for support on non-Christian sources.

The history of the original community ends with the Jewish War (A.D. 66-70). This does not mean that all its members were killed in the war. After the war, there was again a Christian community in Jerusalem (in spite of the extensive destruction of the city). This later community is tied to the earlier one by the fact that kinsmen of Jesus and James held the leadership. But this new community has no more significance for the church as a whole. It is no longer the "original community." The last report about the community *before* the war (Eusebius, CH III. 5.3) tells that on the basis of a revelation they left the city before the outbreak of the war and moved to Pella, a Hellenistic city in the country east of the Jordan. There are reasons for doubting whether this happened. In any case, with the war, the original community disappeared. The echo of its downfall can be detected in the

"Synoptic apocalypse" (Mark 13:14 ff.). Incidentally, the war between Rome
and the Jews in Palestine did not have as a consequence a general repression
of the Jews in the empire. Only *one* general measure was taken against
them, which to be sure they felt as a special offense, the "fiscus Judaicus":
even after the destruction of the temple, Vespasian imposed on them the
payment of the temple tax, to be paid on behalf of Jupiter Capitolinus.

Even for the Christians the war had no general consequences. From the
book of Acts one gains the impression that in Luke's time the Christian
communities in the Palestinian coastal areas and in Phoenicia were flourishing.

CHAPTER XI

The Church down to the End of the
First Century

Through the letters of Paul and his pupils the impression could be created
that the Pauline communities form the main part of the church. But the
majority of Christians lived in the East, in Syria/Palestine. Nevertheless a
survey appropriately begins with the missionary territory of Paul.

1. General survey

The epistles from the school of Paul show the continuity of the Pauline
communities after the apostle's death. Of course there are crises, and at
one point perhaps even an open break. But the Pauline profile remains.
Documents demonstrate the regard in which these communities were held.
A fictitious Pauline letter is addressed to Thessalonica (the second
Thessalonian epistle). The First Epistle to Timothy suggests that Timothy
stayed in Ephesus. Of course the epistle to the "Ephesians" betrays nothing
about the community there; the name "Ephesus" in the address of the
epistle was only later inserted. The expansion beyond the communities
founded by Paul himself is notable. The Colossian epistle is addressed to
communities in the Lycus valley: Colossae, Hierapolis, and Laodicea. The
Pastoral Epistles look toward Crete and Dalmatia. The highly regarded bishop
Polycarp writes to Philippi, to be sure some time after the year 100; but
the continuity of the Pauline tradition is thereby proven even for the follow-

ing period. About 100 the community of Rome writes to Corinth (I Clement); although a crisis has broken out there, Corinth stands in high esteem.

The epistles of Ignatius of Antioch are—not long after 100—addressed to the following communities (all in western Asia Minor): Ephesus, Magnesia, Tralles (according to the traditional arrangement, the epistle to Rome follows here; see below), Philadelphia, and Smyrna. Cilicia is mentioned in Philad. 11.1. The seven letters of Revelation (chaps. 2–3) address the communities in Ephesus, Smyrna, Pergamum, Thyatira, Sardis, Philadelphia, and Laodicea. Revelation has no connection with the theology of Paul. May we infer that his influence was suppressed in Ephesus (and Laodicea)?

The address of I Peter surveys a large part of Asia Minor as territory of Christian communities: Pontus, Galatia, Cappadocia, Asia (in the narrower sense of the Roman province in the western part of the peninsula), and Bithynia. For the double province of Bithynia-Pontus, mentioned in the first and last places in the list above, there is an invaluable non-Christian source:

In the time of Trajan, after 110, the younger Pliny, well known (through his epistles) as an author, was governor there. He engaged in a detailed correspondence with the emperor about problems of his government. Within this correspondence is found a letter about measures against the Christians, and the emperor's answer is given (Appendix II:7). Pliny reports that in many places the shrines were deserted, but that through his intervention the Christian influence had diminished, and that, incidentally, some people already twenty years earlier had again separated themselves from Christianity.

Around the year 130, a Christian from Sinope on the Black Sea, the Marcion who was later so notorious as a heretic, came to Rome. According to credible tradition his father was already a Christian before him.

Close connections appear to have existed between Asia Minor and Palestine. The evangelist Philip is supposed to have moved with his daughters to Hierapolis. Mysterious is the book of "Revelation" and its connection with the "old John" or "elder John": in Asia and especially in Ephesus a "Johannine" tradition appears alongside the Pauline.

In the *East*, Antioch maintains its leading position; in fact, this position now is even stronger since the predominance of Jerusalem is eliminated. Around 100 the bishop Ignatius represents the principle of the monarchical episcopal office there. Paul himself remarks (I Cor. 9:6) that after the separation from Paul, Barnabas continued to work independently; according to Acts 15:39 he went to his homeland of Cyprus (together with John Mark; the latter, however, is later found again in the company of Paul).

Christianity reached *Rome* early. Around the middle of the fifties Paul writes his theologically most important letter to Rome. The community there probably did not develop through a specific missionary effort, but simply came together: in Rome at that time all currents converged, especially those flowing out of the East. The satirist Juvenal makes the reproving remark that the Syrian Orontes empties into the Tiber. The point of entry for Christianity was naturally the strong Jewish contingent in the city. From Rome about A.D. 50 the Jewish couple Aquila and Prisca, presumably already Christian, came to Corinth. Is the edict of Claudius which expelled "the Jews" from the city connected with the penetration by Christianity? It was indeed occasioned by disturbances among the Jews, and these are said to have been instigated by a certain Chrestus (Appendix II:2a). With the pronunciation of Greek then current, "Chrestus" could stand for "Christus." This way of writing the name is even found in manuscripts of the New Testament. In a passage to be discussed later, the historian Tacitus makes a play on this spelling. Of course Suetonius has only a confused picture. He thinks that Chrestus himself had come to Rome. A clear picture can no longer be gained, not even of how many were affected by the edict. At any rate, a few years later, at the time of the Roman epistle, the community is predominantly Gentile Christian; yet there are also Jewish Christians in it. Are there among them also some who returned after the death of Claudius, who in the meantime had been murdered?

An outstanding document about the composition of the community is Rom. 16, if this chapter belongs to the Roman epistle and not rather to an epistle to Ephesus (see above, p. 99). In no other epistle is there such a long list of people to whom Paul sends greetings; among these are found Jewish Christians also. Now historical criticism asks whether Paul can have had so many acquaintances in Rome, where he had never yet been. Among those greeted were also Aquila and Prisca, who had moved from Corinth to Ephesus. Thus they would have to have returned to Rome again, whence they earlier had been expelled. This argument provides support for the thesis that Rom. 16 is a fragment from an epistle to Ephesus. Verses 17 ff. contain a polemic such as one cannot wage in an epistle to a strange community. On the other hand: why should Paul not have a number of acquaintances in Rome, particularly since the fluctuation in population—precisely in the direction of Rome—was so lively? Besides, this could be a case of acquaintances by hearsay. It cannot be held as simply impossible, after Claudius' death, that Aquila and Prisca returned. One could even hold this as likely, since these two, small business people, surely would have left a part of their possessions behind them there. But even on this point there is something to be said on the other side. II Timothy (4:19), written after Paul's death, presupposes that they are still residing in Ephesus. If this epistle should be genuine, the argument would be still stronger. For then it would have to have been composed after a first Roman imprisonment and in any case sometime after the Roman epistle.

The famous dispute as to whether *Peter* came to Rome and died there can be passed over here (on this, see Appendix I, pp. 154-55). This dispute has to do with the personal fate of Peter and with his influence in the later church, but not with the early history of the Roman community. In this, neither Peter nor Paul left a single trace behind—except for the recollection of their martyrdom. The decisive turn of affairs is formed by the persecution under Nero (see below, p. 130), and a further one by that under Domitian. The latter event can be detected in two writings, one of which certainly, the other of which probably, was written about the year 100 in Rome: I Clement and I Peter. The book of Acts further mentions Christians in the port city of Puteoli (28:13-14).

Egypt is, for a time, unknown country. In view of the situation of Alexandria, the second city of the empire, and, above all, of its significance for Jewish-Hellenistic theology, this is surprising. Later John Mark was named as the founder of Egyptian Christianity and first bishop of Alexandria; but this is legend. Apollos comes from there; but unfortunately we do not know whether he became a Christian while still there. It is surmised that Hebrews and the Epistle of Barnabas were written there. They are in fact connected with the Alexandrian-Jewish biblical scholarship. In the second century, two Gospels arose here, of which only scanty fragments still bear witness, the Gospel of the Egyptians and the Gospel of the Hebrews. From Egypt come the two most significant systematic Gnostic thinkers, Basilides and Valentinus. Their achievement does indeed presuppose a certain theological development in this country. Only, we know nothing of it.

2. The form of the church

A general characteristic of this period is that now the system of elders or presbyters comes to prevail, even in Paul's missionary territory. This is shown by the writings from his school: Ephesians, the Pastoral Epistles, the book of Acts; for Corinth, I Clement, and so on. There are still some exceptions: Hebrews, the Didache, and the Epistle of Barnabas are silent as to this office. But the future belongs to it. The so-called Pastoral Epistles (I and II Timothy, Titus) undertake a first systematizing of church order. Of course they pose—in view of the later development—a problem which is not capable of solution. They name alongside each other the two offices of the bishop and the elders (presbyters). For both they give directions about the office. And indeed the bishop is always spoken of in the singular, and the presbyters always in the plural (I Tim. 5:1 is only apparently an exception). Does this mean that in the Pastoral Epistles the monarchical position of the bishop has already been developed? In the past the discussion over this had a confessional character: can the Catholic Church appeal for its organization and its understanding of office to the Bible—perhaps even to Paul himself, if the Pastoral Epistles should prove "genuine"? Today it is clear that the discussion between the different confessions cannot be decided by exegesis, especially since, to repeat, what is found in the epistles is not unequivocal. Even if they are acquainted with one individual as leader of a community, still the position of this one in terms of church order is not identical with that of the later bishop. There is neither the division into clergy and laity, nor the priestly consecration (only an ordination in the presence of the congregation), nor the idea that the bishop receives his power of consecration and teaching by the transferral of the position of the apostles to him. Besides, it is not even certain whether the bishop is the sole leader of the community. It is true that the language appears to indicate that the bishop (see above: singular!) is distinguished from the circle of the elders, somewhat as a president. But a *substantive* distinction between the two offices cannot be discerned. Perhaps the use of the singular for the bishop is explained quite simply and externally by the fact that the author of the epistles has worked-in an already existing "bishop's code" which had the singular, without thereby ruling out a plurality of bishops. Of other congregational offices the Pastoral Epistles name also those of the deacons (I Tim. 3:8 ff.) and the widows (I Tim. 5:3 ff.). In spite of the evident further development, the free Pauline heritage is still there.

In Ignatius things have advanced a step further. Here the gradation in the hierarchy is developed: bishop (community and bishop: Eph. 5.2-3; Magn. 7; Trall. 7.2; Philad. 4; Smyrn. 8; 9.1)—presbyters (bishop and presbyters: Eph. 2.2; 20.2; Magn. 7.1; 13.1; etc.)—deacons (Trall. 2.3). And the hierarchical order is now most closely bound up with soteriology, the doctrine of the Spirit, the doctrine of the sacraments, and the idea of the church, and is justified thereby. The bishop represents God in the community (Ign. Polyc. 6.1; Eph. 5.3; Magn. 3.1).

The rise of the office of bishop can no longer be explained. Its first mention, Phil. 1:1, gives no substantive indication on the matter. Some scholars assume that it developed out of tasks of economic administration. But its later development is hardly explained from this. The most important substantive question now is not whether an individual or a group stands at the head of the community. Besides, at that time this still could vary from one place to another (see below, p. 117). The problem lies in the understanding of office in general and of the office of bishop in particular: what function does it have in the mediation between God or Christ and man, in the application of the salvation event? Are church and salvation connected with certain offices and a fixed order in rank of those offices on the basis of substantive necessity? Is the distinction of clergy and laity, like the figure of the clergyman, only a matter of appropriateness, or a principle of the order of salvation? Is the effect of the saving agencies and powers bound to the hierarchy? Can only a consecrated priest dispense an effectual sacrament and only a bishop consecrate a priest? Is the hierarchy thus inserted as a middle entity between God and men? Does the church become the "agency of salvation"? These questions arise and present themselves out of the later development. In Ignatius the systematic exposition is not yet by any means fully formed, to say nothing of the church as a whole. The development does not progress uniformly. Alongside Ignatius other forms also are found.

In the Didache (Appendix II:11a), there are, alongside the bishops and deacons, the old pneumatic positions of the apostles, prophets, and teachers. The community chooses the required officeholders (15.1-2). In the worship service the prophets pray freely (10.7); the ones chosen utter the prescribed prayers. In Philippi the office of bishop is still unknown at the time of Ignatius and Polycarp. The already monarchically organized Smyrna writes to Philippi: "Polycarp and the presbyters with him to the church of God which dwells in exile at Philippi," and offers the admonition "to be subject to the presbyters and deacons as to God and Christ" (Polyc. Phil. 5.3). This is a slight allusion to a "theological" grounding of the levels of rank, as that grounding is developed in Polycarp's friend Ignatius, nothing more. There is no hint that the office of bishop must be introduced in Philippi also. In the West the office of bishop succeeds only late; in Rome it does not develop until toward the middle of the second century. I Clement is not acquainted with it. But he sets forth a series (42.1 ff.): God — Christ — apostles — bishops (plural: the bishops are identical with the presbyters)—deacons. Thus the offices have their dignity. I Clement is also the first Christian writing which represents the idea of "succession" in office: the offices named are established by the apostles. The dignity is passed on as a legacy from generation to generation (44.2). When the young in Corinth rebel against the elders, Rome intervenes on the side of the authority of the office. Hence I Clement is characterized as the earliest document of the developing Catholic church constitution. This is correct only in a limited sense. The old patriarchal authority of the presbyters is not yet suppressed by the "official" authority; but the office idea is becoming more and more prominent.

Some have sought also to fit into this development the struggle of the "presbyter" who wrote II and III John against a certain Diotrephes, who appears to occupy a monarchical episcopal position. But the proper evaluation of these two brief epistles is uncertain.

There still is not an organization beyond the local community. Some have wanted to find allusions to such an organization already in the Pastoral Epistles: the apostle's pupils, Timothy and Titus, are to give directions to the bishops and presbyters. Thus they are something like archbishops. But this is not intended. The epistles are fictitious; the names of the apostle's pupils serve only to give the stamp of the apostolic tradition.

Luke sets forth in exemplary fashion how people thought of unity: it is established by the origin of the church in Jerusalem. Even when the primitive community no longer exists, it remains present as a model. An overarching organization is not necessary, but the preservation of the legacy of Jesus and the apostles is essential. In all the writings of this time the unity is an ideal unity. The Christians of the whole world form the *one* people of God, the body of Christ. There is "*one* body and *one* Spirit, . . . *one* Lord, *one* faith, *one* baptism, *one* God and Father of all" (Eph. 4:4-6).

A special aspect of this unity is the presence of Jews and Gentiles in the one church (Eph. 2:11 ff.; John 10:1 ff.). The problems and struggles of the Pauline period have died away. The direct confrontation of Judaism, or of Judaizing Jewish *Christianity,* and Pauline freedom from the law no longer exists. The alternative of Jewish Christians—Gentile Christians is no longer current, not even in writings which come out of the Jewish tradition, such as James and Hebrews. Another problem is current: the church has adopted the Old Testament as Holy Scripture and must now adapt it to itself. How is this possible, when at the same time essential contents of the Old Testament are being cast away? Well, it is the book of prophecy concerning Christ (Matthew); it contains God's commandments, which are still valid; it is a prefiguring of salvation in figurative robes (Hebrews; in another way, Barnabas). It contains the prototypes of the Christian life (I Clement). Here too a free abundance of ideas and experiments prevails.

The elements of worship services are still the earlier ones: Scripture reading, preaching, prayer; I Tim. 4:13 enumerates reading, exhortation, and teaching. In this the strong influence of the (Diaspora) synagogue can be discerned. Through lengthy passages I Clement is a collection of excerpts from the Old Testament. The Epistle to the Hebrews develops a typological method of exposition, and the Epistle of Barnabas an allegorical one. The songs and prayers are stamped with the Jewish style. An impression of this may be gained from the numerous hymns in Revelation (even if they are not actually songs of the community), the prayers of the Didache, and the long prayer in I Clem. 59–61 (Appendix II:11*b*). Sunday as the day of meeting is already evident in I Cor. 16:2. Now the indications increase: Acts 20:7; Rev. 1:10; Did. 14.1; Barn. 15.9; Ign. Magn. 9.1; somewhat later, Justin, Apol. I, 67.3. In his letter to Trajan about the Christians (Appendix

II:7a), Pliny knows that they gather "on a certain day before daybreak," and then again for a meal. The morning worship service may be the service of instruction. This explanation is more likely than the other one which says that it was the baptismal service. For Pliny clearly is speaking of a regular custom; but baptism could be performed only when there were candidates ready. The order of service for baptism and the Supper from the Didache and Justin's order of worship are printed in the Appendix (II:11a, c). The laying-on of hands serves to impart the blessing in baptism and ordination (Acts 9:17-18; Heb. 6:2; Acts 13:1-3; I Tim. 4:14; II Tim. 1:6), as well as for the healing of the sick. James 5:14 is acquainted with the ceremony of anointing with oil. Fasting is an established custom. The Didache prescribes (8.1): "Your fasts are not to be at the same times as those of the hypocrites (see Matt. 6:16!); for they fast on Monday and Thursday; but you should fast on Wednesday and Friday."

3. Intellectual achievement

The sources are as abundant in what they tell us about the spirit of the times as they are stingy in yielding historical data. Indeed, an actual history of primitive Christian literature cannot be written, since it rarely is possible to place the writings in their exact time. Yet certain connections and groupings can be recognized. In addition to the genuine epistles of Paul, primitive Christian literature includes all the other writings of the New Testament (some of these even stand already on the outermost boundary of "primitive Christianity"): epistles which are composed under Paul's name and are consciously committed to his legacy, namely the "epistles" to the Colossians and "Ephesians," a second epistle to Thessalonica, and the "Pastoral Epistles." Joined with the composition of the new epistles, there is the collecting and editing of the old ones. The great figures of the past are the established authorities for the present. At this time, the Gospels are formed, more "epistles," and doctrinal writings which ultimately were adopted into the canon as the small corpus of the "catholic epistles," and an apocalypse. The extra-canonical writings of the "Apostolic Fathers" are discussed in another place (pp. 24 ff.). It is evident from fragments of "apocryphal" Gospels that much has been lost; yet their age in individual cases cannot be determined. As a whole, the "New Testament Apocrypha" belong to the time beyond that of primitive Christianity.

The characteristic feature which most clearly shows the spirit of the age is the concept of tradition. Now the idea of the twelve apostles and of the apostolic era is developed. People were aware of belonging to the third generation. Formally, it is true, here and there they still expected the Parousia in the immediate future. At any rate, the prospect of the Parousia as such, of which people were still convinced, was dominant; but the emphasis that it was near at hand diminished, if one did not entirely detach eschatology from cosmology, as the Gospel of John does (see below, p. 121). Incidentally, the occasional assertion that the delay in the Parousia set off a fundamental crisis is not correct. Here and there local discussions and doubts arose, but there was no worldwide shaking of the church. For example, *Colossians* (3:4) indicates the expectation of the Parousia, but does not say that the end of the world is *near*. It is more important to the Colossian epistle to show the believers the heavenly blessings into which they are permitted to look, the powers of salvation which they possess in the church as the body of Christ; to assure them of their participation in the Head, Christ; to lead them to liberty against the powers of the cosmos, to battle against the heretics, and to the right conduct of life. The kindred *Ephesian* epistle develops these ideas further. The church rests on the foundation of the apostles and prophets. It is not the prospect of future events but the penetration into the revealed mystery of God's plan of salvation that actualizes the believers' participation in the salvation, already in the present in an anticipatory way, in their struggle with the evil powers of the world. *II Thessalonians* roundly declares that Paul never taught an imminent expectation. The old anticipation of an immediate end appears somewhere to have become sporadically active again; it could, with good reason, appeal to Paul for support. II Thessalonians must contest this, painstakingly enough. Yet in substance it is—as against the letter of the Pauline statements—in the last analysis correct. For Paul the imminent expectation was not an independent, speculative-cosmological doctrine. Throughout it served the conceptual comprehension of the saving event in Christ. On the other hand, among Paul's descendants, against whom II Thessalonians wages a polemic, it may well have taken on a fanatical characteristic.

The *Pastoral Epistles* concentrate on the preservation of pure doctrine, whose guarantor the apostle Paul is, on the order of the church and the conduct of life, the fending-off of false teaching, which is a sign of the last time; there is nothing said to indicate that this time will be only a brief one.

The *Epistle to the Hebrews* occasionally repeats the old phrase that "the day" is near (10:25; cf. vs. 37). But above all it portrays the church as the pilgrim people of God on a long, weary march to the distant goal, the celestial city.

In two writings the imminent expectation is again intensified, in I Peter and in Revelation. In those places this is connected with the church's situation in persecution. But it is noteworthy that in *I Peter* apocalyptic fantasy does not break out at all. The expectation of the Lord is not an object of speculation. It is a point of orientation which is established from the understanding of the work of salvation. What one has to anticipate and what one already possesses by way of the blessings of salvation is learned from the saving work of Christ, his suffering for our sins. Now of course *Revelation* portrays the end of the world and the celestial world in immense pictures, in the tradition of Jewish apocalyptic, its image of the world and its language. But the point is not the fantastic as such. The entire world of imagery is related to the destiny of the believers.

An interesting special case is *II Peter*. Here disappointment over the delay in the Parousia becomes visible. There are people who are derisive about the imminent expectation. II Peter defends this expectation; but it has difficulty in doing so: in God's sight a thousand years are as a day. Traces of similar discussions are still found in I Clem. 23.3-5 and II Clem. 11-12.

The *Gospel of John* is unique. In it there are sentences which directly rule out the prospect of a future Parousia of the Lord: the Lord *will* not come; he *has* come. He has "come into the world," and this was the coming of the judgment. After his death he has returned to those who are his own. John 3:18-19: no future judgment day is maintained, but "this is the judgment, that the light came into the world, and men loved darkness rather than the light." "He who . . . believes is not judged; but he who does not believe is judged already." But alongside these stand sentences which do point to the coming Last Day (thus in the passages 5:27-29; 6:39 ff.). Now how are the two related? There are scholars who assume that the sentences about the Last Day are later additions. This is possible. For it can be seen from John 21 that the book was not published by the author but by his pupils. Others assume that he preserved the average eschatology of the church, but spiritualized it. In that case both groups of expressions would be original. Only in that case their juxtaposition still is not accounted for. There is agreement that in any case the emphasis is placed on the sentences pertaining to the present, such as 3:18 and 5:24.

In the environs of the New Testament, in the Apostolic Fathers, on the whole the same picture is presented as here. The epistles of Ignatius may be compared with the Gospel of John. It is true that occasionally the future judgment is mentioned (Eph. 11.1); we are living in the last times. But this is only the periphery. The center is formed by the instruction concerning Christ, the incarnation and the saving work, the church's blessings of salvation and mediation of salvation, and thus the understanding of the present and its powers which make possible the highest achievement that the believer can expect, that of martyrdom. Among the Apostolic Fathers it is also true in general that the end of the world and the judgment, eternal life or perdition are expected, but that the *imminent* expectation actually is replaced by the general form of expectation. The thinker who consciously handles the eschatological theme and achieves the solution to which the future belongs is Luke.

4. The church's internal problem

The older and larger the church becomes, the more urgent does it become for the church to find fixed forms of life: for the external organization of the communities, for charity, worship, doctrine, and discipline. These forms can only be *secular* forms. One finds super- and subordination, assessments, church discipline, and therewith compulsion. But is not this also an internal secularizing, a fall from the church's original nature? May the free sway of the Spirit be replaced by legal rules? Would not the church be obliged specifically to strive to prevent this and further to cultivate the vital experience of the Spirit? Must she not rely on the Spirit's revealing to her, from case to case, what is required? These questions will move the church as long as she exists.

Or should one take the "realistic" position that the church could not do otherwise if she wished to exist in the world? But this, in fact, is precisely the question: as *what* does she wish to exist? Surely as the elect community of the Lord in the end-time! And again, from the other side: if the Spirit no longer moves freely, if the church must, so to speak, artificially produce his rule, is this still really the Spirit? Is it still God's Spirit and not rather the believers' own spirit?

The church appears to be between Scylla and Charybdis, in danger of becoming either worldly institution or sect. What are the norms by which the propriety or impropriety of the developing forms of the life of the church are to be measured?

One first indication is provided by the church's origin, the fact that she—because of the appearances of the resurrected One—did not emigrate out of the world, in order to cultivate inner elevation, but remained in the world, in order to proclaim the Lordship of Christ for the world's salvation. We must further remember that the renunciation of worldly forms of life is an illusory renunciation. Even a cloister in the desert is "world." It is not the forms in themselves that are evil. What is evil is the use of force in the church. But can this after all be avoided in the world? In the church, yes! This does not rule out church discipline—but it is to be exercised according to the norm of love. There are criteria for doctrine, for distinguishing truth and error; yet no agency which would enforce the decision by means of force. How, now, are theory and reality related?

The key to the understanding of this period is the changed self-understanding of the church. Her founder belongs to a more remote past. The church, which originally was conscious of facing the end of the world and understood herself as a sign of the end-time, now has acquired a historical dimension and can look back on her own history. The great figures of the founding era become heroes of the faith and authoritative transmitters of doctrine. In view of this, the question suggested above is posed anew: how is this transformation related to the original faith?

One view of history which is influential down to the present sees the development as apostasy: after the period of pure doctrine and love, things went downhill with a dogmatic and organizational hardening. But are not these changes to be judged legitimate insofar as the church is not bound to one particular form of organization and doctrine, because such a binding would again be a law, and achievements of doctrine and life made in conformity to law would thus be raised to the level of a condition of salvation? On the other hand, questions must be raised about the allowable limits, for not every form can be legitimate. How can faith become effective as a criterion? In certain cases it is a simple matter to mark out the boundaries, e.g., when it is a matter of setting forth the difference from the pagan cult. But how is it to be done when within the church the differences of opinion about the faith itself are intensified and lead to a break? When two fronts are formed and each denies the orthodoxy of the other? Thus when norms must be found for the exclusion of "heresy"!

The prelude to the discussion of *orthodoxy and heresy* is Paul's criticism of Corinthian "spiritualism." In this context the first criteria are worked out: the confession (I Cor. 12:3; 15:3 ff.) and the idea of the church ("edification"). In the latter half of the century a new style emerged. It is conditioned by the fact that *tradition* comes into play in a new way; it makes possible the appeal to the guarantors of correct doctrine, the apostles. One must clearly understand how difficult these matters are. Indeed it is not agreed in advance what is orthodox and what is heretical. There are in the church doctrinal statements and persuasions, but still no normative dogmatics and no agency to apply them authoritatively. The groups which gradually are excluded as heretical are at first found in the church and know themselves to be Christians, often even especially enlightened ones. Thus a few features from the varied picture: the *Colossian* epistle attacks people who are pursuing "philosophy." Under this name apparently is concealed a kind of cosmological religion of redemption which interprets Christ as the embodiment of the universe and its elements. From this belief are derived forms for the veneration of the cosmic powers, rites, and rules of continence. The *Pastoral Epistles* contend against similar demands. One doctrinal view of the adversaries is that the resurrection has already occurred (II Tim. 2:18).

Thus it appears that here we have to do with a spiritualistic Gnosticism with a Jewish-ritual element. On the right, asceticism, a practiced renunciation of the world, and on the left, libertinism, a practiced contempt for the world. The book of *Revelation* sees itself faced with this second form of detachment from the world. The adversaries whom *I John* is opposing separate the Son of God from the "flesh," and thus are Docetists; they deny the incarnation of the redeemer and see precisely in his pure divinity the necessary condition of salvation.

What instruments of thought can be offered to aid in illuminating the situation? Can clear alignments be marked out at all? There is indeed nowhere "the" timelessly pure doctrine—from the very nature of faith itself there cannot be such. Faith must be formulated ever again historically, and this also means that it must be conditioned by the times and "worldly." Theses like the one being contested in the Pastoral Epistles about the resurrection existence as a present reality are found also in Colossians (2:12), which so sharply contends against heresy, in Ephesians (2:5 ff.), which reclaims Paul for its teaching, and in the Gospel of John (5:24), following which again I John takes a stand against the Gnostics. Will it come to a struggle of all against all, to a complete relativizing of Christian truth?

Tools for thought are provided first of all by the tradition, not only the teaching of Jesus and Paul which has been put down in writing, but prior to that, the direct and unmediated handing-on of the faith in the communities. New ideas are suspect. This is a handicap for the Gnostics and others, but still not a refutation. For a refutation the heritage must be brought into play. *Colossians* analyzes the position of the opponents with the aid of the Pauline understanding of liberty with respect to the world and the world powers. It rejects the demotion of Christ to the level of a cosmic force. The *Pastoral Epistles* emphatically appeal to the doctrinal legacy of the apostle. They do not offer a refutation of individual doctrines. This is typical of the method of fighting heresy then current: one fought not with arguments but with polemics. One of the most important "arguments" is the constantly reiterated charge of immorality which can occasionally refer to ideological libertinism. It is an objectively more important viewpoint when the Pastorals set the belief in the Creator against all practices of world rejection. The world is not dualistically devalued. The God of the world and the God of salvation are one and the same. What Paul had already held up before the Corinthians (I Cor. 10:25 ff.) and repeated to the Romans—that the earth is the Lord's and the fullness thereof, that therefore nothing is impure in itself (Rom. 14:14, 20)—is taken up by the Pastoral Epistles: "To the pure all things are pure" (Titus 1:15). They, too, independently carry freedom over into the new situation. Especially interesting is *I John*. The author finds himself in a situation where the confession of faith, as far as the wording is concerned, is not in dispute. The adversaries also confess that "Jesus is the Son of God." But they deny that the Son became man. Thus the incarnation of the redeemer becomes the distinguishing sign. Now it comes to light that a formal acknowledgment of the Credo still is no certain indication of orthodoxy. It must also be rightly expounded. Theology is given an expanded task. But to what extent is this dispute over the exposition of the christological dogma the substantive issue? Even Gnostic Christology, in the disputing of the humanity of the Son of God, expressed the tearing-apart of God and world, of salvation and world. Walter Bauer, in his stimulating book entitled *Rechtgläubigkeit und Ketzerei im ältesten Christentum* (1934; 2nd ed., 1964; ET 1971, as *Orthodoxy and Heresy in Earliest Christianity*), poses the question whether it is more than accident that the "orthodox" tendency prevailed (which indeed only by means of this victory became "orthodox") instead of Gnosticism, which at the time had good prospects of becoming the standard form of Christianity. Of course one cannot postulate any historical necessity. But the judgment on Gnosticism which declares it heresy has its substantive, theological justification. All the forms in which Gnosticism was manifested—its asceticism, ritualism, libertinism, theoretical docetism—have this one thing in common, that they separate revelation and world. Salvation is again attained through achievements of man, ascent into the higher world. The church is transformed into a spiritual sect. These points were included in the polemical literature of that time. What can be learned from those battles and their continuation is this: the parting of the ways of orthodoxy and heresy occurs anew in every group which has established itself as orthodox—not because the people are contentious, curious, or narrow-minded, but because orthodoxy is not a possession which can be passed on by inheritance. What can be handed down are doctrinal phrases, explanations of the content of faith, not the content itself. This does not mean that there are not valid criteria; but they must be worked out ever anew, and this in fact must be done in theological self-examination. No one can confirm his own orthodoxy. The criteria must be proved in the internal life of the church as in its relationship to the world, in the attitude of the spirit as well as in the shaping of life.

Heresy is not only a matter of internal politics in the church. In it, voices from the intellectual world in which Christianity lives are heard—a world in which "orthodoxy" also participates. It is compelled from the very outset to be occupied with its intellectual rivals.

5. Rivals

Of course one major rival is Judaism, which at that time was widely scorned and yet also exerted a strong attractive force. Still more immediate competition with Christianity was offered by movements which also offered salvation through revelation and gathered communities together. Such a group were the disciples of John the Baptist (after his death). We know very little of them, but from some polemical passages, especially in the Gospel of John, we can deduce that there were such. For more than once John emphasizes in striking tones that the Baptist was *not* the Light, the Messiah (John 1:6 ff., 19 ff.). Evidently there were people who considered him to be just that. Details are not known. But it may be stated with certainty that this movement did not antedate the Christian movement and did not provide the model for belief in Jesus, but conversely, that it developed its views about the Baptist after the Christian example. The rivalry with this movement also appears in still other passages (e.g., Acts 18:24 ff.; 19:1 ff.). Even in later times there are still references to disciples of the Baptist. Perhaps a part of them still survives in the Mandaeans of today, even though in such a changed form that we can no longer speak of a historical connection.

The only head of a non-Christian sect who is named in the New Testament (but as—at least temporarily—a Christian) is Simon Magus, in Acts 8:9 ff. Here he is presented as a relatively harmless impostor who becomes a Christian in Samaria, but wants to make a business out of the power of the Spirit. Peter pronounces a severe curse upon him and calls on him to repent. Then he disappears from view. Simon actually hailed from Samaria; this is confirmed by his fellow countryman, the philosopher, later Christian and martyr, Justin. But the conversion of Simon is legend. He is not a Christian heretic but a genuine rival. His teaching can be reconstructed only with difficulty and uncertainty. For on the one hand his figure is completely overgrown with Christian legends; on the other hand, his teaching was further developed along Gnostic lines by his disciples. He is said to have led around with him a woman companion, Helena, who represents an element of the revelation, the heavenly "Ennoia," the thought of the divine Spirit, which was imprisoned in the world and was liberated by Simon. It is certain (the book of Acts also goes into this) that he represented himself to be "the great power" (Acts 8:10), that is, the Most High God himself or the revelation of God, and thus the Son; at that time the two were not necessarily mutually exclusive. According to Justin (Appendix II:10), Simon had considerable success in Samaria. In the Christian legend he becomes a magician who is defeated by the superior power of Peter in Rome. The church fathers regarded him as the father of the Gnostic heresy.

CHAPTER XII

The Church and the World

The Roman Empire is not a highly organized territorial state in the modern style. In the provinces the governors rule to some extent as sovereign. Even a province is not a unity. It consists of territories of allies, free cities, domains of vassal princes, whose status again is highly varied, and territories under direct rule. There is, for example, no imperial police force. Thus it is not to be expected that Christianity, once it attracts official attention, is treated everywhere alike. When conflicts arise, at first the local authorities are responsible for dealing with them. The narratives in the book of Acts from Philippi, Thessalonica, and Corinth give a varied picture of this matter. When in Corinth one goes before the governor, this is simply because in the provincial capital people naturally appeal to the highest authority. These political circumstances should be remembered when, in the following, reference is made to the "state."

What are the points of contact and possible irritation between Christian communities and political authorities? What causes the latter to feel prompted to take action, and how do the Christians react?

Public judgment upon Christianity of course is determined in part by the fact that Christianity arose out of Judaism. Judaism was generally known. Jews were scattered over the entire territory of the empire (and beyond). The estimates of their part in the population of the empire run as high as ten percent. They were recognized by their ceremonies, e.g., the observance of the Sabbath, and by their exclusiveness, which by the way was guaranteed by official privileges; it was well known that they rejected the images of the gods. One may read in Tacitus how one Roman judged the Jews: "The Jewish way of life is absurd and repugnant" (*Hist.* 5.5).

The Jewish origin clung to the Christians even after they were recognized as a distinct group. In addition, the fact that the founder of the movement was condemned to death by a representative of Rome was incriminating. This is seen in Luke's efforts: he emphasizes as strongly as he can that Pilate declared Jesus to be innocent (Luke 23:4, 14, 22) and weakened only under pressure from the Jews, when he did not have Jesus executed but rather surrendered him to the Jews, who executed him.

In any case, after Jesus' death Pilate had no interest in the development of Christianity. The same holds true for his successors. Isolated blows in Palestine were not struck by Rome but by Jewish authorities; see Acts 4, 5, 12. From Hellenistic cities like Caesarea we have no reports of persecutions. Important then is the turning point to which the note in Acts 11:26 refers:

in Antioch the "Christians" are already recognized as an independent movement and acquire their own name. It is applied to them by outsiders, which is evident from the Latin form of the word. Occasionally this fact has led to bold constructions: that the designation was bestowed upon them officially by the Roman authorities of the provincial capital Antioch, in other words, that they were officially registered and enrolled in the list of associations, and thus of course were officially supervised. But this is an untenable interpretation of that note. It is important, however, that in the public eye Christianity is distinguished from Judaism.

The attitude of the authorities depends on accidental factors. They must first of all have Christianity brought to their attention, and in addition, in general there needs to be some occasion for this, such as a disturbance. The sketches of the book of Acts again afford illustrative material. According to this, it was almost always the Jews who prompted the authorities to step in (13:50; 14:5, 19, etc.). The concern of the latter is the public peace. Riotous and official proceedings can hardly be precisely distinguished (Acts 14:5, 19). Acts 16 offers an example; even if Luke does not describe the events in Philippi exactly according to the official record, he does give a picture of how it could happen in a provincial capital. Political motives are also indicated: in Philippi—a Roman colony!—the Christians are disseminating non-Roman practices (Acts 16:21); in Thessalonica the belief of the Christians is undermining the position of the emperor (Acts 17:7).

To what extent does the book of Acts in this regard project problems of its own time back into the early period? That it does this can be read from the scene, shaped into a pardigm, before the tribunal of Gallio in Corinth (Acts 18): the Jews drag Paul into court, but the governor declares that he is not interested, since it is not a matter of a judicial and political case, but a purely religious one. For the author of Acts, this is the typical attitude of the Roman officials, whom he commends by means of this portrayal. He can support his view on the fact that in principle Rome is religiously tolerant. Of course we shall have to ask about the limits of tolerance.

The book of Acts indicates still another motive: damage to business (Acts 19: the riot of the manufacturers and sellers of devotional items in Ephesus). This motive is confirmed by the letter of Pliny (Appendix II:7a).

Paul's career shows that from the beginning the Christian mission was exposed to dangers (cf. II Cor. 11:23 ff.). He was conscious of being threatened constantly. He was imprisoned repeatedly. Five times he was scourged in the synagogues; he does not say when or where, but the number of times shows that the intra-Jewish punishments accompanied him on his mission. In addition there was the scourging three times by authorities as official punishment. Once he was stoned; this suggests a riot. In Ephesus he hovered in immediate danger of death (II Cor. 1:8).

Paul's sufferings were climaxed finally in his arrest, transport to Rome, and death. Why he was condemned is not told in the tradition. In any case, the reason lies in his activity as a missionary.

Thus from the outset the mission stands under pressure from without; everyone who becomes a Christian runs the risk of suffering (I Thess. 1:6; 2:2, etc.). The church knows that the persecution is no accident but arises out of the nature of the faith and the church. What consequences did she draw from this? Theoretically, one can imagine several possibilities. It is conceivable that the Christians fanatically seek martyrdom, in order immediately to enter into the heavenly glory. Or they may declare the state to be of the devil. Or they may attempt to convince the state by refuting false accusations, above all those of a political nature: the kingdom which they hope for is not of this world. We shall return to this question later.

What prompted Rome to take action? What is the legal basis?

Rome's point of view is simply that of public security. This is already indicated by certain parallels like Claudius' proceeding against the Jews, which is explicitly accounted for by disturbances. It was not directed against the Jewish religion as such. This is not attacked. Claudius was on friendly terms with the Jewish prince Agrippa, who indeed while abroad behaved like a Hellenist but still protected the Jews and at home was demonstratively pious. Claudius' principles of government appear plainly in a letter that is preserved on papyrus. On the occasion of a tumult between Jews and the rest of the populace of Alexandria, Claudius threatens: "If they (the Jews) do not follow my orders, I shall use every means to prosecute them as people who bring in a pestilence which is scattered over the whole world." Already before Claudius there was an ancient Roman tradition of taking steps against the invasion of foreign cults and "superstition" into Rome. In that case too it was a matter of security for the state; this included seeing to it that Roman custom was not injured. Rome's attitude with respect to Christianity is also to be seen in this perspective. Where the authorities did not see the interest of the state involved, they did not take any action. Contrary to a widely held view, the cult of the emperor did not play a role as a motive for intervention. In the first century this cult involved only small groups. The persecution under Nero was not set in motion by it. Pliny required the Christians to offer sacrifice before the emperor's image. This, however, is not an act of political loyalty, but a sign that they are not Christians or have given up Christianity. That the Christians were required to abjure their confession "Jesus is Lord" with a solemn "Caesar is Lord," is a legend; there is nothing of this in the sources. In the New Testament the imperial cult first comes into view in the book of Revelation, in the time of Domitian.

The first official major action against the Christians is the Neronian persecution. Legend places the death of Peter and Paul in this setting. It was limited to the city of Rome. Tacitus is our major source (Appendix II:5). Suetonius (*Nero*, 16) only remarks: "Death penalties were pronounced against the Christians, a sect which had succumbed to a new superstition that was dangerous to the public." Tacitus is more detailed but obscure. He connects the persecution with the famous burning of Rome, but in such a way that the reader cannot see through: Nero had some Christians arrested "who confessed"—what? when? Was it that they openly confessed their Christianity and were therefore imprisoned? Did they confess *after* their arrest? Then, "on their denunciation a great host" were imprisoned. The investigation indeed did not convict them of arson, but of "hatred of the human race." Thus they were condemned. Nero made a spectacle of the execution in his park (around the present Vatican). Tacitus had no objection to the proceeding against the Christians in itself. For him they were a criminal sect—the founder had already been executed. But he places value upon the declaration that it was not they who had set fire to Rome— let the reader make his own guess. Incidentally, Tacitus also ridicules the stupid populace: they speak not of the "Christians" but of the "Chrestians"; this echoes the Greek "chrestos," which means "qualified, good."

Even in the next persecution under Domitian, a fundamental, legal basis does not become evident. The accounts are scanty (Eusebius following the author Melito of Sardis, around 150; Tertullian). But perhaps one may adduce some indirect indications: I Peter, Revelation, and I Clement all are aware of persecution. These writings may very well have arisen in this time.

There is much puzzlement over Domitian's proceeding against two of his kinsmen, his nephew, the consul Flavius Clemens, and the latter's wife, Flavia Domitilla. According to Dio Cassius (Appendix II:6a), they were accused of atheism; others also who had gone astray into Jewish customs were condemned in great numbers on the same charge. Flavius Clemens was executed, and his wife was exiled to an island. The later legend made Christians of them, and many assume that this contains a kernel of truth, that the "Jewish" customs refer to Christianity.

Why were the Christians persecuted? What is the legal basis, and what was the proceeding against them? Tacitus speaks only in general of crime and hatred of humanity. Nevertheless, intervention could be justified on these grounds: associations by which the state felt itself imperiled were suppressed. Precise juridical definitions were not needed for this.

The governor Pliny (soon after 100) formulated the problem more sharply

(Appendix II:7*a*): Is "the name itself" punishable, or only "crimes which are connected with the name"? In the former case, the confession of a Christian suffices for condemnation, while in the latter case definite offenses against the law must be proven. But even by this alternative a clear legal situation is not created. Pliny avoids it: he has Christians condemned if they do not renounce their faith. The Emperor Trajan approves this (Appendix II:7*b*), but on the other hand decrees that the Christians are not to be sought out, and anonymous denunciations are not to be heeded—with the explanation that has become famous: "nec nostri saeculi est" ("that is not the way of our age"). Hence whether Christians are persecuted depends to a large extent on accident, for example on whether an aroused mob for some reason drags them before the governor (an impressive example from the second century is the martyrdom of Polycarp of Smyrna), and again to what extent the governor yields to pressure.

Connected with the alternative mentioned above (is Christianity in itself punishable or must crimes be proven?) is another which likewise has been much debated: how were proceedings conducted—by criminal trial (because of lawbreaking) or by the so-called police coercion, which the Roman governor exercised by virtue of his dignity as magistrate (in case of the punishability of the "name itself," for the suppression of associations dangerous to the state)? But this alternative also should not be put in this way. In the provinces, jurisdiction was based on the *imperium* of the governor. He pronounces judgment on the basis of his investigation of the facts and his free evaluation of them. And the emperor in his inquiry is "not bound to the laws . . . . He can define new crimes or amend old ones" (J. Bleicken).

Pliny's action and Trajan's approval are in agreement with this. The situation remained the same also under Trajan's successors. For the Christians, this meant that persecution constantly hung over their heads; actual outbreaks of persecution were limited in area and in duration.

Now the effect the persecution had on the church and the Christians' reaction to it are highly significant for the internal development of the church. M. Dibelius formulates the problem thus: Why did the Christians not become enemies of the state?

The reaction of the Christians was prepared in advance: the founder died on the cross. Persecutions had accompanied the church from the beginning, at first by the Jews. Even outside Palestine the Christians had experienced the Jews' activities against them (the book of Acts). But they were not thereby compelled to dissolve the church's connection with Israel in the history of salvation. One of the earliest and most important documents for this is Paul's Epistle to the Romans. The church is exposed to suffering by her faith itself. The world is not her home, but a foreign land (Phil. 3:20, etc.).

In it dwell Satan and his demons, who must be resisted (Eph. 6:10 ff.). The way into the kingdom of God leads through suffering (Acts 14:22). The Gospel of John shows that the world's hatred against the church is not accidental but belongs to the very nature of the church. By means of this hatred it becomes evident that faith does not arise out of the world, but is superior to it. The world can respond to faith only in the weak way of hatred; it cannot escape faith's impact. Thus the entire church has martyrdom before her gaze. Adopting and extending Jewish ideas of martyrdom, the church is convinced that martyrdom has atoning power (I Peter 4:1). Therefore the believers are not merely to rejoice in spite of suffering, but because of it (I Peter 4:12-13). But this joy does not become fanatical. Suffering is not sought out, as by provocation of the public or of authorities. The rule is this: when the confession is called for, then the believer has to take his stand for his Lord, even with his life. But when the missionaries are persecuted in one city, they should flee to another one (Matt. 10:23).

Faith itself makes it impossible for Christians to take the way of "spiritual resistance to Rome" (H. Fuchs), regardless of how obvious this seemed at the time. It was taken by Jewish apocalypticism and by one political group of the Jews. It was followed also by a part of Greco-Roman philosophy in which criticism of the monarchy ("tyrannis") was active then. The extreme Christian possibility is indicated by the book of Revelation (see below). The rule was: "Bless those who persecute you" (Rom. 12:14; cf. Matt. 5:44).

The most important document from the early period about the relationship to political actuality (next to Mark 12:17, "Give unto Caesar that which is Caesar's, and unto God that which is God's") is the passage in Rom. 13:1-7 (cf. the related passage in I Peter 2:13-14). It would be a mistake to regard this "Be subject to authority" as the basic outline of a Christian doctrine of the state. Paul does not have this in mind at all, particularly not of developing the doctrine of the state as a divine salvific agency. Not a trace of the state as possessing God's grace! Certainly the political power for keeping order is instituted by God. This appertains to the ordering of the world. But it belongs to the old world. In this old world it is necessary as a factor in an ordered society, and therefore it is to be respected. The entire passage is constructed out of ideas and expressions which were in common use at that time. It contains no specifically Christian ideas but is expressly civil. It shares this feature with large sections of the ethical instruction: because the world is eschatologically measured, the Christians do not emigrate from it, not even in a political theory. On the other hand, they have no idea of a revolution in God's name. It cannot be objected at this point that they in fact lacked tne power for such a revolution. They could nevertheless have cultivated it intellectually, and elevated it to the position of a program. After all, every revolutionary movement begins somewhere. In Palestine, revolutionary Jewish tendencies and groups were immediately evident. It was faith which cut off this route.

In Rom. 13, Paul does not touch upon the case in which the state requires a religious confession to itself or at least demands the abjuring of the Christian faith. But I Peter 2:13 utters the "Be subject . . ." with the persecution in view.

The next step can be discerned in the Pastoral Epistles (I Tim. 2: 1-2) and in I Clement (chap. 61—in view of the persecution! Appendix II:11*b*): the supplication of Christians for the (non-Christian) authorities. In this also the Christians are following Jewish tradition. They pray, by the way, not for the ruler's conversion but for his well-being. Presupposed in this is the ancient idea of the prosperous state: the ruler's well-being includes his good conduct; thereby the welfare of the people is assured. The church also prays for a prosperous life for itself. This is not in contradiction with readiness to suffer martyrdom. As said earlier the church was not to provoke martyrdom. She rather defended herself against false accusations and provided information about the faith (I Peter 3:15).

The church can be politically loyal because the Kingdom which she expects is not of this world. Jesus is the Messiah, but his messiahship is not political. This is set forth in the passion narrative especially by Luke and John. Thus in the book of Acts Luke can show in repeated scenes that from the Christians' side there is no disloyalty to the state. The state can be well satisfied with them, whether they are citizens or subjects.

The book of Revelation forms the dividing line in the judgment concerning the state. Here full-scale war is raging: the beast—unmistakably the Roman *imperium*—has risen out of the abyss and demands worship. A second beast follows it. Spiritual force, the ability to persuade, comes to power. Only martyrdom remains for the Christians (chap. 13). They know that the beast has its number—the number of a man. In the second picture, Rome appears as the great Babylon, the harlot on the beast, drunken with the blood of the saints; but the Lamb will be victorious (chap. 17). The judgment is painted in glowing colors (chap. 18). God avenges the blood of his servants (19:2). Thus he heeds the cry of the martyrs' prayer (6:10). It should be noted that this is the cry of those who have been slain. What is portrayed here is a scene in heaven, not a direction to the martyr as to what he is to wish for his persecutor.

CHAPTER XIII
Jewish Christianity After the Jewish War

1. On the concept "Jewish Christianity"

Here too the presentation again must begin with a remark about the usual dominant picture of the history. In this, Jewish Christianity is a sect on the very periphery of the church—substantively and geographically: these sectarians live on the boundary of the Roman Empire and of the arable land in Transjordan. Once again this picture is not accidental; the sources which we possess have had a part in molding it. The book of Acts follows only Paul's mission, the road to the west. No sources about the mission are preserved from the east, and incidentally not even any that are Gentile Christian ones. One must painstakingly dig for buried sources. In later times a flourishing Jewish Christianity existed in Syria. This makes it likely that from the outset it pursued missionary work in far greater scope and with greater success than can be discerned from scattered reports. It is extremely difficult to investigate this mission, particularly since it is by no means certain what all can serve as sources. For example, for the theological currents in Jewish Christianity, may we cite writings like Hebrews and Revelation? These certainly were written by Jewish Christians. But are they representative of groups of Jewish Christianity? Particularly since the latter does not form a unity! Even the term "Jewish Christianity" is loaded in advance and can be misleading. This is related to the position of the church fathers, which is one-sided and polemical. Since Irenaeus, this part of Christendom is stamped as heretical. The author Hegesippus distinguishes between orthodox and heretical Jewish Christians; he finds the derivation of heresy in the Jewish sects. The judgment of the church fathers has its effect down to present-day writing of history. Under the impact of Paul's theology and of the freedom of Gentile Christianity from the law, people see in the Jewish Christians the representatives of the vanquished narrow and false standpoint of legalism. Typical of this view is the judgment of a modern historian (H. Lietzmann, *Geschichte der Alten Kirche*, I [1932]:192) concerning a Christian author (Ariston of Pella) of presumably Jewish origin in whom no narrow legalism is visible: the conclusion is that he does not represent Jewish Christianity. Here the concept is narrowed in keeping with that ancient prejudice. Lietzmann explains further that after the year 70 Jewish Christianity moved into the sphere of influence of the Jewish sects of Transjordan. Here Hegesippus' presentation, which has the Christian sects arise out of the Jewish sects—a thoroughly tendentious picture—exerts its influence. Moreover, Hegesippus presupposes that the mass of Jewish Christians are not heretical, a fact which the modern historian ignores. Thus it is important that dogmatically determined categories be avoided. This applies above all to the attitude toward the law. The Jewish Christians' keeping of the law is their original style of life, which had been explicitly confirmed at the apostolic council. Seen from the perspective of the beginnings of the church, it is the emancipation from the law that is the innovation. Certainly the holding fast to the law can become heretical—if thereby the universality of salvation is limited and the binding character of the law is extended to the Gentiles as well. There were such groups; yet the concept "Jewish Christianity" may not be narrowed to include them alone. The Gospel of Matthew, for example, is also a Jewish Christian document. Even one who disputes this will concede that it at least reworks Jewish Christian traditions. But it does not subject the Gentiles to the law. Besides, even the community in which it arose appears to have detached itself from the Jewish ceremonial law.

That Irenaeus and his successors give a one-sided picture may still be seen in the earliest church father who discusses the Jewish Christians, Justin Martyr (himself from Palestine; around 150). He makes a distinction between those who indeed keep the law for themselves but do not wish to impose it upon the Gentiles, and those who declare that it is universally binding. In Justin's opinion only the former can be saved. Thus if one takes the concept broadly, in accordance with the historical state of affairs, then the Gospel of Matthew, the book of Revelation, etc. also belong to the sources. A further special problem is attached to the latter. This book was not composed in the East, but in western Asia Minor. Philip the evangelist settled in Asia Minor. Bishop Papias of Hierapolis (before 150) shows how lines run from there to Palestine. People were already speaking of an "invasion" of members of the original community into Asia Minor and found the cause of this in the Jewish War.

Only when one considers all this does one gain an accurate judgment as to the particular manifestations. These can at least be intimated from some fragments (excerpts from Jewish Christian writings). A special position among the reports of the church fathers is held by the fragments from Hegesippus about the church of Jerusalem which Eusebius inserted into his church history. Further, some church fathers mention Jewish Christian Gospels and quote some sentences from them. We hear of a Gospel of the "Hebrews," and of Gospels which the "Nazarenes" and "Ebionites" use. It is not clear whether this has to do with two or three different writings. The report in the church fathers is in part a confused one. Many scholars assume that the Gospel of the Hebrews and that of the Nazarenes are identical. Yet the doctrinal views in the fragments do not coincide. Therefore it is better to assume that they belong to different groups. One can summarize with caution thus:

(1) The Nazarene Gospel, employed in the Aramaic (or Syriac) language, is a variant form of the Gospel of Matthew (and thus translated from the Greek); it is not heretical.

(2) The Ebionite Gospel, written in Greek, likewise is related to the Gospel of Matthew. But it only begins with the appearance of John the Baptist. The reason for the omission of Matt. 1 and 2 can only be that the content, namely the doctrine of the virgin birth, was disputed. The Son of God appears by the Spirit's being united with the man Jesus at the latter's baptism.

(3) The Gospel of the Hebrews is likewise written in Greek. It is more strongly syncretistic than the other two: at the baptism "the entire fount of the Holy Spirit" descends upon Jesus. The latter is carried away by his mother, in other words, the Spirit. The understanding of the Spirit as Jesus' mother shows a Semitic background: in Semitic language the word for "spirit" is feminine. This book was perhaps the Gospel of the Egyptian Jewish Christians.

2. The church in Jerusalem

Our information comes essentially from Hegesippus (around 180), whose work Eusebius excerpted. In this connection a distinction is to be made in using the material between literal quotations and free rendering by Eusebius.

Even after the Jewish War, Rome allowed the Jews a certain amount of internal self-determination. It is true that the temple was not rebuilt. Thus the high priesthood and the sacrificial cultus came to an end. But through the initiative of the Pharisee scribe Jochanan ben Zakkai, a new Sanhedrin was constituted, to be sure no longer in Jerusalem but in the small town of Jamnia (near Joppa). Judaism was reformed in conformity with Pharisaic scribalism. The influence of the Sadducees was broken. The authority not only of the law but also of tradition was assured. The canon was closed. The Apocrypha, which were accepted in the Greek canon, remained excluded. The last book to be accepted was the book of Daniel. Non-orthodox biblical manuscripts were destroyed. With these measures not only was it positively determined what would thenceforward qualify as Jewish, but also a barrier was consciously raised against heresy. The malediction of (the "Nozrim" and) heretics was adopted in the chief Jewish prayer (Appendix II:9).

Of course the Jews under Roman rule could not at will use force against the Christians. But they could expel them from their still existing religio-social commonwealth (John 9:22; 12:42; 16:2). This situation is reflected in the Gospel of Matthew. This book makes the claim for the Christians that they are the true Israel. It is engaged in a bitter struggle with the dominant Pharisaism.

In spite of the destruction, after the war Jerusalem was again partially inhabited. In schematizing fashion Eusebius writes that half of the city was ruined under Titus, and the other half under Hadrian (through the uprising led by Bar Cochba). A Christian community also existed there once again. Anyone who holds the flight to Pella to be historical must assume that the refugees returned. This is probable anyhow. Hegesippus presents the history of the community in harmony with his view of history. For him James was the first bishop of Jerusalem. After his death in the year 62, Simon, son of Clopas, a kinsman of Jesus, was unanimously chosen to be his successor. He led the community to Pella and back again. He is said to have been crucified in the year 107 on the denunciation of Jewish heretics. What actually happened can no longer be discerned, since the accounts are confused. We learn that Vespasian had all the descendants of David tracked down. Hegesippus knows that Domitian had grandnephews of Jesus, grandsons of his brother Judas, brought to Rome, but released them again as politically harmless (Appendix II:6b). Perhaps Hegesippus got things confused: did Simon fall during Domitian's reign, and were those grandnephews brought to Rome under Trajan? The tradition is, after all, unclear. An unbroken succession of fifteen bishops from James down to the time of Hadrian was finally constructed.

It is historical that the community existed down to the second Jewish War, and apparently also that kinsmen of Jesus played a role in it. The war brought an end to the Jewish settlement in Jerusalem as well as to its Jewish Christian community. The Jews were forbidden to stay at all in the city which was newly established as Aelia Capitolina. Already during the war the Christians had been persecuted by the leader of the revolt, Bar Cochba. From this we must infer that they did not take part in the uprising.

3. Jewish Christianity outside Jerusalem

The distribution of Jewish Christianity is not limited to Palestine. From Matthew's Gospel one can infer Syria, without learning any particulars. Where did the community which based its tradition on Peter await the onset of the powers of hell (Matt. 16:17-19)? To what does the curious rivalry of a "Petrine" and a "Johannine" community in John 20–21 point?

The church fathers name some centers. The significance of Pella is shown in the statement, discussed above, that the original community fled thither. If this is historical, then the Jerusalemites must have succeeded in winning natives there. If it is legendary, it apparently developed because Pella was the seat of a significant community. The name of an author (Ariston) who came from Pella has been handed down. As other centers, Cochaba (in Hauran) and Beroea near Antioch (Aleppo) are named. Jerome claims to have visited the communities there; it may be that there he became acquainted with the Gospel of the Nazarenes. Yet there is reason for doubting his assertions.

The designations of two groups are handed down: "Nazarenes" (also given as "Nazorenes") and "Ebionites" (from the Hebrew word for "poor"). The Nazarenes are located by Epiphanius and Jerome in Beroea. They used the complete Gospel of Matthew in the "Hebrew" language (see above, p. 136: the so-called Gospel of the Nazarenes). The Ebionites are said to have used a Gospel of Matthew without chaps. 1 and 2 (see above: the so-called Ebionite Gospel). Thus the church fathers. Yet it is questionable how precisely one may define the individual groups. In essence the reporters say nothing concrete about the Nazarenes; they do not have precise information. In many passages they identify the two groups. Thus in Epiphanius, Pella is one time named as the seat of the Nazarenes, and another time of the Ebionites. But on the other hand, certain distinctions appear to have existed, chiefly in the attitude toward the law—is it binding also upon the Gentiles?—and in Christology—the virgin birth is a point of contention. Many regarded Jesus as a man who because of the conduct of his life was declared righteous. The title "Son of Man," which was significant in the primitive community but disappeared in Hellenistic Christianity because non-Jews could not understand it, appears again to play a role. For one group, apparently baptism and meals took the place of the law, along with ablutions and rules of abstinence (vegetarianism). The primitive Christian ideal of poverty was further cultivated. The unity of piety and ethics is expressed in the role of the concept "righteousness." James "the Just" is an ideal figure. Two quotations may illumine the moral ideal: "If you are on my breast and do not do the will of my Father, I will thrust you from my breast" (Gospel of the Nazarenes). According to the Gospel of the Hebrews, "anyone who has disturbed his brother's spirit" is among the worst of sinners.

There were Jewish Christians who revered the city of Jerusalem, that is, apparently so: they prayed facing Jerusalem. To all appearance they maintained that the temple was the true place of prayer, even after its destruction. This is distilled in the legend of James: James is said to have stayed there incessantly in prayer. The fate of the city is interpreted as punishment for his murder. A syncretistic special group are the Elkesaites. They too maintain the law, but reject the sacrificial cultus. Their doctrine displays some elements of cosmological speculation.

The Emergence of the New Testament Canon

1. In the presentation of early church history, it has been necessary to ask repeatedly: What norms are there for doctrine and the regulation of life, of the church as well as of the individual Christian? Doctrine indeed does not consist simply of a collection of propositions which were coined and handed down unaltered. Doctrine exists only in perennially new exposition and application, in the constant relation to the life of the believers and to the task of the church in the world: it is actualized in confession and mission, in the understanding of the faith, in the illumination of the forms of life, in comfort and promise, in the debate with Judaism and paganism, and more and more within the church in the distinguishing of orthodoxy and heresy, churchliness and sectarianism. Now how are the preservation of Christ's legacy and the perennial newness of the message related to each other? By what does one measure what is "Christian"? How does one define it without its becoming rigid?

In the beginning period, the content of the teaching and its norm coincide: in the confession of faith, which is summed up in brief formulas (see above, p. 45). Its authority is not that of a "sacred formula"; the wording is fluid. What matters is the substance, the saving event, Christ. The authority is that of the dead and risen Jesus Christ himself. Steadfastness of doctrine and its specific actualization belong together. Indeed, preaching and teaching are nothing other than the exposition of the authority of the Lord, for the salvation of the world.

The *writings* of the Christian teachers also get their recognition from their content. For a long time they still were not "Holy Scripture" in the sense of a dogmatically defined, formal authority. Still lacking also was the conception that they had arisen by means of a special inspiration.

The Holy Scripture of primitive Christianity is the Jewish Bible, our "Old Testament." As shown above, the primitive community did not "withdraw" from the Jewish religious fellowship. The God in whom they believed is he who speaks in the Scripture. This is expressed in the language: as "Scripture" or "Scriptures" one designated only Old Testament writings or passages taken from them. It was not until II Clement that a saying of Jesus was first introduced under this rubric. Finally, the expressions, familiar to us, of "canon" and "Old Testament" and "New Testament" come from a much later time. It is true that Paul already speaks of the old and the new "covenant": the Greek word employed was translated into Latin with the

139

word "testament." But it was a long time before people spoke of the "books of the old covenant" and soon thereafter also of those of the "new covenant," and still longer before "Testament" directly denoted the collection of books.

Except for individual disputes in Judaism over the validity of some books, the scope of the Old Testament canon at that time corresponded to the one recognized today.

2. For *Paul* the Old Testament was unconditionally valid. He could adduce it as an example for a doctrine: the election of Isaac and Jacob demonstrates the truth of God's free gracious choice (Rom. 9:7 ff.). It offers warning examples (I Cor. 10:1 ff.). Hebrews and I Clement both compile lists of examples from it (Heb. 11). The history of Israel sheds light on the present (Acts 7). The Old Testament is the book of prophecy, whose fulfillment the believers recognize and with which in turn they explicate the saving event (I Cor. 15:3-5). This form of the "proof from Scripture" is frequently expanded and varied. The passion narrative in particular is thus elucidated. From the Scripture one can show that Jesus' death is not his defeat but the saving deed willed by God. Indeed, one can look up therein, as in a reference book, the details of the course of events. Thus one learns from Psalm 22 what were Jesus' last words (Mark 15:34). Matthew in particular employed proof from Scripture throughout his entire book. "This happened so that it might be fulfilled . . . ."

Thus the Scripture was not only cited, as formal evidence, but interpreted. What was considered the correct interpretation is shown, for example, by passages like Luke 4:16 ff.; 24:25 ff.; 24:44 ff.: the key to the understanding is the Lord himself. The formal methods of interpretation are the Jewish methods of that time, e.g., allegory (Gal. 4:24) and typology (the Epistle to the Hebrews). What is "Christian" in the use of the methods does not lie in the methods themselves, but in the church's self-understanding as the true people of God (see above, pp. 37-38). Incidentally, there is no prescribed norm of exposition. It suffices that "Christ" is the canon of interpretation. One gains an impression of the multiplicity of possibilities in interpretation by looking beyond the New Testament and comparing the Epistle of Barnabas with I Clement: in the former, extravagant allegory plainly dominates, while in the latter the Old Testament serves primarily as a textbook in morality.

Since the authority of the Old Testament is acknowledged and since it is practiced, people hardly trouble themselves with its formal justification. Only in the later New Testament writings is it given protection by means of the (Hellenistic) Jewish idea of the inspiration of the Scripture (II Tim. 3:16-17; II Peter 1:21).

Incidentally, the scripture is not "necessary" in the sense that one could proclaim the message of Christ only with an explicit dependence on it. In long sections of Paul's epistles it hardly appears at all. It is not to be concluded from that, as A. v. Harnack does, that in essence the Old Testament is unimportant for Paul and that it serves only as a weapon in the discussion with Judaism. The state of things shows rather that Scripture does not "function" mechanically; that faith of course comes first and now sheds new light upon Scripture.

3. In the early period, there still was no awareness of one particular problem which necessitated some reflection in a later time. And yet one would expect it to arise, not for the first time with Paul, but already in pre-Pauline Hellenistic Jewish Christianity: if one no longer expects salvation from the fulfilling of the law and detaches oneself from the Jewish prescriptions, how can one then at the same time retain the Jewish religious document as Holy Scripture? For primitive Christianity the solution of the problem, as surprising as it may sound, lies in the Old Testament itself. Where the tradition of Jesus' teaching was cultivated, one had a support in Jesus' association with the Scripture. In addition, the tie with the Scripture is established in the belief in Christ as such, insofar as the "Messiah" is a figure of the Israelite salvation history. The assertion, now, that he has already come, implies both a positive acceptance of the Scripture and a critical debate with Judaism's interpretation of the Scripture. *Paul* characteristically makes use of the Old Testament in his argument precisely where he is justifying his doctrine of freedom from the law (e.g., in Rom. 10; Gal. 3), and thus is of the opinion that precisely in this doctrine the true sense of the Old Testament finds its expression (cf. Rom. 3:31). The *Epistle to the Hebrews* demonstrates from the Old Testament that with Christ's saving act the Old Testament cultus is at an end. Up until Christ it was commanded; but for faith it is only a shadowy prefiguring of the office and sacrifice of Christ as the true high priest. Its meaning, therefore, was to point beyond itself. Thus the Old Testament becomes the instrument of the theoretical debate with Judaism.

Around the middle of the second century, the author Justin Martyr produces a certain systematizing: in the Old Testament he distinguishes, first, the still valid moral law; second, the prophecy of Christ; and third, the cultic law, which was once valid for the Jews but now is a thing of the past. This systematizing presupposes a change in the framing of the question as compared with the earlier time (H. v. Campenhausen). Originally the authority of Scripture was undoubted. But in time the problem shifted to the question: how can the law ever have been God's revelation? When one raises the question thus, then the rights of Scripture must be explicitly proved. The time is ripe for Justin's solution on the one hand, but also for that of Marcion on the other hand (see below).

4. How does the formation of a *New Testament canon* come about? If one reflects on it abstractly, leaving out of consideration the actual position of the Old Testament in the church, which is already confirmed by tradition, in essence two possibilities may be conceived: a Christian collection of writings either *supplements* the Old Testament, or it *replaces* it. The first possibility lies along the line of development. The second, curiously and noteworthily, was the first to be actualized, by Marcion.

We noted above that for the church the authority was simply the Lord. This means first of all that faith is tied to Jesus as to him who fulfills the saving work, to the Christ of the confession of faith, the dead and risen and exalted One, who in the present not only guides his church by means of the tradition, but illumines her through the living Spirit.

The words of Jesus that are handed down have an unconditional validity. This is especially worthy of note in Paul, in whose theology the earthly history of Jesus, with the exception of his crucifixion, plays no role. In his epistles he cites only very few of Jesus' *words,* but these are presented as absolutely obligatory, e.g., the tradition of the Supper (I Cor. 11:23 ff.), and direct commandments (I Cor. 7:10).

Elsewhere people collected the teaching of Jesus as fully as was possible, in the sayings source ("Logia") and in the Gospels (on this, cf. Luke's program described in Luke 1:1-4). An impressive documentation of what the Lord meant for the molding of life and also for the understanding of the Old Testament law are the "antitheses" of the Sermon on the Mount with their "But I say to you" (Matt. 5:21 ff.), especially if this formula should be a creation of the community. There are arguments favoring such an interpretation.

The individual stages of the way from the original free form of the authority of the Lord to the canonizing of the books which transmit the account of his work cannot be traced out. This is due, for one thing, to the sources. Down to the middle of the second century there are no documents on this process. This is no accident, but is quite in harmony with the state of things. Down to that time there still was not even the idea of a canon of Christian writings. One can only infer from isolated allusions how Christian authorities—always under the presupposition of the absolute position of the Lord—were formed. But this still does not mean the authority of a *book* as such. With the passage of time, points of crystallization can be recognized: an earlier one, "the apostle" Paul and his epistles, and another, later one, the Gospels. At first, the development of the collection in these two groups ran two independent courses, until the two groups were combined; when this is done the first Christian canon is there. In both cases the common presupposition is the interval that has come to separate people from the early period, which now, from the new perspective, is characterized as the "apostolic" period (see above, Introduction). Even though for the *literary* collection Paul is utterly authoritative, still the general presupposition is the conception of the unity of all apostles, on the foundation of whom the church is built (Eph. 2:20). How the authority of the Lord is related to the role of the apostles is shown by passages like II Peter 3:2 (the apostles transmit the Lord's commandment) and I Clem. 42 (the apostles received the gospel from Jesus). They, on their part, preached the gospel and installed bishops and deacons. Thus the line to the present is laid.

5. The person of *Paul* was under attack after his death as it had been during his lifetime. Yet the development of the canon is first of all to be understood not from the rejection of his epistles (on this, see below) but from the esteem which he enjoyed. This is shown in several occurrences: new epistles are composed under his name (we call them deutero-Pauline; see above). Then, his epistles are collected and published; the individual stages in the emergence of this collection again cannot be traced out. Yet II Thessalonians already presupposes that letters of Paul—and even already forged ones?—are well known. The Ephesian epistle appears to know several of them. An important witness is II Peter 3:16: it speaks already of a collection of epistles and laments the fact that they are used by the heretics. In fact they were read and interpreted by Gnostics. Now there may be some connection between that fact and the fact that some "orthodox" writers are strikingly silent about Paul: Papias and Justin, for example (W. Bauer). Around the year 100, epistles of Paul are cited by authors (outside the deutero-Pauline literature:) Clement, Ignatius, and above all, Polycarp of Smyrna. It is possible that at first one or more smaller collections appeared (I Clement mentions only I Corinthians and is acquainted with Romans). Yet the details are unknown. In any case, soon after 100 the collection of the ten epistles which stand in the canon today (the epistles of Paul without the three epistles to Timothy and Titus; these emerge only later) may well have appeared. It is a pity that whoever edited them does not provide a foreword with information as to how he arrived at these epistles.

There are many conjectures about how this came about. Two examples: one is related to the order of the epistles. These appear in essence to be arranged according to length, with Romans at the head. But now there are ancient documents in which the Corinthian epistles are named in the first position: Tertullian and the Muratorian Canon (see Appendix II:12). From this fact, many conclude that the collection was brought together in Corinth. Yet it is uncertain whether the Corinthian epistles actually stood in first place in manuscripts. The order in the Muratorian Canon appears not to be that of manuscripts, but the order in time, as assumed by the author, of the emergence of the individual epistles.

Another hypothesis is: the Ephesian epistle is modeled after other epistles of Paul, and it is the only Pauline epistle which (possibly) is directed to no particular address. It was produced by the editor of the collection in order to introduce it and to set it forth as "ecumenical."

The impact of Paul's epistles, finally, is shown in the fact that (with minor exceptions) all the primitive Christian epistolary literature is shaped according to their pattern or betrays their influence.

One reaches firmer ground with Marcion (around 140), who adopted the ten epistles into his canon.

6. The *tradition of Jesus* is first passed along orally, but soon also put down in writing. The earliest collections are completely displaced by the Gospels. The oldest Gospel is the one traditionally ascribed to Mark. It becomes the model for all the later ones. But of course it is not "canonical." What it does is provide the stimulus for further collecting and editing. The authors of Matthew and Luke not only supplement but also vigorously reshape Mark's material. Luke gives (1:1-4) information explicitly about the principles of his work and thereby also suggests a criticism of his predecessors. The author of the Gospel of John is particularly free in his dealing with the tradition. Obviously the form and wording of the tradition are not sacred.

The oral tradition of Jesus' sayings is not ended by the composition of the Gospel books. It can be traced until well into the second century, in the Apostolic Fathers, and perhaps in Justin, who of course knew and used gospel writings. About the same time, Bishop Papias of Hierapolis in Asia Minor, who was acquainted with the Gospels of Matthew and Mark, declared that he esteemed the oral tradition more highly than the books.

There is disagreement as to how the four Gospels which have become canonical came to be collected. Undoubtedly the point of departure is the simple fact that they were available and enjoyed high regard, even though this differed from one country to another. But the multiplicity of presentations of Jesus also brought difficulties: indeed, they disagreed on some points. Would not the obvious thing have been to select *one?*

Here too the traces are scanty. In the first half of the second century, Clement knows either Matthew and Luke or a collection of sayings of Jesus which is based on these two. Polycarp may very well have been acquainted with the same two Gospels. Papias occupies himself with Matthew and Mark. Justin works with Matthew and Luke—not with John. Even Papias is silent about John.

Further traces are found in "apocryphal" writings, that is, those that represent themselves to be apostolic but (rightly) are not recognized. Examples are the "Gospel of Peter," fragments of an otherwise unknown Gospel, and the "Epistle of the Apostles" (texts in Hennecke-Schneemelcher-Wilson, Vol. I, with an indication of the gospel passages used).

On the whole, one has the impression that the traces steadily become clearer during the first half of the second century. But the idea of a canon of four Gospels is not yet present (particularly since the position of the Gospel of John still is uncertain). For the idea of the canon there is still lacking, as the decisive impetus, the formalizing of authority, and, included with this, the exclusion of the unrecognized writings as "apocryphal."

7. However one may evaluate the traces and find in them the presuppositions of the formation of the canon, the idea of the Christian canon was produced in one single, conscious act by Marcion, in order to establish his teaching:

The God of Jesus is not the same as the God of the Old Testament. The latter is the creator of the world, the God of righteousness. The good God dwells beyond the world. Out of compassion for men, who are enslaved by the law, he reveals himself in Jesus. Redemption is redemption from the world and from the law. This original teaching of Jesus, which Paul also held, then was adulterated with the Jewish interpretation, for one thing by means of other doctrinal writings, but then also by the action of some in falsifying the documents of the pure doctrine. Now Marcion sets up the canon for pure doctrine: the Gospel of Luke and the ten epistles of Paul. Whatever does not fit in with his teaching is excised as a forgery; for example, he strikes out Luke 1 and 2, the narrative of Jesus' birth. For the redeemer was not born as man. He appeared from heaven (in the fifteenth year of the Emperor Tiberius: Luke 3:1).

Thus the first Christian canon excludes the Old Testament. Now the battle revolves around the substance of the faith: the idea of God, namely the relation of God and world, creation and redemption, God and Christ; the nature of Christ; the validity of the tradition which for the church guaranteed the truth. One can anticipate that the "orthodox" canon will soon stand opposite Marcion's canon. Of course this was not produced in a single, organized action. At that time the presuppositions for such were lacking. There was not yet a supra-regional ecclesiastical organization. Nevertheless, toward the end of the second century the idea of the canon was present throughout the church, a canon in which the Old Testament is joined with a normative collection of Christian writings. There was extensive agreement about the central elements of this canon. The differences of opinion, which continued for a long time, had to do with peripheral elements. To be precise, one could say that full agreement was never reached. This is in itself correct, but in view of the scope of the agreement, it is of no substantive weight.

Over against Marcion's *one* Gospel stands the canon of the *four* Gospels. The "Muratorian Canon" (see Appendix II:12) presupposes the latter. The church father Irenaeus accounts for the necessity of the four: as there are four winds, four points of the compass, so also four Gospels; the number agrees with the number of the heavenly beings in Rev. 4 (Ezek.1): man/angel (Matthew), lion (Mark), ox (Luke), and eagle (John). Yet it is still true that the book as such is not sacred. The Syrian Tatian, a pupil of Justin, wishes to preserve the entire heritage and at the same time eliminate the inconsistencies by working the four Gospels into one book (a harmony of the Gospels). For a long time his work was the Gospel canon of the Syrian church. When here and there objection was raised to the Gospel of John, this has no great significance. It is interesting, however, that those who raised the objections were not at all branded as heretics.

In the "apostle" part of the new canon, the ten epistles of Paul are undisputed; in addition, there are the three Pastoral Epistles (the two epistles to Timothy and one to Titus). The apostolic canon is expanded beyond Paul to include "catholic" epistles. This happened to a varying extent in different places. Generally recognized are I Peter and I John. The others gradually gain their way, up to the finally accepted seven. The judgment on Hebrews similarly fluctuated. In the East around 200, it was accepted as one of Paul's epistles. In the West, it prevailed as an epistle of Paul only slowly, under the influence of the East. Two other writings round out the whole collection: the connection of the Gospels and the apostle section was achieved by the book of Acts, which is related to the third Gospel through the author and to the apostles through its contents. In the West, finally, the book of Revelation is acknowledged. In the East this did not happen until the fourth century, when Athanasius pleaded its cause. But opposing voices were still heard for centuries.

The "Muratorian Canon" shows how open the fringes of the canon remained. It recognizes not only the Apocalypse of John but also the Apocalypse of Peter. Elsewhere still other writings, for example the Epistle of Barnabas, were recognized.

The collection of the canonical at the same time signified the exclusion of the "apocryphal." In this connection a distinction is to be made: many writings were thoroughly accepted as orthodox and useful for reading, only they were not among the official writings read in worship services. Others, on the other hand, were rejected as heretical. The "Muratorian Canon" offers examples of both.

8. What were the standards for recognition or exclusion? Did the formation of the canon first of all mean as extensive as possible a collection of the extant writings from the early period, or primarily a critical sifting for the elimination of the proliferating "apocryphal" literature? Finally: did the churches with the canonizing process definitively renounce any further creative achievement and classify themselves as epigoni?

The second of the three questions above may not be formulated in this absolute alternative. The first step is the gathering together of the legacy. It begins already in the time when the production of still more Gospels was not yet thought of as a threat. People wanted to have good, old traditions about Jesus. After the sharp delimitation by Marcion it was all the more important to have a broad basis of accounts of Jesus. If the author of such a book is an apostle (i.e., passes for an apostle), so much the better. But the authority of his book is not bestowed by the idea of apostolic *office,* but by the fact that he is an eyewitness and well informed. Indeed, the books of the two non-apostles Mark and Luke are likewise accepted on the basis of their reliability. The idea of inspiration also plays no role. It is only in the next period that this idea is transferred by Origen from the Old Testament also to the New. That also answers the question of whether the church substituted the rule of a book for the free sway of the Spirit. This question is a modern formulation, not one of the ancient church. It presupposes a long process of formalization of Scripture and Spirit. In the period in which the canon was formed, there was no idea of a possible conflict between Spirit and Book. For one read the Book as current communication, in connection with the life of the church.

Persons (History and Legend)

It was necessary for us to present the life and work of Paul after his conversion in a connected fashion. All other persons have been mentioned only occasionally. This corresponds to the state of things in the sources. But it is rewarding to assemble the scattered notices. The lack of a closed tradition made possible the proliferation of legends. Hence we must attempt to separate truth and fiction.

1. The "twelve apostles"

We must keep in mind that the Twelve and the apostles were different groups. Only in the course of time did they come to be identified. In the present section we are concerned with the members of the circle of the Twelve, who down to the present time are "the apostles" in the public mind.

Who were they? What were their names? What did they do? With few exceptions they appear in the Gospels as inactive. They are simply Jesus' companions, who often disappear from the narrative when Jesus goes into action (e.g., Mark 1:21-28). This curious fact is explained by means of literary-critical analysis. It can be shown that many old bits of tradition did not take into account this group at all, and that the "disciples" were first mentioned upon the later combination of the individual narratives into a cluster of narratives. Alongside these are also ancient narratives in which they appear. Occasionally their conduct is reported: they do not fast. Once they pluck some grain, contrary to law, on the Sabbath. But such narratives are not intended to preserve for later generations an image of the disciples; they serve rather to impress upon the community, and to account for, one of Jesus' maxims. Only in a few scenes is their later role reflected: that of Peter above all in the scene of his confession of Jesus as the Messiah (Mark 8:27 ff.), and that of the sons of Zebedee in their proposal to Jesus that he assign to them the places of honor in the kingdom of God (Mark 10:35 ff.). Again and again Mark emphasizes the disciples' lack of understanding with respect to Jesus' deeds and teachings, although they are constantly being taught by him. Now this must not be explained by the suggestion that Jesus apparently gathered around him a group of dullards. The disciples' lack of understanding is connected with Mark's central theological idea, the "messianic secret." Mark presents them thus in order to mark the transition from the earthly ministry of Jesus to the time after his death and resurrection and to demonstrate the paradoxical character of the revelation: it is only the resurrection that discloses his true nature. Hence even his closest followers could not comprehend him. Because Mark pursues first of all

148

theological interests, not psychological or biographical ones, personal features hardly become visible. The disciples appear for the most part as a collective entity. When one or another is singled out, these are in the main those who after Easter enjoyed the greatest esteem in the church, yet without any character sketch being given: Peter and the two sons of Zebedee. One can still trace out how certain names made their way into the narrative. According to Mark 14:13, Jesus sends "two of his disciples" into Jerusalem to prepare the Passover meal; according to Luke they were Peter and John (Luke 22:8). It is not that Luke has some more exact tradition at his disposal. It is rather that in time the notion arose that it must have been these two, as the most famous ones.

The group embraces the following names:

At the head stand two pairs of brothers: *Simon* and *Andrew;* and *James* and *John,* the sons of Zebedee. The tradition has it that the father of the former pair is Jona (Matt. 16:17) or John (John 1:42). In the lists of the Twelve these four are regularly named first, though with variations in the order (cf. Mark 3: 16-17 with Matt. 10:2; Luke 6:14; Acts 1:13, and on the founding of the group, Mark 1:16-20). Further, there is uniformity in the tradition on the following names: *Philip, Bartholomew, Matthew, Thomas, James* the son of Alphaeus, *Simon* "the Canaanean" (i.e., "the Zealot," member of the group of nationalist activists), and *Judas Iscariot* (or "the Iscariot"). *One* name varies in the tradition: in Mark one is called *Thaddaeus* (he is listed after the second James), and in Luke on the other hand, *Judas,* son of James (here he is placed after Simon the Zealot, before Judas Iscariot; thus the two Judases form the conclusion of the list; cf. also Acts 1:13). In Matthew the tradition in the manuscripts is not uniform. The best ones, in agreement with Mark, have Thaddaeus, but some manuscripts, and church fathers as well, read Lebbaeus; and most of the manuscripts smooth it out thus: Lebbaeus with the surname of Thaddaeus. Apparently the original is "Lebbaeus." Later an attempt was made to eliminate the contradiction with the other tradition. The Gospel of Matthew has caused much racking of the brain because it places Matthew (Matt. 9:9; cf. 10:3) in place of the tax collector Levi (Mark 2:14). The Gospel of John, which does not assemble a list of the Twelve, mentions by name Simon Peter, Andrew (not the two sons of Zebedee), Philip, Thomas, the two Judases, and (beyond the Synoptics) Nathanael (John 1:35 ff.).

Later, attempts were made to remove the contradictions and, above all, to save the number twelve. These speculations have no historical value, although they determine the Catholic Church's saints' calendar down to the present day. In Syria, Thomas was equated with the one Judas. But the simplest way was to identify this Judas with Thaddaeus. Since the Middle Ages, Nathanael has been regarded as a second name of Bartholomew. Since Origen and Tertullian, another line of reasoning has also appeared: Judas is identified with the brother of Jesus of the same name; the further description of him as "of James" is interpreted to mean "brother of James" (namely, the Lord's brother). Similarly, then, Simon the Zealot also becomes the brother of Jesus.

Some are said to have been fishermen by trade (Mark 1:16-20, etc.). Luke casually remarks (Acts 4:13) that they possessed no scribal education. From none of them has anything written come down to posterity, if one denies the genuineness of the two epistles of Peter and the five Johannine writings. About most of them nothing at all is known except the name. Yet of one, the "Canaanean" or "Zealot," this surname preserves an allusion to his political past; but we do not learn how he came to Jesus or anything about his later activity as a member of the circle of the Twelve.

Since after a little while nothing more was known about them, legend had free play. It begins already in the New Testament, with the episodes of Peter sinking beneath the waves (Matt. 14:28 ff.) and of the unbelieving Thomas (John 20:24 ff.). Only one remains at least largely excluded from the legend-building, James the son of Zebedee, who was put to death about the year 43 (Acts 12:2). Nevertheless, the feature which is also typical of other martyrdoms was invented concerning his martyrdom, that the soldier who conducted him to the court was converted and was likewise beheaded. And in spite of the New Testament, the Spanish church succeeded in connecting him with her country and in preparing a burial place for him which is venerated down to the present (Santiago de Compostela).

Passages from the New Testament became sources for the legend-building: from Jesus' missionary commandment arose legends about the mission of the "apostles" "into all the world." The notion was formed that they divided up among themselves the missionary territories. From Jesus' words which predict to the disciples their following him into suffering grow the legends of the apostles' martyrdoms. Especially abundant is the legendary tradition (apart from Peter and John, to whom a special section is to be devoted; see below) about Andrew, Thomas, and Philip.

Andrew is given for his mission territory the land around the Black Sea, the lands of the lower Danube, and Greece. He is said to have been executed on September 30 of the year 60, in Patras, on a diagonal cross ("St. Andrew's Cross").

Thomas is regarded as the apostle of Parthia and India. The name "Thomas" means "twin." He is identified with Judas, and the latter again is identified with Jesus' brother of the same name. The culminating point then is that Thomas/Judas even becomes the twin brother of Jesus. An abundant body of literature is attached to his name: the recently discovered "Gospel of Thomas," a collection of sayings of Jesus; and an entirely legendary book about Jesus' childhood. His activity is related in the legend-filled Gnostic Acts of Thomas.

An interesting special case is *Philip*. A Philip is one of the Twelve. In addition, the book of Acts knows a Philip who belongs to the circle of the seven (Hellenists: Acts 6:5). The significance of the latter is evident from his honorary name: he is called "the evangelist" (Acts 21:8). He perhaps is the most important pioneer of the primitive Christian mission (Acts 8). He worked in Samaria and in the coastal regions. He was surrounded by a "pneumatic" atmosphere. His daughters were prophetesses. Later he is said to have gone to Hierapolis in Asia Minor and to have died there as a martyr.—It is not surprising that the legends now confuse the two Philips. On the other hand, incidentally, modern scholarship has occasionally asked whether they were not in actuality identical.

Of course the traitor *Judas Iscariot* also affords abundant material. Even the New Testament already knows two different legends about his frightful end (Matt. 27:3 ff.; Acts 1:15 ff.). A fragment from Papias, full of repulsive fantasy, shows how the legends grew further. The motive for his deed is said to have been greed (cf. Mark 14:10 with Matt. 26:15; cf. John 12:6). This too must be adjudged legendary. Even the surname gives us no information, for it cannot be interpreted with certainty. Suggestions are: a) "the man from (the city of) Kerioth"; b) "the deceiver" (in this case the name would have to have been attributed to him subsequently); c) "the Sicarian" (from the Latin *sica*, "dagger"); the Sicarii were a group of active revolutionaries. In this case the surname would characterize his past as did that of the "Zealot" Simon. Incidentally, in time Judas came to be described as having red hair.

2. *Simon "Peter"*

According to Mark 1:16-18, Simon and his brother Andrew were the first ones called by Jesus to be his "disciples," who shared his wandering life with him. This does not mean that they were always on the move. Jesus appears rather to have had a fixed residence in Capernaum. The two brothers also lived there (Mark 1:29), though of course according to John 1:44 they lived in Bethsaida. Peter was married (I Cor. 9:5); his mother-in-law is mentioned once (Mark 1:30-31). His name, in Hebrew Simeon (transcribed in Greek as Symeon: Acts 15:14; II Peter 1:1), is assimilated to the Greek name Simon. Their father was called Jona (Matt. 16:17) or John (John 1:42).

It can be inferred from his later position in the church that he moved to the head of those who were called to be disciples. John 1:40 has a different order of the first calls: two disciples of the Baptist, one of them Andrew, are the first to join Jesus; Andrew then also brings his brother Simon to him. Yet even this is not a historically reliable report. In any case, the lists of the Twelve in which Peter regularly stands at the head were formed after Easter and correspond to Peter's position in this circle. The story of the calling in Mark 1:16 ff. also acquired its form after Easter. This can be recognized in the saying about fishers of men; by means of this saying the calling became a sending forth; this is a post-Easter interpretation. One can read the rapid growth of the legend in the Lukan version of the call, the story of the miraculous catch of fish (Luke 5:1 ff.).

It became of decisive significance for his career that he was the first one to whom the resurrected Jesus appeared. One might find it strange that this event, foundational for the church, is only incidentally mentioned, not portrayed. It is true that Peter is present, together with others, in other appearance stories. But this *first* appearance has not been transposed into a narrative. This is not surprising, but rather typical: the narrative elaboration belongs to a later time.

There are many conjectures as to why it was Peter who first experienced such an appearance. The only one which we may explore arises out of the question:

how is this appearance connected with Peter's "denial" of Jesus after the latter's arrest? If this denial is historical, then Peter is rehabilitated by the Lord himself. But is it historical? In favor of its being historical, one can argue thus: How could this story, which lets the leading man of the church appear as weak of character, indeed, attributes to him the gravest sin, have been invented? One can only read it in the light of Jesus' words about confessing and denying him before men (Mark 8:38 par.). Some respond to the question by saying that it was an invention of Peter's adversaries. We see in other passages that he had such. But this explanation is unlikely. For in that case this story would not have been preserved in the church and incorporated into the Gospels. And who are these adversaries supposed to be? Of course one could let his imagination run on: Peter disappears from history in mysterious fashion. A brother of Jesus appears in his place in Jerusalem. Were the disciples pushed aside by Jesus' kinsmen, who indeed then are said to have stood at the head of the community for a long time (see above)? Did the story of the denial arise out of these rivalries? Hardly; for there is no prevailing tendency in it in favor of Jesus' kinsmen and none against the rest of the disciples. It is told rather precisely as a foil to Peter's later position of leadership. And precisely this prompts us to note: does it actually speak *against* Peter? Does it lay bare his character?

If we start out, not from our impressions, but from the mentality of the early church, the picture changes. The early times did not glorify any heroes of the faith. This is only a later tendency. Originally the picture of the disciples is not shaped by the feeling of admiration, but it rather serves to further the understanding of the person of Jesus. They do not understand him—not because they were stupid; rather, in this fashion the mystery of the revelation is elucidated, the way to the cross, which only by the resurrection is disclosed to be the way of salvation. It is from this perspective also that the scene of Peter's *confession* (Mark 8:27 ff.) is shaped: he confesses Jesus as the Messiah—the first one to do so. But he wants him in his glory, and must hear the words, "Get thee behind me, Satan!" Did the story of the denial arise in some sort of combination with that of the confession? The latter is hardly historical; for Peter is uttering the confession of the post-Easter community.

Anyone who assumes that Peter's denial is historical can explain his development thus: Although Peter had broken his loyalty to his Lord, the impression which Jesus had made upon him remained in effect, more than in the other disciples; indeed, he was motivated precisely by the consciousness of his failure. Of course this consideration does not offer much satisfaction; in essence it explains an X by means of a Y. More substantial is another suggestion: Peter was the first confessor after Easter. Now, by means of this scene, this is transposed back into the life of Jesus. If now a connection with the denial can be shown, a similar inference should be drawn concerning it. Was it intended precisely to emphasize the confession?

A further argument *for* the historicity of the denial is this: the author of Mark's Gospel, John Mark, is said to have stood close to Peter personally (I

Peter 5:13). He is even supposed to have been his interpreter and to have written down his reminiscences (Papias). But what Papias writes is twaddle. First of all, it is not known who wrote the Gospel of Mark. And if it really was John Mark, it is true that he hailed from Jersalem, but outside I Peter 5:13 nothing is known of any closer connection with Peter. The First Epistle of Peter does not come from Peter. At times Mark worked together with his kinsman Barnabas. Thus he comes into contact with Paul; in spite of temporary separation, he appears to have gone back to him and remained with him.

If one does not take the person of Mark as the point of departure, but the narrative as it stands, it shows no indication that it goes back to a narrative of Peter himself. And yet it would have had to do so, because no other eyewitness from the circle of the disciples is supposed to have been present. Only the Gospel of John introduces such a person, "another disciple," but this person remains a shadowy figure.

We have spoken earlier of the conclusions which Peter drew from the appearance. Now we must go into the picture which the book of Acts draws in representing his activity. After the ascension, he takes the leadership of the community in hand and has the circle of the Twelve filled out again (Acts 1:15-26). At the outpouring of the Spirit, he is the spokesman, with the striking success which the Spirit vouchsafes. He performs miracles (3:1 ff.; cf. 5:12-16) and is the instrument of the divine intervention against Ananias and Sapphira (5:1-11). He speaks in the trial before the Sanhedrin (5:26 ff.). At the direction of the Spirit he opens the door into the church for the Gentiles (chap. 10).

Certain items must be eliminated from this picture. It was the Hellenists who took the first steps toward the Gentile mission, as the book of Acts itself shows (11:19-20). But the fact remains that for a long time Peter was the leading man in the church, apparently not only with the rights of the "firstborn" but also with the recognition of the one who had grasped the meaning of the appearances and molded the church's thought. When Paul traveled to Jerusalem for the first time after his conversion, he did so in order to meet Peter (Gal. 1:18). In addition he mentions James (the brother of Jesus) only in passing, and declares that he saw no other of the "apostles."

As was set forth earlier, Peter later is one of the three "pillars," along with James and John. At the apostolic council these three are the representatives of the community. An agreement assigns to Peter the "department of foreign affairs" for the Jewish Christians, probably on the basis of his achievements as a missionary. He is the only one of the Twelve of whom there are reliable reports about an activity also outside Palestine. But when and why he left Jerusalem is unknown. Much discussed is one sentence in the book of Acts: according to Acts 12 he was once imprisoned (by Agrippa I) and was to be executed. But he was set free by an angel and "went to another place" (12:17). One can find in this an allusion to his final departure from the city. But this is not intended. Subsequently, at the council, he is there again. Or was the sentence supposed to have had that meaning at least in one of Luke's sources? Hardly. It says nothing but that Peter first went to a safe place. After the early death of Agrippa, when Judea again came under direct Roman administration, he must have returned. Another explanation is yielded if one dates the council as early as 43/44. In that case it has already taken place before the imprisonment, and in Acts 12:17 the final departure was meant (in the source). But the reservations discussed above are against the early dating of the council.

Later, apparently not long after the council, he appeared in Antioch; this must have been connected with the agreement reached at the council. Here we get an interesting glimpse of his behavior (Gal. 2:11 ff.). On the one hand, the council had preserved the unity of the church, and on the other hand, it had maintained the relative separation between Jewish and Gentile Christians. This agreed with the standpoint of the Jerusalemites as well as with that of Paul. The one maintained the law, and the other did not adopt it. But from this arose the problem of whether Jewish Christians may take meals with Gentile Christians. Opinions about this were divided. Peter and Barnabas answered the question in the affirmative, the group around James in the negative. Thus at first Peter and Barnabas maintained the fellowship at table; but they let themselves be frightened off by followers of James. Thus it came to the clash (discussed above); apparently Peter remained the tactical victor.

About his further work as missionary, there is in addition only the brief note in I Cor. 9:5, that on his travels he was accompanied by his wife. May we conclude from this passage that he once came to Corinth? It is true that he had disciples there (I Cor. 1:12). But the traces are too faint for us to be able to say.

The most vigorously debated problem of his biography or of the boundary between biography and legend is that of his stay in Rome. The dispute was kindled anew by the new excavations under St. Peter's which were expected—in vain—to uncover his tomb. According to Catholic tradition he was bishop of Rome for twenty-five years. Since he is supposed to have been executed under Nero in the year 64, he would have to have come there as early as about the year 40. But this is impossible. At the time when Paul wrote his letter to Rome, in the mid-fifties, Peter cannot yet have been there. Otherwise Paul could not have completely ignored him. There is still no full agreement among scholars as to whether Peter was ever in Rome at all. For a long time the dispute over this question was, to a large extent, one between confessional groups. Today the lines of battle are not so rigidly drawn. Both sides are agreed that even if one could prove that Peter never set foot in Rome, the Catholic Church would not be unhinged. Today the majority even of Protestant scholars are of the opinion that Peter in fact stayed for a time in Rome and that he suffered death there. The swing of the pendulum to the current opinion was brought about by a book of the Protestant church historian Hans Lietzmann in 1915 (*Petrus und Paulus in Rom*). He concluded from some reports from the early church that already around 200, people were showing the tombs of the two chief apostles, that of Peter in the Vatican gardens, beside Nero's circus, and that of Paul on the road to Ostia. Lietzmann argues (*Geschichte der Alten Kirche*, I:201; ET, *Begin-*

nings of the Christian Church, p. 192) that the two burial places "lie in sites apart from those of all other cults of early Christian Rome, so that there can be scarcely any doubt of their genuineness." This logic is not absolutely conclusive. One could also deduce that if the place of martyrdom was known, people later sought the tomb also in the same vicinity. That would at least make martyrdom in Rome historical. What are the *sources?*

(1.) I Peter, according to well-founded opinion composed in the time of Domitian, purports to have been written in "Babylon" (5:13). This is certainly a code name for Rome. Thus the anonymous author assumes that Peter spent some time there.

(2.) I Clement is dated in the same time. This work looks back on a persecution. At the outset it enumerates, in order to strengthen the believers, examples of heroic endurance of martyrdom, and as the most outstanding of these it lists Peter and Paul (Appendix II:4). It is true that the author does not say explicitly that they died in Rome, but the assumption that he meant this is an obvious one.

(3.) In his letter to Rome around 110, Ignatius of Antioch, looking toward his own forthcoming martyrdom, likewise recalls these two. He too fails to say that they suffered in Rome. But it is striking that he mentions them precisely in his epistle to Rome. Of course objections can be raised to the conclusiveness of I Clement and Ignatius. The former says explicitly of Paul that he came to the West, but it does not say this of Peter. And Ignatius is on the way to martyrdom in Rome. Thus it could be that he mentioned the two martyrs in this particular epistle simply because for him "Rome" means "martyrdom."

Nevertheless, I Peter remains as a witness that around the year 100 the connection of Peter and Rome was known. Further: there is no competing tradition that he died elsewhere (however, see below).

None of the other witnesses is substantial. Whether Rev. 11 refers to Peter and Paul and their death in Rome is at least doubtful. All the rest are legends (in the apocryphal Acts of the Apostles).

Perhaps there is after all one counter-argument: Jesus' word to Peter in Matt. 16:17-19. The linguistic foundation of this is Semitic. It must have arisen in a community in the East which was conscious of a special tie with Peter and which already was looking back on his death. Does it presuppose that he died in the vicinity of "his" church, in the East?

It is certain that Peter was not bishop in Rome. The office of monarchical bishop did not yet exist at that time. And precisely in Rome it was especially late in developing, around the middle of the second century. On the positive side, the only established fact is that he died as a martyr. This is further confirmed by John 21.

The legend about his death is connected with the denial: Peter yields to the urging of concerned friends and leaves Rome in order to find safety. At the gate of the city Jesus meets him. To Peter's question, "Where are you going, Lord?" (*quo vadis?*), he answers that he is going to Rome to be crucified. Shamed, Peter turns around. He is crucified head downward.

3. James "the Just"

James is the only person (other than Jesus himself) of primitive Christianity who is mentioned by an early non-Christian source, namely the Jewish historian Josephus in his *Antiquities of the Jews* (Appendix II:3*a*). This book appeared in the year 93/94. Josephus comes from Jerusalem, is of priestly lineage, and during the Jewish War was in command in Galilee. The fact that he mentions James shows what recognition the latter enjoyed even among the non-Christian Jews. His position in the church had a twofold ground: he was a brother of Jesus (Mark 6:3; Gal. 1:19; Josephus), and the resurrected Jesus appeared also to him (I Cor. 15:7). Apparently it was not until this appearance that he was converted to Jesus' cause. Presumably it was he who led into the church the other kinsmen who became Christians. Sometime, apparently early, he came to Jerusalem. His career crossed that of Peter. When Paul visited Jerusalem for the first time, James was already a well-known personality, but he still stood behind Peter. At the time of the apostolic council he was, *along with* Peter and John, one of the three "pillars"; many assume that he was already the leader, since Paul mentions his name first. Yet this conclusion is not compulsory (see above, p. 55). In any case, together with Peter he determines, on the Jewish Christian side, the course of the negotiations.

Of course his success is grounded not only in his lineage but also in his own achievement and bearing. He represents the consistent point of view that the Jewish Christians must continue to keep the law. But he does not wish to limit the church to Jews, nor does he wish to impose the law upon Gentile Christians. He is no "Judaizer." Judaizers appear in Galatia and appeal to James—unjustly, as Paul shows (Gal. 2). Unlike Peter, he remains in Jerusalem and comes to head the community there. But his influence extends far beyond the city. In Antioch Peter beats a retreat before James's people (Gal. 2:12). After his death his personality continued to exert an influence in the memory of the people. His conduct earned him the surname of "the Just." His piety (legend was able to elaborate it) must have been acknowledged even by the Jews. For up to the year 62, he could appear in Jerusalem and lead the community there. Josephus shows that esteem for him continued after his death even outside the community.

The background of his violent death was formed by the intensification of the political crisis in Palestine which preceded the war of the years 66-70. The political attitude of the Christians ("render unto Caesar that which is Caesar's") had to excite the radical nationalists. In the year 62 the governor Festus died in office. The (Sadducean) high priest Annas II used the vacancy before the arrival of Festus' successor to strike: James, along with others, was stoned (Josephus; Hegesippus already relates his martyrdom in a legendary version; Appendix II: 3*b*). After his death he became the patron of a group within Jewish Christianity. He appears in this role in the Gospel of Thomas (Saying 12). There the role is accounted for by means of a saying of Jesus: "The disciples said to Jesus, 'We know that you will go away from us. Who then is to be great over us?' Jesus said to them, 'In the place to which you have come, you will go to James the Just, because of whom heaven and earth have come to be.' " Writings also were attributed to him, e.g. the "Epistle of James," which was accepted into the canon; and he became the patron of Gnostic writings. A Gnostic sect, the "Naassenes," was traced directly back to him. All such things were possible then.

4. John, the son of Zebedee

According to Mark 1:16-20, John, together with his brother James, was called, after Simon and Andrew, by Jesus to "discipleship." The two pairs of brothers are described as fishermen on the Sea of Tiberias ("Sea of Galilee"). John 1:35 ff. gives a different tradition: two disciples of John the Baptist join Jesus; one is Andrew, and the other is unnamed. It is frequently conjectured that John is meant. According to this view, his name is not given because he is identical with the author of the Gospel of John, who deliberately keeps himself in the background. Indeed, in the entire Gospel the name of John (and of his brother James) is passed over. Similarly, it is said, it is John who is concealed behind the disciple "whom Jesus loved." These suggestions are possible, but they remain only conjectures.

The two brothers must have had a significant position in the community. In the lists of the apostles they stand in second place. They were given a surname (according to Mark 3:17, Jesus himself did it): Boanerges, which is translated in Mark as "sons of thunder." The actual meaning of the word has never been explained with certainty. Together with Peter they appear as Jesus' three closest confidants. Some light is shed on them by a scene in Mark 10:35-45; they desire to occupy the places of honor beside Jesus in the kingdom of God. This story is a legend which first arose after Jesus' resurrection. What is to be deduced from it? Rivalries over the leadership of the community, an effort on the part of these two to place themselves at the head, which however did not succeed? Yet they must have maintained a prominent position. James was put to death in the year 43; thus he appeared to the public as one of the representatives of the community. And John was one of the three pillars. Unfortunately, we do not know his role at the apostolic council, except for the fact that he approved the agreement.

This is all that we know about him. At this point begin the puzzles, more than about any other of the Twelve (even including Peter). His life and death are completely woven about with legend. According to Mark 10:39, Jesus prophesied to him and his brother their martyrdom. Thus we must assume that he actually suffered martyrdom; but already in John 21 it is cloaked in enigmatic fashion. The occasion, time, and place of his death are unknown. Some (relying on an obscure note) have assumed that he was killed at the same time as his brother, in the year 43. This is unlikely. Apart from the fact that then one would have to place the apostolic council earlier, it leaves unexplained why the book of Acts is silent about his death.

The legend develops in the opposite direction: in it, John is the apostle who reaches a great age and connects the time of the apostles with the later generations until he dies a natural death in Ephesus. He appears as a battler against Gnosticism. He is said to have been exiled to the island of Patmos under Domitian. This is inferred from Rev. 1:9. According to the tradition, John is the author of the Gospel, the three Epistles, and the "Revelation." But even from these alleged writings of his, "John" remains an enigma. The obscure "Revelation" purports to have been written by someone named John on the island of Patmos—but who is this? The fourth Gospel, which is attributed to him, resists every attempt to fit it into church history. It is a document of a community which cannot be pinned down anywhere. Can one establish it as historical kernel that this community had elevated John to be its patron (yet without any concrete knowledge about him to hand down)? At any rate it is aware of being in competition with a group whose watchword is "Peter" (John 21), without branding these others as heretics.

Papias, bishop of Hierapolis, contributed a great deal to the confusion of the tradition—the historian Eusebius already testifies to his intellectual weakness. Papias names two Johns, the disciple and the "Elder." What he has to relate about them is unclear and without any historical value.

Later, John acquires the surname of "the theologian." Throughout church history he becomes the patron of a spiritualistic religiosity: the church father Clement of Alexandria venerates him as such. The Gnostics interpret the Gospel of John in their sense.

Also to be mentioned is the connection with the legends about Mary. According to John 19:26-27, the dying Jesus entrusted his mother to his favorite disciple. When this disciple was identified with John, the legends about John drew the legends about Mary along with them. When John went to Ephesus, Mary also had to be relocated there.

5. Joseph Barnabas

The surname "Bar-naba(s)" is supposed to mean "son of consolation," according to Acts 4:36.

The couple of fragmentary notes about him do not correspond to his actual significance. In truth he was one of the most important personalities of the primitive church. He hailed from the Jewish Diaspora, from Cyprus. Apparently he, like many Jews of the Diaspora, had moved to Jerusalem. He must have become a Christian early and achieved a highly regarded standing. The book of Acts knows (4:36-37) that he gave his possessions to the community. This fits in with a remark of Paul (I Cor. 9:6); as a missionary, Barnabas holds to the same principles as does Paul—and since Barnabas is the older, he is Paul's teacher: Barnabas and Paul renounce the right of missionaries to be supported by the communities.

Although a Jew of the Diaspora, he appears not to have belonged to the circle of the "Hellenists." At any rate he was not a member of the leading group in this company. He also remained in Jerusalem when this circle was dissolved.

In Acts 14:4, 14, the title of apostle is assigned to him. Since elsewhere Luke uses this title only for the Twelve, it is possible that here an early source is showing through. His activity becomes visible after he has moved to Antioch. The book of Acts has him coming there on official business for the Jerusalem community. In any case he keeps up the connection with Jerusalem and communicates this attitude to Paul also. But his role in Antioch does not rest primarily on an official mission, but on his own religious attainments. In Acts 13:1 he appears at the head of the leading men, the "prophets and teachers." He is chosen with Saul to extend the mission. Later the two of them represent the Antiochian community in the delivery of a collection (Acts 11:27 ff.) and then in the apostolic council. Apparently Barnabas grew in Antioch along with the development of affairs. He affirms the Gentile mission and—this is to be inferred with certainty from the facts, from the course of the apostolic council, and from Paul's assertions—the freedom of the Gentile Christians from the law.

Thus already in Barnabas are displayed the basic features of the idea of church and mission which Paul then developed conceptually: law-free Gentile church and maintenance of the unity of the church by means of ties with Jerusalem, and therewith preservation of the salvation-history connection. His influence reaches still further. The common life of Jewish and Gentile Christians in the new fellowship poses problems, even immediately after the council. At first they are passed over, since the Jews apparently without scruple set aside their law and maintain table fellowship with the Gentiles. It is true that in this respect the Hellenists had already led the way. After the council, Barnabas bows to the letter of the agreement and binds himself as a Jewish Christian to the ceremonial law again. Paul makes this a grave charge against him. But obviously Barnabas with Peter won his way in Antioch. He remained a missionary to the Gentiles, and Paul speaks of him (if one excepts the collision in Antioch) without criticism, indeed, can even emphasize their agreement.

In church history, attention has been given above all to Barnabas' collaboration with Saul/Paul. According to Acts 9:27, the older man introduced the younger in Jerusalem. Later he brought him from Tarsus to Antioch (Acts 11:25-26). In their mission together he was at first the leader. He worked out the principles to which Paul then held all through his life (I Cor. 9). Yet at the apostolic council Paul already appears as the superior. He decides on the companion, the Gentile Christian Titus. He appears to have conducted the discussion with the "pillars"; indeed, he is even officially acknowledged as *the* missionary to the Gentiles and to this extent as being of equal rank with Peter. Later Paul and Barnabas separated, as a result of the conflict which Paul relates in Gal. 2. The book of Acts (15:36 ff.) reduces the dispute over principle to an innocent difference in personal opinion. But Paul's respect for Barnabas remains—or is restored. Paul indicates this clearly in I Cor. 9. Galatians and I Corinthians likewise show that in the Pauline communities also, Barnabas was a generally well-known and esteemed personality.

After the separation, Barnabas betook himself, with John Mark, to his homeland of Cyprus. There legend seized upon him. People attributed to him the Epistle to the Hebrews (Tertullian) and the "Epistle of Barnabas" (see above, pp. 27-28).

6. Apollos

This name is an abbreviated form of Apollonius or something similar. He became a Christian after Paul, but asserted himself in the latter's missionary territory independently alongside him. In I Corinthians, Paul treats him as a partner, not as a pupil, even though he clearly maintains his own precedence (I Cor. 3:6). He hails from Alexandria, the famous center of Jewish scholarship (the philosopher Philo taught there, on into the forties). If we only knew whether Apollos became acquainted with Christianity while still in Alexandria! What the book of Acts tells about him (18:24 ff.) is somewhat unclear: he is said at first to have been only imperfectly acquainted with Christian doctrine, to have known only the baptism of John (thus not the baptism of the Spirit). He had then been instructed in Ephesus by Paul's two fellow laborers, the couple Aquila and Priscilla.

After Paul had moved from Corinth to Ephesus, Apollos went to Corinth. This can have happened only with Paul's agreement. Indeed, in I Cor. 3 the latter describes the work of Apollos as a continuation of his own. Apollos must have made a great impression. His followers formed a group and were in rivalry with Paul's and Peter's admirers. Paul denounces these groupings and holds firm to cooperation with Apollos. At the time when Paul was writing I Corinthians, Apollos was once again in Asia Minor, in Paul's vicinity (I Cor. 16:12).

This is all that has been handed down. In spite of his highly esteemed scholarship, no literary work from his hand is existent or extant. Luther believed that he could see in Apollos the author of the Epistle to the Hebrews.

7. Paul's co-laborers

a) *Silas/Silvanus.* The name Silas is the Aramaic form of the Hebrew Saul; thus he is a namesake of Paul. He hails from Jerusalem. According to Acts 15:32, he was a prophet. In I Thess. 1:1, Paul names him along with Timothy, as joining him in sending the letter. The two were with Paul in Macedonia as well as in Corinth, where the letter was written. Personal traits do not emerge. This is due to the book of Acts, which indeed suppresses the significance of Paul's co-workers. According to I Peter 5:12, he later became secretary to Peter. How this came about and what stands behind this exchange of Peter tradition and Paul tradition cannot be explained (see also above on John Mark).

b) *Titus* is passed over completely by the book of Acts. He was a Gentile Christian; Paul remarks this in his account of the apostolic council as a demonstration that there the freedom from the law was actually acknowledged (Gal. 2:3). Titus must have been especially gifted in dealing with people. It was he who in the Corinthian crisis achieved the final change in Paul's favor, after Paul shortly before this had accomplished nothing. When he arrived at Paul's side (in Macedonia) with this report, the latter immediately sent him back to Corinth to prepare the way for Paul's visit and to organize the collection. He was successful with this mission also. Paul was able to spend the winter in Corinth and in the spring to travel to Jerusalem with the collection. But why is Titus missing from the list of salutations in the Epistle to the Romans? Is this a further argument for saying that this list is addressed not to Rome but to Ephesus? II Timothy (4:10) has Titus working in Dalmatia, and the Epistle to Titus (1:5) has him in Crete.

c) *Timothy* apparently is the one who stands closest to Paul. He was one of Paul's own converts (I Cor. 4:17). Several times he names him as sharing in the sending of an epistle. Paul entrusts to him an important mission to Corinth, which to be sure was not successful. Titus appears to have been the better diplomat. The recollection of Timothy is preserved by two pseudonymous letters of Paul to him. In them there already appears a trace of legend: the piety of his mother and his grandmother is extolled. If the book of Acts is correct (16:1-3), this is questionable: his Jewish mother was married to a Gentile, and Timothy had remained uncircumcised. Paul allegedly had performed the circumcision belatedly. Scholars disagree over whether this is correct. Pro: according to Jewish law, the son of a Jewish woman is a Jew. If the law remained in force for Jewish Christians, Paul did nothing but make Timothy what he really was in the terms of the law. And only thus, as one circumcised, could Paul employ him as co-laborer among the Jews.—Contra: for one to abide by the law as a Jew is not the same thing as for one as a Christian to be subjected to the law.

d) *Prisc(ill)a and Aquila.* The book of Acts uses the longer form of the woman's name, and Paul uses the shorter. The order in which the man and the woman are named varies. What we know about them has been drawn together above (pp. 97-98, 114).

8. The evangelists (authors of the Gospels)

Anyone who has traveled in Italy knows at least one of the symbols which are assigned to the four evangelists, the lion of Mark, the national emblem of the republic of Venice. The other symbols are: Matthew, an angel or a man; Luke, an ox; and John, an eagle. One can remember how they are correlated thus: the four symbols come from Rev. 4. Around the heavenly throne stand four beings; they resemble a lion, an ox, a man, and an eagle. These now are allocated to the individual evangelists according to the beginning of their respective books. Matthew begins with the genealogy of Jesus, thus with his becoming *man.* Mark begins with the appearance of John the Baptist in the wilderness; the wilderness attracts the *lion.* Luke 1 shows the priest Zacharias at the sacrifice in the temple; hence Luke gets the sacrificial animal, the *ox.* Thus for John with the exalted prologue there remains the creature of lofty flight, the *eagle.*

a) We have dealt with *John* above (pp. 157-58), with the conclusion that the "Johannine writings" hardly were composed by the son of Zebedee. The "Elder" John of whom Papias knows is an utterly intangible figure.

b) *Matthew.* The Gospel of Matthew is said to have been written by the "apostle" Matthew (Mark 3:18; Matt. 9:9; 10:3). According to the book itself, Matthew is a former tax collector. It is unlikely that he actually is the author of the book. For this is not written by an eyewitness of the history of Jesus. It is based on written (Greek!) sources (among them, the Gospel of Mark).

Other than the name in the list of the Twelve, nothing is known about Matthew.

c) *(John) Mark* is mentioned in Paul's letters and in the book of Acts. He comes from Jerusalem, and is a kinsman of Barnabas (Col. 4: 10). Acts 12:12 has preserved a local tradition about the house of his mother Mary. Luke relates that he had accompanied Barnabas and Paul on their first missionary journey for a distance, but then had turned back. Hence the next time Paul did not want to take him along. For this reason, it is said, a division arose between Paul and Barnabas. One learns the actual reason from Gal. 2. Again, we are not told how long Mark remained with Barnabas and why he left him. But he must have returned to Paul, for Paul mentions him as his fellow laborer (Philem. 24; cf. also Col. 4:10; II Tim. 4:11). In the same unexplained way as in the case of Silvanus, Mark also is made by the tradition into the companion of Peter (I Peter 5:13). In Papias he is promoted to Peter's interpreter, who wrote down Peter's reminiscences. Finally he becomes the first bishop of Alexandria, which therewith acquires at least a semi-apostolic tradition. As to the way the combination of Peter and Mark came about, may one offer the following conjecture? The name of Mark is found in the prison epistles. According to the general view in the early church, these were written in Rome (see above, p. 99). Then the association of "Peter and Paul in Rome" can suggest itself.

Down to the present day, the view is represented in scholarly circles that he actually wrote the Gospel of Mark. But there are counter-arguments: the author is not familiar with the geography of Palestine. And above all: he knows the Jewish customs only imprecisely. In substance the book has nothing to do with specifically Petrine tradition.

d) *Luke the physician.* According to legend he is an Antiochian. Col. 4:14 discloses his profession. The so-called Muratorian Canon from the end of the second century knows him as a jurist; in the legends the picture of a painter is dominant. Luke, like Mark, is found in the vicinity of Paul the prisoner. He is named in the same passages as Mark (Philem. 24; cf. Col. 4:14; II Tim. 4:11). The third Gospel and the book of Acts are attributed to him. Both books undoubtedly stem from the same author, but hardly from a companion of Paul. Many wish at least to trace back to him those sections of Acts which are written in the first person plural. But even these appear to be already somewhat far removed from the events. According to legend, he lived at the last in Boeotia.

APPENDIX II
Sources

1. The death of Agrippa I
(Josephus, *Antiquities of the Jews* 19. 343-350)[1]

19.343. The third year of his rule over all Judea had ended.[2] He betook himself to the city of Caesarea, which was earlier called Strato's Tower. There he established shows in honor of the emperor, since he knew that this festival was celebrated for his well-being.[3] To this festival came together in great numbers those throughout the province who held office and places of honor. 344. On the second day of the shows, Agrippa came into the theater at daybreak. He wore a garment which was made entirely of silver, of a marvelous texture. When the first rays of the sun fell upon it, the silver flashed and shone amazingly, so that its sparkling splendor produced awe in all who saw it. 345. Immediately the flatterers on all sides raised their clamor—though not for his benefit—and called on him as a god[4] and said: "Be gracious to us! Though we hitherto have feared you as a man, from now on we confess you as a supraterrestrial being." 346. The king did not silence them or reject their blasphemous flattery. But just then, when he looked up, he saw the owl[5] sitting on a rope above his head. He understood immediately that this one-time messenger of good news had become a messenger of bad news, and gloom filled his heart. He began to have sharp pains in his body which immediately became violent. 347. Then he sprang up and said to his friends, "I, your god, now must depart this life. At this very moment fate is overruling your lies of a moment ago. You called me immortal, and already I am being led away to death. . . ."

350. For another five days he was torn by the pains in his body, and then he died.

2. Claudius and the Jews in Rome[6]

a) Suetonius, *Claudius* 25.4

He expelled the Jews from Rome because they, incited by Chrestus, were constantly creating an uproar.

1. Cf. Acts 12:20-23 (where Agrippa is called "Herod").
2. He had gradually acquired his territory from Caligula and Claudius.
3. Is this a reference to the games which his grandfather Herod the Great had established for the well-being of the emperor? They were held every five years.
4. Acts 12:22.
5. It had already appeared to him once (18.195).
6. Acts 18:2.

b) Dio Cassius, *Roman History* 60.6.6 (on the year A.D. 41)

The Jews had once again increased so greatly that because of their great numbers it would have been difficult to bar them from the city without creating a tumult. So he did not drive them out, and even allowed them to continue their traditional manner of life, but forbade them to hold meetings.

He also disbanded the clubs which Gaius[7] had again permitted.[8]

3. The death of James, the brother of Jesus

a) Josephus, *Antiquities of the Jews* 20.200

Josephus is picturing the situation between the death of the governor Festus (A.D. 62) and the arrival of his successor Albinus.
He characterizes the high priest Ananos (Annas II) as bold and as a Sadducee, thus a member of the strictest group in political and legal matters. He gives an entirely different picture of Ananos' character in *Jewish Wars* 4.319 ff.

This was the character of Ananos. Since Festus was dead, and Albinus was still on the way, he considered the occasion favorable. He called a meeting of the judges (the Sanhedrin) and brought before them the brother of Jesus, the so-called anointed one (Christ), James, and some others. The charge against them was that they transgressed the law; he handed them over to be stoned.

b) Hegesippus (in Eusebius, *Church History* II, 23.4-18)[9]

The (leadership of the) church was taken by James, the brother of the Lord, together with the apostles. From the time of the Lord until today he is called by everyone "the Just," since there are many named James; he was holy from his mother's womb. He did not drink wine and strong drink, nor did he eat meat. No razor touched his head, he did not anoint himself with oil, and he did not frequent the baths. He alone was allowed to enter the holy place, for he wore nothing of wool, but only linen. He used to go into the temple alone and kneel and pray for forgiveness for the people, so that his knees became as hard as a camel's because of his constant kneeling, worshiping God and praying for forgiveness for the people. So, because of the great abundance of his righteousness, he was called "the Just" and "Oblias" (which means[10] "rampart of the people")[11] and "righteousness," as the prophets disclose concerning him. Some from the seven sects among the people . . . now asked him: "What is the door of Jesus?"[12] He answered, "He is the Savior." Some of these came to believe that Jesus is the Christ. . . .

7. His predecessor Gaius, called Caligula.
8. On this, cf. the letter of Pliny in Appendix II:7.
9. Eusebius is quoting from the second book of the "Memoirs" of Hegesippus. The text displays many obscurities. It is a mixture from various traditions.
10. I.e., in the original Greek.
11. "Oblias" is incomprehensible. The original reading here probably was "Abdias," which is the Greek transliteration of Obadiah, "servant of God."
12. Is this a reference to John 10:9? Or "door (Greek *thura*) to salvation (Hebrew *jeshua*)"? Or "law (Hebrew *torah*) of Jesus"?

Now since many even of the rulers believed, there arose an uproar among the Jews, the scribes, and the Pharisees who said that the whole people was in danger of looking for Jesus as the Christ. So they went to James and said, "We beg you to restrain the people, for they have strayed off after Jesus, as though he were the Christ. We beg you to persuade concerning Jesus all who have come to the Passover, for we all have confidence in you. For we and all the people bear witness of you that you are righteous and have no respect of persons. So persuade the people concerning Jesus not to be led astray; for we and all the people have confidence in you. So stand on the pinnacle of the temple so that you may be clearly visible up there and that your words may clearly be heard by all the people. For because of the Passover, all the tribes, along with the Gentiles, have come together."

The afore-mentioned scribes and Pharisees therefore placed James on the pinnacle of the temple and called out to him and said, "Just One, whom we all ought to heed, since the people are going astray after Jesus, who was crucified, tell us what is the door of Jesus?" And he answered with a loud voice, "Why are you asking me about the Son of Man? He is seated in heaven at the right hand of the great power, and he is about to come on the clouds of heaven."

And many were convinced and gave glory at the testimony of James and said, "Hosanna to the Son of David." Then again the same scribes and Pharisees said to one another, "That was a mistake to provide such a testimony for Jesus. Let us go up and throw him down, so that they may be afraid and not believe him." And they cried out, saying, "Oh, oh, even the Just One has gone astray." And they fulfilled the Scripture which was written in Isaiah,[13] "Let us remove the Just One, for he is a burden to us. Yet they shall taste the fruits of their works."

So they went up and threw down the Just One, and they said to one another,[14] "Let us stone James the Just." And they began to stone him, since the fall had not killed him. But he turned and knelt, saying, "I beseech thee, Lord God and Father, forgive them, for they do not know what they are doing." And while they were thus stoning him, a priest from the family (of Rechab, of the sons) of the Rechabites, of whom Jeremiah the prophet bore witness,[15] cried out and said, "Stop! What are you doing? The Just One is praying for you." And a certain one of them, one of the laundrymen, took the club with which he beat the clothes, and struck the Just One on the head, and thus he died the martyr's death.

And they buried him in the place beside the temple, and his gravestone still remains beside the temple. Thus he became a true witness to Jews and Greeks alike that Jesus is the Christ. And immediately thereafter Vespasian began to besiege them.

4. The martyrdom of Peter and Paul
(I Clement 5–6)

Context: warning against "jealousy." Its devastating effects are illustrated by a number of examples from the Old Testament.

13. Isa. 3:10.
14. Clearly a composite passage, in which various versions are interwoven.
15. Jer. 35:1 ff.

5. *1*. But to cease from the examples of long ago, let us come to those who contended (athletes) of the most recent past. Let us take the noble examples of our own generation. *2*. Because of jealousy and envy the greatest and most righteous pillars[16] were persecuted and contended unto death. *3*. Let us set before our eyes the good apostles: *4*. Peter, who because of unrighteous jealousy endured not one or two but many trials, and thus gave his testimony, reached the place of glory which was his due. *5*. Because of jealousy and strife Paul showed (the way to) the prize for endurance. *6*. Seven times he was in bonds, pursued, stoned, a herald in the East and in the West,[17] he received the glory befitting his faith. *7*. He taught righteousness to all the world, and having reached the limits of the West[18] and having given his testimony before the rulers, he departed from the world and was taken up into the holy place, the greatest example of steadfastness.

6. *1*. Associated with these men, with their holy manner of life, was a great throng of elect ones,[19] who because of jealousy suffered many torments and tortures, and thus became a splendid example in our midst. *2*. Because of jealousy women were persecuted and as Danaids and Dircae suffered fearful and wicked indignities.[20] Thus they reached the certain goal of faith[21] and received the noble prize, in spite of the weakness of their bodies.

5. The persecution of the Christians under Nero
in the year A.D. 64
(Tacitus, *Annals* 15.44)[22]

Context: the burning of Rome; reconstruction; ceremonies in order to appease the gods.

But no human effort, no gifts of the ruler, no ceremonies to placate the gods, could stifle the suspicion that the fire had taken place by command. In order to dispel the rumor, Nero shifted the blame to others and imposed the most refined punishments upon people despised for their vices, whom the populace called "Chrestians." The name is derived from Christ; he had been executed by the procurator Pontius Pilate during the reign of Tiberius. For the moment the pernicious superstition was suppressed. But it broke out again, not only in Judea, the home of the disease, but in the capital itself, where everything atrocious and shameful from everywhere comes together and finds a following.

16. Gal. 2:9.
17. II Cor. 11:23-30; Acts 9:23-24, 29; 13:50; 14:5-6, 19; 16:20 ff.; etc.
18. Spain (Rom. 15:24)?
19. Cf. Tacitus (Appendix II:5).
20. Scenes from mythology were enacted in the circus; Dirce was dragged to death by a bull.
21. The passage is saturated with the language of the contest; it is a favorite instrument of philosophy. Paul uses it (I Cor. 9:24 ff.; Phil. 3:14).
22. Also mentioned by Suetonius, *Nero* 16: "The death penalty was enforced against the Christians, a sect which had succumbed to a new and dangerous superstition."

First, then, they arrested people who confessed,[23] and then following their leads, a great throng, who were convicted not only of arson but also of hatred of humanity. Those condemned to death were made a spectacle; they were clothed in animals' skins and were torn to pieces by dogs; (or they were fixed on crosses or were burned) and when darkness came they served as torches. Nero made his gardens[24] available for this spectacle and presented an exhibition in the Circus. Dressed as a chariot-driver, he mixed with the people or stood in his chariot. Hence the victims, although they were guilty and deserved the harshest punishment, were pitied, because they were being sacrificed not to the general welfare but to the cruelty of one individual.

6. Domitian

a) Dio Cassius, *Roman History* 67.14.1

In the same year (A.D. 95), besides many others, Domitian had the consul Flavius Clemens executed, although the latter was his cousin and was the husband of Flavia Domitilla, who was also related to the emperor. The charge of atheism was made against both of them. For this reason also many others who had strayed off into the Jewish religion were condemned. Some were put to death, and others at least lost their possessions. Domitilla was only exiled to Pandateria.

To the later tradition both were represented as Christians. This opinion is still shared today by many students of the matter. In favor of it may be cited the fact that Dio Cassius on principle avoids any mention of Christianity.

b) Eusebius, *Church History III*, 18.4–20.7

18.4. In the time mentioned (i.e., of Domitian), the teaching of our faith already radiated so far that even writers who were alien to our cause did not hesitate to tell in their historical works of the persecution and the martyrdoms that occurred in it. They even gave the time accurately, telling that in the fifteenth year of Domitian (A.D. 95), along with many others, Flavia Domitilla, a daughter of the sister of Flavius Clemens, who at that time was one of the Roman consuls, was exiled to the island of Pontia because of her confession of Christ.

19. The same Domitian gave orders for the execution of the descendants of David. According to an ancient report, some heretics denounced the descendants of Judas, a brother of the savior according to the flesh, as descendants of David and kinsmen of Christ himself. Hegesippus tells this exactly thus: *20. 1.* "Of the kinsmen of the Lord there were still surviving the grandsons of Judas, said to be a brother of the Lord according to the flesh. These were denounced as descendants of David. The officer brought them to the emperor Domitian, for he, like Herod,

23. Confessed what? That they were Christians? Then how do they denounce the others? Or that they had set the fire? Then why did police first catch those who confessed, and subsequently the purely innocent? In any case, Tacitus knows how to gain attention and to suggest something to the reader.
24. In the vicinity of the present-day Vatican.

feared the coming of the Christ. 2. He asked them if they were descendants of David, and they admitted it. Then he asked them how much property they had and how much money they possessed. They said that altogether they possessed only nine thousand denarii, half of it belonging to each, and even this, they said, was not in money but was the value of some ten acres of land on which they worked in order to pay taxes and to gain a living from it." [25] 3. Then they showed him their hands and as proof of their labor called attention to the hardness of their bodies and the callouses on their hands from their unceasing toil. 4. When they were asked about Christ and about the nature, place, and time of the appearing of his kingdom, they explained that it was neither worldly nor earthly, but celestial and angelic, and that it would come at the end of the world, when Christ would appear in glory to judge the living and the dead and to reward every man according to his deeds.

5. Thereupon Domitian did not condemn them, but scorned them as simple fellows. He released them and issued a decree to cease the persecution of the church. 6. After their release they were leaders of the church, since they were confessors and kinsmen of the Lord. After peace was restored they survived until the time of Trajan.

7. So much from Hegesippus.

7. The proceedings against the Christians
(Pliny the Younger, Letters X. 96)

a)   C. Pliny to the Emperor Trajan. It is my rule, sir, to refer to you all doubtful cases.

I have never taken part in proceedings against the Christians. Therefore I am unfamiliar with the object and the extent of both punishment and examination. 2. And I am in considerable uncertainty: should a distinction be made according to age, or should those quite young be treated exactly as are the older ones? Does remorse remit the penalties, or does it not avail anything if one who was once a Christian no longer is one? Is the name (of Christian) itself culpable, even if there is no crime connected with it, or only the crimes which are connected with the name?

In the meantime, I have proceeded thus with those who were denounced to me as Christians: 3. I asked them whether they were Christians. If they confessed, I asked them a second and a third time, under threat of the death penalty. If they persisted, I had them led away (to death). For I had no doubt that, whatever they had to confess, their stubbornness and unbending obstinacy deserved punishment. 4. Some who had fallen into the same madness were Roman citizens. These I had noted to be sent to Rome. As it developed, my judicial intervention caused the number of denunciations to increase, and several cases came before me. 5. An anonymous pamphlet of accusation listing many names was submitted.

25. End of the quotation. The continuation is Eusebius' discussion of Hegesippus.

To those who denied that they were or had been Christians I stated the formula and had them call on the gods and do reverence to your image, with incense and wine, together with the images of the gods which I had brought together for this purpose, and moreover to curse Christ. Thereupon, in my opinion, they could be set free; for it is said that true Christians cannot be compelled to do all this. 6. Others who were named by the accuser confessed themselves to be Christians, but then at once retracted their confession: they had been Christians, but had given up Christianity, many of them three years ago, many others still earlier, and some even as much as twenty years ago. All these also did reverence to your image and to the statues of the gods and cursed Christ. 7. They assured me that the sum total of their guilt or their error consisted in the fact that they regularly assembled on a certain day before daybreak. They recited a hymn antiphonally to Christ as (their) God and bound themselves with an oath not to commit any crime, but to abstain from theft, robbery, adultery, breach of faith, and embezzlement of property entrusted to them.[26] After this it was their custom to separate, and then to come together again to partake of a meal, but an ordinary and innocent one.[27] After my edict they discontinued this practice; in it, on the basis of your command, I had forbidden secret societies (hetairia). 8. I regarded it as all the more necessary further to use torture to learn the truth from two maidservants, who were called "deaconesses."[28] I found nothing but depraved and boundless superstition. 9. Therefore I postponed the matter in order to get your decision. It appeared to me that this inquiry was justified, particularly because of the large number of the people accused. For many of every age, of every station, and of both sexes are coming and will come before the court. For the contagion of this superstition has spread not only through the cities, but also in the villages and in the open country. Yet it seems possible to stop its spread and to root it out. 10. At any rate, it is certain that the temples, which were almost deserted, are beginning to be frequented again. The long-neglected sacrifices are again being offered. The meat of the sacrificial animals, for which previously a buyer could hardly be found,[29] is on sale everywhere. From this one may confidently conclude how many could be set straight if they were allowed to recant.

b) Trajan to Pliny. The procedure which you have followed, my dear Secundus,[30] against the people who are accused to you as Christians is a proper one. No general rule can be laid down which would be, so to speak, a fixed standard.

They are not to be sought out. If they are accused and convicted, they are to be punished. Yet this reservation applies: anyone who denies being a Christian and attests this by his action, namely by praying to our gods, shall be pardoned on

26. An echo of the Ten Commandments and of New Testament "catalogs of vices," e.g., I Cor. 5:11; I Tim. 1:9-10.
27. Among other things, the accusation was made against the Christians that in their meetings they ate the flesh of infants and practiced incest.
28. *Ministrae.*
29. Acts 15:29.
30. Pliny's name was C. Plinius Caecilius Secundus.

the basis of his recantation, regardless of the suspicion about his past. Accusations published anonymously may not be considered in any proceeding. They set a very bad example and are not in keeping with the spirit of our age.

8. Inscription in the forecourt of the temple at Jerusalem[31]

No Gentile may tread the area within the enclosure and the fence around the temple. Anyone caught violating this rule is to blame for his own death.

9. The twelfth petition of the Eighteen Benedictions

May there be no hope for the apostates and mayest thou quickly root out the kingdom of violence in our days. And [32] may the Nazarenes[33] and heretics perish in an instant. May they be blotted from the book of life and not be enrolled with the righteous.

Praised be thou, Jahweh, who humblest the violent.

10. Simon Magus
(Justin, Apology I, 26.1-3)

26. 1. After Christ's ascension into heaven the demons[34] also incited many men to represent themselves as gods. These not only were not persecuted by you,[35] but were even honored. 2. Thus a certain Samaritan Simon, from the village of Gitta. Under Claudius Caesar, by virtue of the influence and the art of the demons he practiced magical arts. Hence in your imperial city of Rome he was held to be a god and was honored by you as a god with a statue. This statue is erected in the Tiber[36] between the two bridges and bears this Latin inscription: "Simoni deo sancto" ("to the holy god Simon").[37] 3. And almost all the Samaritans, but also a few even of other nations, confess and venerate him as the most high god. And a certain Helena, who at that time went around with him—she had previously been a prostitute—, they call the first thought,[38] standing beneath him.

31. Cf. Acts 21:27 ff. Gentiles were permitted to enter the outer part of the forecourt.
32. This sentence and the next were inserted near the end of the first century.
33. Is "Nazarenes and" a still later addition?
34. Traditionally, demons influenced people toward pagan degeneracies; Justin had previously spoken of these.
35. Justin is complaining that the Christians are forbidden what is allowed to others: namely, to revere a man as God.
36. On an island in the Tiber.
37. This is a (naïve or intentional?) grotesque interpretation. This statue (it has been rediscovered!) bears the inscription: *Semoni Sanco Deo Fidio sacrum*. . . . Semo Sancus is an ancient Italic god.
38. The Greek word (*ennoia*) is feminine in gender.

11. Documents of primitive Christianity outside the New Testament

a) Order of worship and of community life (*The Teaching of the Twelve Apostles* 7 *ff.*)

7.1. On baptism. Baptize thus: After you have rehearsed all this,[39] baptize in the name of the Father and the Son and the Holy Spirit[40] in living[41] water. 2. But if you have no living water, then baptize in other water; if you are unable to do it in cold water, then in warm. 3. But if you have neither, then pour water three times on the head, in the name of the Father and Son and Holy Spirit. 4. But before baptism the one who baptizes and the one who is to be baptized are to fast, and if possible, others as well. Require the one who is to be baptized to fast one or two days beforehand.

8. *1.* Your fasts[42] are not to be at the same time with those of the hypocrites. For they fast on Monday and Thursday;[43] but you shall fast on Wednesday and Friday. 2. And do not pray as do the hypocrites.[44] But you are to pray as the Lord commanded in his gospel: (then follows the Lord's Prayer).[45] For thine is the power and the glory forever.[46] 3. You shall pray thus three times daily.

9.1. On the Eucharist. Give thanks thus (Greek *eucharistesate*): 2. First concerning the cup: We thank thee, our Father, for the holy vine of David, thy servant, which[47] thou didst make known to us through Jesus, thy servant. To thee be glory forever. 3. Concerning the broken bread: We thank thee, our Father, for the life and knowledge which thou hast made known to us through Jesus, thy servant. To thee be glory forever. 4. As this bread was scattered upon the mountains and was gathered and made one, so may thy church be gathered from the ends of the earth into thy kingdom. For thine is the glory and the power through Jesus Christ forever. 5. But let no one eat and drink of your Eucharist but those who are baptized in the name of the Lord. For concerning this, the Lord said, "Do not give what is holy to the dogs."[48]

10.1. After you are satisfied with food, give thanks thus: 2. We thank thee, holy Father, for thy holy name which thou hast caused to dwell in our hearts, and for the knowledge and the faith and the immortality which thou hast made known to us through Jesus, thy servant. To thee be glory forever. 3. Thou, Lord

39. I.e., the foregoing basic ethical instruction.
40. Cf. Matt. 28:19.
41. I.e., running water.
42. Cf. Matt. 6:16.
43. These are the Jewish fast-days.
44. Cf. Matt. 6:5.
45. With slight variations from Matt. 6:9-13.
46. The "closing doxology" was not originally a part of the Lord's Prayer. It is lacking in the best manuscripts of the Gospel of Matthew. It developed in the course of usage in worship. The earliest witness for it is the *Teaching of the Twelve Apostles;* here, of course, it still has only two parts.
47. The vine!
48. Matt. 7:6.

Almighty, hast created all things for thy name's sake. Thou hast given food and drink to men to enjoy, that they may give thanks to thee. But to us thou hast given spiritual food and drink[49] through thy servant. *4.* We give thanks to thee for all things, for thou art mighty. To thee be glory forever. *5.* Remember, Lord, thy church, to deliver it from all evil and to perfect it in thy love, and gather it, the sanctified, from the four winds into thy kingdom which thou hast prepared for it. For thine is the power and the glory forever. *6.* Let grace come, and this world pass away. Hosanna to the God of David.[50] If any man be holy, let him come. If not, let him repent. Maranatha. Amen.[51] *7.* But let the prophets give thanks as they will.[52]

11.*1.* Now if one comes and teaches you all that has been said, receive him. *2.* But if the teacher himself has turned aside and teaches a different doctrine, to destroy (these things), do not hear him. But (if he teaches) for the increase of righteousness and the knowledge of the Lord, receive him as the Lord. *3.* Concerning the apostles and prophets, act thus according to the ordinance of the gospel: *4.* Every apostle who comes to you is to be received as the Lord. *5.* But he is to remain only *one* day, and if need be, a second day as well. But if he remains three days, he is a false prophet. *6.* When the apostle travels on, he is to take nothing but bread till his next night's lodging. If he asks for money, he is a false prophet. *7.* You shall not test or examine any prophet who speaks in the Spirit.[53] For every sin will be forgiven, but this sin will not be forgiven.[54] *8.* But not everyone who speaks in the Spirit is a prophet;[55] (he is one) only if he practices the way of life of the Lord. Thus the false prophet and the (true) prophet will be known by their way of life. *9.* And any prophet who orders a table to be set does not himself eat of it; otherwise he is a false prophet. *10.* Any prophet who teaches the truth but does not practice what he teaches is a false prophet . . . .

14.*1.* On the Lord's Day you shall come together, break bread, and give thanks, after you have first confessed your sins, so that your sacrifice may be pure. *2.* But no one who has a quarrel with his neighbor should join in your meeting until they have become reconciled, so that your sacrifice may not be defiled . . . .

15.*1.* Thus select for yourselves bishops and deacons. . . . *2.* . . . For they are your honored ones together with the prophets and teachers. *3.* Correct one another, not in wrath, but in peace, as you have it in the gospel. And no one is to speak to anyone who has done a wrong to another, nor is he to hear (a word) from you, until he repents.

49. Cf. I Cor. 10:3-4.
50. Cf. Matt. 21:9.
51. Cf. I Cor. 16:22.
52. They are not bound to the wording and the scope of the stipulations that have been given.
53. On the following, cf. I Cor. 14.
54. Cf. Matt. 12:31.
55. There are also demonic ecstasies; cf. I Cor. 12:1-3.

b) A prayer (I Clement 59–61)[56]

59.2. We . . . will pray with constant pleading and entreaty that the creator of
the universe may preserve unharmed the number of his elect who are numbered
throughout the world, through his beloved servant Jesus Christ, our Lord, through
whom he has called us out of darkness into light,[57] out of ignorance into the
knowledge of the glory of his name.

3. (Address)[58] that we may hope in thy name,
the source of all creation,
thou who hast opened the eyes of our hearts, that we may know thee,
alone the Most High among the most high ones,
the Holy One, resting among the holy ones,[59]
who dost humble the pride of the haughty ones,[60]
who dost nullify the plans of the heathen,[61]
who dost lift up the humble and put down the haughty,[62]
who dost make rich and make poor,
who dost kill and make alive,[63]
the only benefactor of the spirits and the God of all flesh,[64]
who dost look into the underworld,[65]
who dost oversee the works of men,
the helper of those in peril,
the savior of those in despair,
the creator and overseer of every spirit,
thou who hast multiplied the peoples on the earth
and out of all hast chosen those who love thee,
through Jesus Christ, thy beloved servant,
through whom thou hast taught us, made us holy, and honored us.
4. (Petition) We beseech thee, Master,
to be our helper and protector.
Save those of us who are afflicted,
lift up the fallen ones,
show thyself to those who pray,
heal the sick,
bring back those of thy people who have gone astray.

56. The prayer is marked by numerous allusions to the Old Testament. Examples of
these are indicated in the first part.
57. Cf. Acts 26:18; I Peter 2:9.
58. Beginning of the prayer (transition to the use of the second person).
59. Isa. 57:15.
60. Isa. 13:11.
61. Psalm 33:10.
62. I Sam. 2:7; Job 5:11; Luke 1:52.
63. Deut. 32:39.
64. Num. 16:22; 27:16.
65. Dan. 3:55 Septuagint.

Feed the hungry,
set our captives free,
raise up the weak,
comfort the fainthearted.
Let all the peoples know that thou alone art God, and Jesus Christ thy
Servant, and we thy people and the sheep of thy pasture.

60.1 (Renewed address) Through thy works thou hast disclosed the eternal
order of the world.
Thou, Lord, hast created the earth, thou who art faithful in all generations,
righteous in judgment,
marvelous in power and majesty,
wise in creation, and knowing in maintaining what is created,
good in things that are visible, and gentle with those who trust in thee.
(Petition) Merciful and compassionate one,
forgive us our wrongdoing, unrighteousness, transgressions, and failures.
2. Do not count every sin of thy servants and handmaids,
but purify us with the cleansing of thy truth,
and make our paths straight,
that we may walk in purity of heart
and may do what is good and well-pleasing to thee and before our rulers.
3. Yea, Lord, let thy face shine upon us for good in peace, that we may be protected by thy strong hand and may be preserved from every sin by thy uplifted
arm, and keep us from those who hate us unjustly. 4. Give harmony and peace to
us and to all inhabitants of the earth, as thou hast given to our fathers, when they
called upon thee piously in faith and truth. Make us obedient to thy almighty and
glorious name, and to our rulers and governors upon the earth.
61.1. Thou, master, hast given to them the authority of rule, by virtue of thy
exalted and ineffable power, that we may acknowledge the glory and honor which
thou hast given to them, and may submit to them, in nothing resisting thy will.
Give to them, Lord, health, peace, harmony, steadfastness, that they may exercise
their rule which thou hast given them without offense.
2. For thou, heavenly master, king of the eons, dost give to the children of men
glory and honor and power over things that are on the earth. O Lord, direct their
will to that which is good and well-pleasing to thee, that they may piously exercise in peace and gentleness the authority which thou hast given to them, and may
gain thy praise.
3. Thou who alone art able to do this and yet much more that is good to us, we
praise thee through the high priest and protector of our souls, Jesus Christ,
through whom be glory and majesty to thee now and through all generations and
forever. Amen.

c) Worship (Justin, *Apology I*, 65–67)

Context: Baptism. The baptized person is brought into the assembly of the brethren,
who pray for him and for all.

65.2. When the prayer is ended, we greet one another with a kiss.[66] 3. Then bread and a cup with water and wine are brought to the president of the brethren. He takes them and gives praise and glory to the father of the universe in the name of the Son and of the Holy Spirit and utters a long thanksgiving that we were counted worthy of these gifts by him. When he has ended the prayers and the thanksgiving, all the people present express their agreement by saying, "Amen." . . . 5. After the thanksgiving by the president and the assent of all the people, those who among us are called "deacons" give to each one present some of the bread, wine, and water for which thanksgiving was said, and some is taken also to those who are absent.

66.1. This food is called among us "eucharistia." No one may partake of it but one who holds our teachings to be true and has received the washing for the forgiveness of sins and rebirth and lives according to Christ's directions. . . .

67.3. On the day called Sunday there takes place an assembly of all who live in the city or in the country. There the memoirs of the apostles or the writings of the apostles—a suitable amount—are read. 4. Then when the reader has ended, the president delivers a discourse for edification and exhortation to be zealous for these good things. 5. Then we all rise together and pray. And, as was mentioned earlier, after the prayer, bread, wine, and water are brought . . . (see above).

d) Christian-Gnostic poetry (*Odes of Solomon,* Ode 6)

> As the hand wanders over the harp and the strings sound,
>> so sounds in my members the Spirit of the Lord, and I resound in his love.
> For it destroys what is alien,
>> and everything is of the Lord.
> For thus it was from the beginning
>> and will be to the end,
> that nothing should oppose him,
>> and nothing rise up against him.
> The Lord increased the knowledge of himself,
>> and he was zealous that what was given to us by his goodness should be known.
> And he gave us the praise of his name;
>> our spirits praise his Holy Spirit.
> For a brook sprang forth and became a great wide river;
>> for it flooded everything and carried away the temple.
> And the hindrances made by men were not able to stem it,
>> not even the arts of those who dam the waters.
> For it spread over the surface of the whole earth,
>> and it filled everything.

66. Cf. I Cor. 16:20.

And all the thirsty of the earth drank,
and their thirst was quieted and quenched.
For the draught was given from the Most High.

Therefore blessed are the ministers of that draught,
those to whom the water is entrusted.
They have refreshed the parched lips,
and the faltering will they have lifted up.
And the souls that were near departing
they have snatched back from death.
And the members that had fallen
they have set upright and established.
They have bestowed strength, that they can come,
and light for their eyes.
For everyone has known them in the Lord,
and by means of the water they live forever.
Hallelujah!

12. The earliest list of the canonical writings (Muratori Canon)[67]

This fragment of an eighth-century manuscript was published in 1740 by the Italian scholar Muratori. It has been translated from Greek into atrocious Latin and barbarously copied; parts of it cannot now be translated with certainty. As can be seen from this Canon itself, it dates from about the year 200.
The beginning is lost. Yet is can be inferred that it was concerned with the Gospels of Matthew and Mark, since the Canon introduces the Gospel of Luke as the third.

at which however he was present and so he has set it down.
The third Gospel book, that according to Luke.
This physician Luke after Christ's ascension (resurrection?),
since Paul had taken him with him as an expert in the way (of the teaching),
composed it in his own name
according to (his) thinking. Yet neither did he himself see
the Lord in the flesh; and therefore, as he was able to ascertain it, so he begins
to tell the story from the birth of John.
The fourth of the Gospels, that of John, (one) of the disciples.
When his fellow-disciples and bishops urged him,

67. Latin text: Alexander Souter, *The Text and Canon of the New Testament*, 1913, pp. 208-10. The above translation from *New Testament Apocrypha*, Volume One, edited by Edgar Hennecke and Wilhelm Schneemelcher. English translation edited by R. McL. Wilson. Published in the U. S. A. by The Westminster Press, 1963. Copyright © 1959, J. C. B. Mohr (Paul Siebeck), Tübingen. English translation © Lutterworth Press. Used by permission. I:43-45.

he said: Fast with me from today for three days, and what
will be revealed to each one
let us relate to one another. In the same night it was
revealed to Andrew, one of the apostles, that,
whilst all were to go over (it), John in his own name
should write everything down. And therefore, though various
rudiments (or: tendencies?) are taught in the several
Gospel books, yet that matters
nothing for the faith of believers, since by the one and guiding (original?)
   Spirit
everything is declared in all: concerning the birth,
concerning the passion, concerning the resurrection,
concerning the intercourse with his disciples
and concerning his two comings,
the first despised in lowliness, which has come to pass,
the second glorious in kingly power,
which is yet to come. What
wonder then if John, being thus always true to himself,
adduces particular points in his epistles also,
where he says of himself: What we have seen with our eyes
and have heard with our ears and
our hands have handled, that have we written to you.
        For so he confesses (himself) not merely an eye and ear witness,
but also a writer of all the marvels of the Lord in
order. But the acts of all the apostles
are written in one book. For the "most excellent Theophilus" Luke
summarizes the several things that in his own presence
have come to pass, as also by the omission of the passion of Peter he makes
quite clear, and equally by (the omission of) the journey of Paul, who
   from
the city (of Rome) proceeded to Spain. The epistles, however, of Paul
themselves make clear to those who wish to know it which there are (i.e.,
        from Paul), from what place and for what cause they were written.
First of all to the Corinthians (to whom) he forbids the heresy
of schism, then to the Galatians (to whom he forbids) circumcision,
and then to the Romans, (to whom) he explains that Christ
is the rule of the Scriptures and moreover their principle,
he has written at considerable length. We must deal with these
severally, since the blessed
apostle Paul himself, following the rule of his predecessor
John, writes by name only to seven
churches in the following order: to the Corinthians
the first (epistle), to the Ephesians the second, to the Philippians
the third, to the Colossians the fourth, to the Galatians the

fifth, to the Thessalonians the sixth, to the Romans
the seventh. Although he wrote to the Corinthians and to the
Thessalonians once more for their reproof,
it is yet clearly recognizable that over the whole earth one church
is spread. For John also in the
Revelation writes indeed to seven churches,
yet speaks to all. But to Philemon one,
and to Titus one, and to Timothy two, (written) out of goodwill
and love, are yet held sacred to the glory of the catholic Church
for the ordering of ecclesiastical
discipline. There is current also (an epistle) to
the Laodiceans, another to the Alexandrians, forged in Paul's
name for the sect of Marcion, and several others,
which cannot be received in the catholic Church;
for it will not do to mix gall with honey.
Further an epistle of Jude and two with the title (or: two of the above
     mentioned)
John are accepted in the catholic Church, and the Wisdom
written by friends of Solomon in his honour.
Also of the revelations we accept only those of John and
Peter, which (latter) some of our
people do not want to have read in the Church. But Hermas
wrote the Shepherd quite lately in our time in the city
of Rome, when on the throne of
the church of the city of Rome the bishop Pius, his brother,
was seated. And therefore it ought indeed to be read, but
it cannot be read publicly in the Church to the people either among
the prophets, whose number is settled, or among
the apostles to the end of time.
[There follows an obscure and in part erroneous comment about heretics
whose writings are not recognized.]

Bibliography

Note: in the original German edition of the present work, the author included works in English, French, and German. They were arranged in two sections, general presentations, and works pertaining to individual themes, corresponding to the chapters. Further division was made between those works designed for the specialist and those suited to the non-specialist reader. In the list below, only those works available in English are given, in alphabetical order, without further classification.

The Apostolic Fathers, translated by Kirsopp Lake, in The Loeb Classical Library, 2 vols., 1948, 1952.

Bauer, Walter, *Orthodoxy and Heresy in Earliest Christianity*, 1971, edited by Robert Kraft and Gerhard Krodel, ET from the 2nd ed., 1964, with added appendixes by Georg Strecker, of *Rechtgläubigkeit und Ketzerei im ältesten Christentum.*

Bousset, Wilhelm, *Kyrios Christos*, 1970, ET by John E. Steely from the 5th German ed., 1965.

Bultmann, Rudolf, *Primitive Christianity in Its Contemporary Setting*, 1956, ET by R. H. Fuller of *Das Urchristentum im Rahmen der antiken Religionen*, 1949.

————, *Theology of the New Testament*, 2 vols., 1951, 1955, ET by Kendrick Grobel of *Theologie des Neuen Testaments*, 1948, 1953.

Campenhausen, H. v., *Ecclesiastical Authority and Spiritual Power in the Church of the First Three Centuries*, 1969, ET by J. A. Baker of *Kirchliches Amt und geistliche Vollmacht in den ersten drei Jahrhunderten*, 1953.

Cullmann, Oscar, *Peter: Disciple, Apostle, Martyr*, 1962, ET by Floyd V. Filson from the 2nd rev. and enlarged ed., 1960, of *Petrus.*

Dibelius, Martin, *Paul*, edited and completed by Werner Georg Kümmel, ET by Frank Clarke, 1953, of *Paulus.*

Filson, Floyd V., *A New Testament History: the Story of the Emerging Church*, 1964.

Finegan, Jack, *Handbook of Biblical Chronology*, 1964.

Foakes Jackson, F. J., and Lake, K. *The Beginnings of Christianity*, 5 vols., 1920-33.

Goguel, M., *The Birth of Christianity*, 1953, ET by H. C. Snape of *La naissance du christianisme*, 1946.

————, *The Primitive Church*, 1964, ET by H. C. Snape of *L'église primitive*, 1947.

Goppelt, L., *Apostolic and Post-Apostolic Times*, 1970, ET by Robert A. Guelich of *Die apostolische und nachapostolische Zeit*, 2nd ed., 1966.

———, *Jesus, Paul and Judaism: an Introduction to New Testament Theology*, ET by Edward Schroeder, 1964, from *Christentum und Judentum im ersten und zweiten Jahrhundert*, 1954.

Haenchen, E., *The Acts of the Apostles*, 1971, ET by Bernard Noble and Gerald Shinn, under the supervision of Hugh Anderson, and with the translation revised and brought up to date by R. McL. Wilson, of *Die Apostelgeschichte*, 14th ed., 1965.

Harnack, A. v., *The Mission and Expansion of Christianity*, 2 vols., 1908, ET by James Moffatt of *Die Mission und Ausbreitung des Christentums in den ersten drei Jahrhunderten*, 2nd ed., 1905.

Hennecke, Edgar, *New Testament Apocrypha*, 2 vols., 1963, 1965, ET edited by R. McL. Wilson, of *Neutestamentliche Apokryphen*, 3rd ed., 1959, 1964, edited by Wilhelm Schneemelcher.

Lietzmann, H., *Beginnings of the Christian Church*, 1949, ET by Bertram Lee Woolf of *Geschichte der alten Kirche*, Band 1, 1932.

Marxsen, W., *The Resurrection of Jesus of Nazareth*, 1970, ET by Margaret Kohl of *Die Auferstehung Jesu von Nazareth*, 1968.

Schweizer, E., *Church Order in the New Testament*, 1961, ET by Frank Clarke of *Gemeinde und Gemeindeordnung im Neuen Testament*, 1959.

Weiss, J., *Earliest Christianity*, 1959, reprint in 2 vols. of ET (originally published in 1937 under the title *The History of Primitive Christianity*) by Frederick C. Grant and others, of *Das Urchristentum*, 1917.

Index of New Testament Passages

Selected Index of Persons and Subjects

(The index contains only those references which
would not be evident from the Table of Contents)

189